COMPLETE & UTTER FAILURE

ALSO BY NEIL STEINBERG

If at All Possible, Involve a Cow:
The Book of College Pranks

COMPLETE & UTTER FAILURE

~

A Celebration of
Also-Rans,
Runners-Up,
Never-Weres
and
Total Flops

·

NEIL STEINBERG

PAVILION

First published in Great Britain in 1995 by
PAVILION BOOKS LIMITED
26 Upper Ground, London SE1 9PD

Text © 1994 Neil Steinberg
Design by Susan Yuran

A CIP catalogue record for this book
is available from the British Library.

ISBN 1 85793 696 5
Printed and bound in Great Britain by
Hartnolls Ltd, Bodmin

2 4 6 8 10 9 7 5 3 1

This book may be ordered by post direct from the publisher.
Please contact the Marketing Department.
But try your bookshop first.

To Bill Thomas

CONTENTS

—

Here the author lubricates friends, relatives and associates from whom he hopes to sponge, emotionally and perhaps financially, for years to come.

In which fellow authors who might otherwise consider legal action are given praise and recognition.

There are many ways to fail.
—Aristotle

INTRODUCTION

The Siren Beauty of Ruin

CAPTAIN KANGAROO betrayed me. He had demonstrated a magic trick to his legion of little followers: how to pass a knotted string through a toilet paper tube and remove the string, magically unknotted, from the other end. The secret involved first poking a hole in the cardboard tube just big enough to fit a finger through. Holding the tube so that no one could see the inserted digit, the magician mesmerized the audience with mumbo jumbo, cleverly untying the knot with his hidden finger while slowly drawing the string through the tube.

I could hardly wait to amaze and dazzle the world with my newfound talent. Our garage served as a theater. Assembling some pathetic band of neighborhood children as an audience, I grandly opened the garage door—ta-da, curtain going *up*—to present the magic trick, a trick I had not properly mastered and could not do.

My magician's cool quickly evaporated into a face-contorting, squirming, flailing of finger in tube. The trick had seemed so easy when the Captain did it. My friends drifted off, and I pulled shut the garage door. I was four years old and had to put my full weight into the rope to make that garage door come down. It closed with a bang. End of show.

The garage was still pretty clean back then—the house was

younger than I—and I stood for a while in the quiet dimness, the cool of the gray concrete floor, the tube still stuck on my finger. The emptiness of the two-car garage was immense.

Though I wasn't aware of it, whole avenues of life were closing off to me at that moment. Inner faults of personality—lack of confidence, short attention span, inability to plan, impatience, underestimation of obvious difficulties—were now beginning to manifest themselves. Nobody was ever going to stand on a chair and applaud, hands clapping ecstatically overhead, then whistling between index fingers, in response to something I had done. Groupies were never going to embroider silk panties with their phone numbers and fling them at my feet. The feeble stratagems yet to come—piano lessons, cornet lessons, guitar lessons, Little League practice, dance class, drama club, debate, wrestling, track, choir—were but desperate rearguard actions meant to forestall what had already been decided.

The year was 1964. In Minnesota, Prince Rogers Nelson was banging on his mother's piano. Bill Gates was reading *The Big Wonder Book of Science*. George Stephanopoulos was just out of training pants. Bret Easton Ellis was an undescended egg. And I was standing in an empty garage on Carteret Court in Berea, Ohio, toilet paper tube stuck on my finger, feeling like an idiot. A new feeling, but one that would become familiar.

A FEW YEARS before I began and ended my career as a magician, Courvoisier cognac started a long-running series of full-page magazine advertisements featuring classic paintings of the libation's mascot, Napoleon Bonaparte. In most of the paintings the Emperor of the French was posed triumphantly—Napoleon seizing the tattered French flag to lead his men to victory at the Battle of Arcola; Napoleon astride a huge, rearing white stallion; Napoleon crossing the

Alps into Italy; Napoleon making an expansive gesture skyward, surrounded by cheering soldiers; Napoleon at his desk, hand tucked demurely within his shirt, a faint Mona Lisa smile on his lips.

The scenes were generally images of glory. But one ad in the series didn't fit. It showed Napoleon and the ragged remnants of his army slouching back from Moscow in defeat, the Little Corporal hunched forward in his saddle. You could see his breath.

A strange image to use in an ad. But then, it was a cognac ad. Napoleon appeared miserable and cold. He looked as if he could have used a cognac. Perhaps that was the subliminal message behind the advertisement: If you foolishly invade Russia, bog down in a killing winter and decimate your troops, the least you can do once you drag yourself back to Paris is bolt the door, pour a healthy snootful of Courvoisier, and muse over the entire fiasco. That's what cognac is for.

Musing over failure is not a particularly American activity, however. Sure, it's big in Europe, where every nation, at one time or another, has had a lock on greatness, only to fritter it away smothering monster palaces in gold leaf and commissioning jeweled Fabergé eggs by the dozen. England had her empire; Spain, her Armada; France, her Napoleon; Germany, its unspeakable zenith. Even Belgium had a moment of glory, though, true, things haven't been quite the same since the death of Charles the Bold in 1477. For those nations, remembering and bitterly analyzing greatness are about their only connection to it anymore. Why do you think they have all those pubs and outdoor cafés?

Not us. Americans are still moving forward, winning, doing, scheduling meetings. The gales of decline may be rattling the windows, but we're still snugly ensconced in our Great Period, at least in our own minds, with a frontier to be explored, a world to be set right, money to be made, and the losers and complainers to be shunted into oblivion. Those who fail, who come in second, whose sales figures disappoint, who do promising initial work but then compromise—in other words, the majority—are lost and forgotten. Tough luck, buddies.

That's a pity. Because, with hindsight, one realizes that the second-placers and also-rans were sometimes better, more interesting, even more worthy, than those whose combination of luck, effort and circumstance for some reason brought success. George Leigh Mallory was a handsome, romantic figure who knew the Latin names of mountain flowers and wrote poetry as he trekked up the side of Mount Everest. Edmund Hillary was a rather drab New Zealand beekeeper, squintish and gangly, with the dramatic flair of an accountant. But it was Hillary who made it to the top of Everest and back, immortalizing his name, while Mallory is the answer to a trivia question, his body still on the side of Everest, mummified in a crevasse somewhere, if not crushed to dust under shifting tons of ice. Lots of bodies are there, actually—more than a hundred—forgotten to history because they failed. But not because they were uninteresting.

MY APPRECIATION OF failure springs, I believe, from the arid surroundings in which I was raised. The new suburban subdivision where I grew up in the 1960s lives in my memory the way sub-Saharan Africa must be recalled by a Sudanese living in New York—heat shimmering off treeless plains; high, cloudless, painfully blue skies; small figures moving far away in the vast distance.

Since the subdivision had been a field the year before we moved in, it hadn't had time to become the cluttered and crumbling jumble that marks most areas populated for any length of time by human beings anywhere in the world. Nor did it have any of the dense randomness of nature—there were trees, but seldom in pairs. The large tree off to the side of our house was surrounded by a neat oval of pebbles, like a pedestal. In the beginning, it was our only tree.

There just wasn't much there, and what *was* there was clean and from-the-box new—the light poles, the fire hydrants, the lawns, the bushes, everything. Flaws were readily apparent—a crack in the sidewalk, a slight depression in the yard—and thus took on special significance.

The people basically fit their surroundings. Everyone had a mom and a dad. Everyone was white. The men all had jobs. There were no particularly old people. There were no lunatics.

But children are creative, and they will supply what is missing if they need it badly enough. I needed, apparently, to be raised in some feverish Tennessee Williams clan, rattling around its familial gothic ruin: high, peeling ceilings; a sloping, rotted veranda; and bougainvillea overrunning the gnarled oak in the front yard.

I would have liked my father to be a minor functionary at the court of the Medici, coming home for dinner, his honorary gold medallion bobbing against his red velvet doublet as he sawed into a mutton chop, regaling us with tales of betrayal and intrigue. Instead, he was a scientist.

To those who have actually undergone disaster—whose homes have been washed away in floods, or who have fled into the night from invading armies, running blindly down pitch-black hillsides, with the dogs baying somewhere near—this next confession will no doubt seem a grotesque perversity on my part.

But I, too, wanted that. I was afraid of the dark, but I loved to have the lights go out. Sitting at the dining room table, around the flickering candles, I would imagine we were huddled, pathetic, in some abject garret, the rain pelting down outside. The electric company had broken down, not temporarily but forever. Soon we would be divvying up the canned food, skulking between the houses, using snow shovels to hunt squirrels. My sister, Debbie, and I had a game we called "Joe and Mack." Basically, Joe and Mack were two poor souls struggling in a torn-up world, constantly fleeing someone or something; and the entire game involved imagining the details. A typical episode, I recall, played while waiting in front of the house to be picked up for Sunday school, had the bushes as a bonfire and us warming our hands and cooking potatoes. Another time, in the back of the station wagon, on our way home from Grandma's house, we entertained ourselves by having Joe and Mack bathe their wounds in buckets of iodine.

But my sister became adept at ditching me and going off with her friends, so most of my play was solitary. Bobby and Ricky and Tommy and Danny and the other kids on the street were nice enough, I suppose, but I found their games pointless and tiresome and not at all tinged with the Grand Guignol I expected from playtime. Once the neighborhood coalition knocked on our door and asked me to come out to play kickball. I turned to my mother. "The guys are here," I said, sotto voce. "I have to go out. But wait twenty minutes, then call me in."

That's the sort of boy I was. "In" was where I wanted to be, playing in some corner by myself. Being trapped in some dire circumstance was a favorite pastime; often I would just roll into the small gap between the bed and the wall and lie there, happily pinned. My mother once frantically rushed outside, calling my name. I was inside, of course, in the kitchen, having climbed into a cabinet and pulled the door shut behind me. The cell was small and very dark.

When I did go outside, it was to continue conducting my own private investigation into the possibilities of disaster and ruin. One snowy day I had my mother pack me a tuna sandwich wrapped in foil. Dressed in my snowsuit, I placed the sandwich on the center of my Flexible Flyer sled and pulled it to the far corner of our third-of-an-acre yard.

Reaching that remote spot, I lay down in the snow and pulled the sled over me. Trapped, I spent a while savoring the acuteness of my plight, then groped for the sandwich, unwrapped and ate it, nourishing myself until my rescuers would arrive.

Similar in tone was the set-piece battle I fought with toy soldiers until so late in childhood—twelve, maybe thirteen—that toward the end it struck me as something obscene, a retardation.

Toy soldiers have a way of lagging a generation or two behind actual developments in military strategy. While doughboys were being slaughtered in trenches in World War I, their children back home were still massing battalions in geometric formation for the suicidal assaults of the Civil War. In the 1940s, lead soldiers still had World War I helmets; in the 1960s, we were still refighting World War II, an infinitely more satisfying conflict than the one going on at the time in Southeast Asia. Soldiers were rendered in colored plastic—green for the Americans, gray for the Germans, yellow for the Japanese. The Russians were blue, but they were hard to find. (Shortly after G.I. Joes were introduced, also in 1964, they were divided into the Allies and the Axis. I had a Wehrmacht infantryman G.I. Joe, who came complete with a MP38 submachine gun, a potato-masher grenade and his own little border-crossing station. My parents gave him to me for Hanukkah.)

Despite the army men being outfitted to fight at Salerno, or Anzio, or Normandy Beach, that was not the task I set out for them. My battles—identical and scripted as invariably as a Japanese Noh play—placed them in the medieval role of defending a castle against invaders.

First I constructed as elaborate a fortress as my store of blocks would permit. Every block was used, every time. Then I deployed my entire force of soldiers, half defending, half besieging. This alone could take several hours of careful setup.

The battle would begin. Soldiers were eliminated by my lightly touching the muzzle of a weapon and drawing an imaginary line to an opponent, who fell over dead. I had hundreds of men, and they killed each other one at a time.

In the process, the fortress would be quickly destroyed. Not utterly, not to rubble, but to a cluttered mess I viewed as a scenic ruin. I loved a good breached wall, a crumbling arch, a collapsed tower, a stairway to nothing. The battle would wind down amidst the wreckage, and would always end the same way—down to the last two soldiers, one from each side. One would kill the other, and the last would stand victorious for a moment, before a loose block from above would break free, crushing him. Finis.

AT THE OTHER end of the spectrum from the tiny, private flop of my magic trick was the sprawling, operatic disaster of the 1964 New York World's Fair, which my parents took me to the summer it opened, unaware they were handing me a facile literary transition to use thirty years later. They thought they were showing me Michelangelo's *Pietà*.

I did not know the fair was a dud at the time—all I remember are the antique car ride, the Orange Julius stands and the enormous U.S. Royal Tire Ferris Wheel. My Uncle Morty had a toy replica of the wheel on his basement bar, and I lusted after it. The *Pietà*, if I saw it, made no impression.

Despite enormous hype, the fair was pretty much a disappointment from day one, when fewer than 100,000 of the predicted 250,000 people attended the opening ceremony, itself a near fiasco, with miserable, rainy weather, chanting protesters and President

Johnson being forced to stop his speech for nearly half a minute while a New York Airways commuter helicopter passed low overhead.

Like the magic show, the fair's failure was due to blind imitation. The 1964 World's Fair was dreamed up by a quartet of New York business executives who, reminiscing at a 1959 luncheon over how great the 1939–40 World's Fair had been, decided to do it over again. All the changes in the meantime—World War II, the cold war, television, the space race, the civil rights movement—didn't affect the decision nearly as much as the neat symmetry of marking the twenty-fifth anniversary of the 1939 fair with another fair. Nor did anyone remember that the 1939 fair, despite its wild popularity, had paid back its investors thirty cents on the dollar.

The reprise fair was held at the same spot—Flushing Meadow, in Queens—and utilized some of the same buildings as the earlier fair. The same giant corporations that had delighted visitors in 1939 with "The World of Tomorrow" and its visions of gleaming cities and superhighways, trotted out the same, now-frayed images of a high-tech, high-consumption, concrete-and-plastic world. Bell Telephone unveiled Picturephones. General Motors predicted automobiles on the moon and in Antarctica, and pictured robot "jungle-road builders" automatically laying down superhighways through the rain forests, using laser beams "to saw off the age-old trees at their base." Westinghouse buried a time capsule, the unspoken implication being that our descendants will need clues as to what our culture had been like, after all traces of it are wiped from the earth in some self-induced cataclysm. Anthropologists of the future will think that our gods were a Beatles 45, a bikini, a Corning Ware platter and a box of detergent—some of the items in the capsule. Maybe they'll be right.

But 1964 was not the same as 1939. Life had changed. With urban problems beginning to manifest themselves, the fair's vision struck many, not as a dazzling promise to be worked toward, but as a futuristic nightmare to be avoided. "I saw no parks, no grass, no trees, though there may have been a few buried away on some sunless level below the soaring belts of concrete," wrote one critic, wondering "why the people of the future would be so willing to court acrophobia on the mountaintop or claustrophobia in the vasty deep."

The 1964 fair, whose theme was "Peace Through Understanding," had no blacks or Hispanics on its administrative staff of two hundred. In fact, few minorities were hired at any level, even as maintenance workers, and the fair became the focus for civil rights demonstrations. One reason for the low opening day attendance was that the Congress of Racial Equality was threatening to "block every street that can get you anywhere near the World's Fair and give New York the biggest traffic jam it's ever had," according to Isiah Brunson of CORE's Brooklyn chapter. To prevent this, the City of New York positioned tow trucks every few hundred yards along the expressways leading to Flushing Meadow, and conspicuously set up iron-barred detention cages to handle the rioters, who did not show.

The irony, of course, was that the racial protest and protoecological criticism swirling around the fair were a far closer approximation to what the next few decades held than any of the gleaming, homogenized Futuramas and Atomsvilles cooked up by far-seeing futurists who had planned the financial bomb.

FEW THINK ABOUT the 1964 New York World's Fair anymore, except perhaps motorists stuck in traffic near Flushing Meadow, forced to ponder the fair's hulking Unisphere, whose rings of orbiting satellites make it seem like a big atom, gleaming in the acid rain. Perhaps the fair's most enduring legacy is an episode of "The Flintstones" set at the fair. (Don't ask. A time machine was involved.)

The fair also gave birth to the "It's a Small World" pavilion, still delighting children at Disneyland and providing their parents with a fairly convincing preview of what Hell will be like.

The fair's twenty-fifth anniversary in 1989 passed with little note—no nostalgic businessmen this time planning an anniversary fair. By then, fairs had become outmoded tourist gimmicks. Anyone attend the 1982 fair in Knoxville? Anyone remember there *was* a fair in Knoxville?

While history obscures failure on the grand stage, within one's own personal life the opposite is true. Just as ancient insects that led full, productive lives disappeared without a trace, and those that bumbled into amber and died are still around in a tangible form, so our personal failures remain, sharp and clear, long after the day-to-day routine and minor victories fade into nothingness.

In fact, sometimes failure burns so brightly in memory, producing a shiver of shame whenever a particular incident is recalled, that many years must pass before it can be stared at directly.

In August 1973, my family went to Montreal for a summer vacation. Having grown up in a suburb of Cleveland, an American League baseball town, I of course wanted to see the Montreal Expos of the National League play, and hounded my parents during the long road trip. My mother, thinking she was being clever, agreed that if the Atlanta Braves were playing in Montreal, we could go see a game—Henry Aaron was racing toward Babe Ruth's all-time home run record at the time, and even a mom could understand the utility of seeing Aaron hit a home run.

The odds were heavily in her favor, but she lost. Not only were the Braves playing, but they were staying at our hotel, the Queen Elizabeth. This was before greed ruined baseball, and kids could mingle with the players freely, hovering around and getting autographs. Freddy Velazquez, a second-string catcher, carried my little brother, Sam, on his shoulders. Henry Aaron graciously paused from his breakfast to sign a baseball. Phil Niekro hit me in the mouth. He didn't mean to. A group of Braves were standing around the lobby, talking. I was swooning at their elbow. Niekro came up and told one of them he had a phone call. The player asked where. Niekro shot an arm out, pointing, into the space where my head happened to be. He was very apologetic. (I was delighted.)

So we went to the game, hoping to see Aaron hit a home run. As Aaron stood at the plate in the sixth inning, waiting for a pitch, I for some reason noticed Sam's shirt was hiked up in the back, underwear showing. Looking down, I reached over to pull his shirt into place. There was a crack of the bat. The crowd roared. I looked up, to see Henry beginning to round the bases. A home run.

At the time, I was mortified. He hit the home run and I missed it. Fussing with my little brother's shirt, I failed my chance to witness history.

But in doing so, I memorialized a small gesture—one that I had no doubt performed hundreds of times, but that was now seared into my brain, coupled with the horror of having missed Aaron's mighty swing. Today, of course, I value the image of that small tug of prissy older brother concern much more than I would value having seen the slash that led to home run No. 703.

But it took me years to realize that.

FAILURE IS, above all else, a function of time, of framework and perspective.

Much failure is self-assigned, an interpretation open to debate. "I must make some great efforts during the next few years, however, if I wish not to have been on the whole a failure," Henry James wrote in his diary at age thirty-nine, already internationally famous, having written *Daisy Miller* and *The Portrait of a Lady*, among other works. "I shall have been a failure unless I do something *great!*"

Everyone feels this to some degree. Most of my friends, upon discovering the subject of this book, immediately said, in a jokey and embarrassing way, "Well, I'm sure you're going to include *me*." I always took this as a plea for compliments and uttered something soothing. But I was tempted to say, "Why, yes, *of course*, it wouldn't be a failure book without *you* in it. In fact, *you're* going to be the central element, the leitmotif, as it were . . ."

These friends are all leading basically happy and productive lives. What they meant was that, in a Henry James sense, they had not done their particular great thing, whatever it was they had decided at one point they were destined to do. Neither did I; I was supposed to write the 1980s version of *This Side of Paradise* while my mom left sandwiches outside my door, just as F. Scott's mom did. Only I never got around to finishing the task, despite many beginnings, and now it's too late.

No matter how perceived failures sting, however, they do not have the consequences of real failure. That is something of a tautology, since the definition of real failure is the presence of true consequences—a fall, as opposed to a neglect to climb.

In 1813, Napoleon was emperor of France. He lived in the Tuileries Palace above cellars of gold and enjoyed the perquisites of a king. In 1814, he was a prisoner of the British, exiled to the island of Elba. The difference was real.

Courvoisier was on to something when they chose Napoleon as their poster boy for cognac. Napoleon encompasses the thorny, tangled nature of failure, the way it can uplift while it destroys, the quizzical pairing of downfall and glory, the siren beauty of ruin.

Napoleon is buried in Paris in a massive sarcophagus of dark red Finnish porphyry under the great Dome des Invalides, which used to be a royal chapel and was, in that adaptive way the French have, changed into a tomb for the emperor's remains when they were returned from St. Helena in 1840.

The Invalides isn't the best place for a tomb. The sarcophagus is in a wide circular pit and you can't see it until you walk inside and peer over a rail. It's as if the statue of Lincoln in the Lincoln Memorial were at the bottom of a well and you had to stand on a box and look down to see it.

But with its crustings of gilt and crystal, its stained glass, its lush stone Doric columns and human hearts in marble boxes, the Invalides is the perfect spot to contemplate the shifting frameworks of failure.

Was Napoleon a failure? Well, he did fail mightily, grasping for the world, ending up with dust. But on the other hand, one could argue, he did grow up from humble Corsican origins to rule all of France and most of Europe, seizing the crown from the Pope's hands to place it on his own head. Not every corporal who graduated from Napoleon's military academy got to rule France. In fact, just Napoleon.

On the other hand, he tried to conquer Europe and ended up caged like a beast (metaphorically, that is) on Elba, exiled in disgrace, the Ogre, hated by millions. A failure.

But then he got away and almost pulled off an amazing comeback, with his exciting sprint back to Paris, until the British recaged him and sent him to an even more remote spot, St. Helena, where he read a lot and took long baths and wrote his memoirs and complained about the food and sniped at his jailer until he finally died in 1821.

So he ended up a failure. With our love of narrative and our blurring of fact and fiction, we tend to judge lives by how they end, as if they were a story. Napoleon's turned out badly in the end. He failed.

But what about his reputation? After a few short years of ignoring his legacy, the French decided that maybe Napoleon hadn't been so bad. They fetched his body from St. Helena and, with maximum pomp and honors, interred it in Paris.

So he ended up a hero, which he remains today. He is certainly among the handful of historical characters who have captivated the imagination of the world—some writers compare him to Jesus. That's success, isn't it?

The question is not whether Napoleon was an overall "failure" but, rather, why we still care. The answer is, if a historical failure takes place on a grand enough scale, it assumes the emotional impact of failures within our own lives. Napoleon himself recognized that his exile would elevate him and keep his name vibrant and real as the centuries passed. Had he taken a musket ball at Waterloo, he would have become just another lifeless nineteenth-century historical figure. Wellington. Talleyrand. Metternich. Napoleon. Yawn.

The failure, the suffering, the banishments to Elba and St. Helena, beatified him, giving us common people something to relate to. Defeat does that. Lincoln, Martin Luther King, Joan of Arc, Moses —all the truly great figures in history end in some sort of failure or tragedy. (Moses, for those who've forgotten, irked God once, so He let him die just short of the promised land. Kind of mean, really.) Christianity might not have become as popular as it did if, at the end of the New Testament, Jesus had got down from the cross, retired to Samaria and raised figs.)

The dark shades of failure illuminate a different and enlightening brand of history. The world seen through the screen of failure appears more genuine, more human, more funny. Past events seem more real, less mythical, less polished. Failure can be a guide, helping us shake off erroneous generalities and briskly contemplate the face of things that otherwise are too often ignored—a handy tool to dredge up the forgotten and to celebrate the shunned. Too often we are satisfied with parsing the tired minutiae of the familiar and famous, rolling in the memories of Elvis and Marilyn and Madonna, scraping every detail from the successful. It is both a duty and a joy to turn our gaze away occasionally, to seek out failure and to probe its mysteries.

—Neil Steinberg
January 3, 1994
Chicago

ONE

Tragically Defunct

Product Failure

FOUND THE large green bottle years ago on the dusty bottom shelf of a grocery store in Weirton, West Virginia. After pouring out the soda, I wrapped the bottle and carefully transported it home. Since then, I've displayed it like a trophy, sometimes on a shelf in my office, sometimes in the kitchen.

The bottle—a hefty 28-ounce container for 7-Up—is a relic from another time, long before the company's irritating, upside-down Uncola imagery, or the idiotic, mischievous Dots. The design still has the clean tang of the 1920s about it, with a square orange art deco shield proclaiming "7-Up" amidst seven little rising bubbles.

And three times, twice on the neck and once on the back, is emblazoned what, to me, has to be the most brash and engaging, twee and ridiculous slogan in the entire history of advertising: "You like it. It likes you."

There are many reasons to love that slogan. The first sentence is pure moxie: "You like it." A direct statement of fact, bordering on a command. Nothing more is really necessary. But then comes the second, incredible bit of anthropomorphism, "It likes you," striking with all the impact of a surprise valentine from a secret admirer. The soda *likes* you, loves you even, and is sitting in the store, pining away, wondering where you are, when you are coming by. Yearning for the touch of your lips.

That pretty much sums up my view of consumer products, especially foods. I like them; they like me. I know it's a childish irrationality, but there you are.

I want to say immediately that these feelings weren't packed into my head by some slick advertising agency. Ads rarely affect me—they're always babbling on about salt and calories and wholesome goodness and other things I don't care a bit about. If memory serves, I've never seen an ad for Hostess Sno Balls—those familiar hemispherical marshmallow domes, furred with white coconut, lined with chocolate cake and centered with a heart of creme. Yet I have feelings for them. They extract a certain sympathy, hunched there in the store. So artificial; so without corollary among the foodstuffs of the planet. Their odd peripheral nature is underscored by the fact that Hostess thinks nothing of dyeing production runs for holidays—pink for Easter, orange for Halloween, green for St. Patrick's Day. What other product can even be considered a relative? Cupcakes? Macaroons? No, Sno Balls are unique to the point of freakishness.

The most popular and heavily advertised products—Coca-Cola, for instance, or Wheaties—do nothing for me. They are arrogant; they lack the sense of marginality, of quaintness, that inspires ardor. McDonald's, for instance, is too much of the whore to love—ubiquitous, tarted-up in plastic and primary colors, trying to please everyone. How could something so promiscuous ever hope to compete with, say, the anachronistic pale gleam of a White Castle, with its risible corporate motto ("Buy 'Em by the Sack") and its narrow, unchanging product line of tiny sebaceous, cubelike burgers?

Even more affecting are products that are no longer manufactured, items whose personalities have been intensified by rarity and failure and a sense of time passed. I'm not referring to old ads, plastered on the walls of prefab, faux-Irish megapubs. They are too artificially invigorated by the circus of pinewood rec rooms and ladies in crinoline skirts and men chomping on pipes, all fawning over the extinct product, plus the copywriter's hyperbole, still echoing, if hollowly, after all these years—"It's Branderschläger beer time!"

Rather, my affection is reserved for the products themselves, or at least their containers. They no longer belong to platoons of identical soldiers lined up shoulder to shoulder on grocery racks, ready for duty, but are the lone survivors of decimated battalions, stragglers cut off from their units, unexpectedly discovered hiding in odd places—dismal curio shops; back shelves of basement closets; stockrooms of fading businesses—like those Japanese holdovers from World War II who for a time kept popping up on remote South Pacific islands.

Nicholson Baker, a novelist whose exacting eye notices everything except perhaps atoms flitting through air, sums up this feeling perfectly when he describes the "black, weighted Duesenberg" of an old Scotch tape dispenser as being "grandiose and Biedermeier and tragically defunct."

The tragedy lies not so much in the lost personalities of failed products—which in most cases weren't in actual use long enough for people to become familiar with. Rather, it is the mist of doomed hopes, aspirations and attitudes enveloping these products that tugs at the heart.

In the late 1960s Ronson, the lighter-fluid company, started selling a line of candles that ran on butane. They came in brushed aluminum, copper and rosewood finishes and were dubbed Varaflame Butane Candles. They were intended, if the box is any indication, to replace wax candles on festive occasions.

Take a moment to savor the assumptions underlying such a

product. First, some Ronson executive had to conclude that the problem with selling butane for cigarette lighters was that they are used so momentarily. Cigarettes are too easy to light. The heaviest smoker can be expected to light a lighter for only a second or two at a time, even on windy days. If only a way could be found to get people to burn their lighters continuously, for hours at a time. Think of the butane they'd use.

What would you call a lighter that needed to be lit for long stretches? Of course—a candle.

You have to admire such yearning, wistful greed—it's as if a margarine company started dipping their product in chocolate and selling it in the freezer section along with Eskimo Pies and Popsicles. Since no one could reasonably be expected to buy fake candles for themselves, the candles were presented as something to give to others at Christmas. Ronson was trying to position itself as a maker of gifts (butane-burning gifts, mostly, such as fondue sets), and thus the candles fit perfectly into its general marketing strategy.

In order for Ronson to have a chance at repackaging lighters as brushed-aluminum faux candles, they first had to find fault with traditional wax candles, a product unchanged for millennia.

Here the engorged futurism of the times revealed itself in full poignant bloom. Apollo rockets were bravely traveling to the moon, a destination where we had convinced ourselves we would all someday live in mazes of interconnected geodesic domes. Couples would dine on artificial food while Moog synthesizers burbled on the quadra-phonic stereo. Wax candles, of course, would not fit in—they are messy, they drip, they smoke, they burn down to nothing and, worse, you can't adjust their flame to suit your changing mood.

Varaflame.

"Low for intimate dinners," read an ad. "Medium for dinner parties . . . high for swinging soirees."

The candles did not flop, in and of themselves. People bought them. It was Ronson that flopped, turning out overengineered products nobody wanted to pay for. The candles cost as much as $30 and were abandoned, along with Ronson's entire consumer goods business, in 1981.

Given the times, the Ronson executives cannot be faulted too severely for birthing such a quizzical product. The future was here. About the same time that Ronson introduced Varaflame candles, Pillsbury came out with Space Food Sticks, foil-wrapped fingers of chocolate, vanilla and strawberry candy with the consistency of clay —sort of like a mushy Tootsie Roll. They were supposed to be similar to what astronauts ate, and did quite well for a number of years. And Tang orange drink substance—invented in 1959 but forever associated with the space-race era—is still with us today, a puzzling contradiction to all familiar concepts of gustation.

Despite occasional success, businesses that introduce futuristic products are generally hobbled by a form of flawed thinking more subtle and complex than mere optimism-stoked greed. This pervasive, enduring fallacy I have long referred to as the Arthur C. Clarke Syndrome.

Clarke, the science fiction writer best known for *2001: A Space Odyssey*, was a particular favorite of mine when I was in my mid-teens. I read at least a dozen of his novels and short story collections— such as *Earthlight*, *Childhood's End*, and *A Fall of Moondust*—and in my quest for more titles, I stumbled upon *Report on Planet Three*, Clarke's nonfiction musings on what he sincerely believed the future held for mankind. Written in 1972, perhaps by the light of Varaflame candles, *Report* saw a world of limitless growth and potential, where people lived on the moon, and on Mars; where they didn't have to work because machines did everything; and where the only problem was encouraging everybody to consume hugely and quickly enough so that the products pouring out of automatic factories would not start to pile up and create a clutter.

I could never read Clarke again. What was entertaining as science fiction struck me as unforgivably stupid when presented as fact, even as a prediction of potential fact. Though just fifteen years old and as worldly as a minnow, I was able to marvel at Clarke's naive and blinkered point of view, one that ignored a basic reality: the bulk of the world's population is scratching in the dust with a stick to get by and always will be. How could even the most starry-eyed Pollyanna contemplate the massive national concentration of money and energy required just to get a handful of joyless Air Force colonels to the moon and then extrapolate it endlessly into the future? Clarke's vision was so utopian, so dripping with hubris, that it made me fear backlash. All his predictions of space colonies and miracle inventions forced me to sadly conclude that I would end my days crouched at the mouth of a cave, scoffed at by my berry-smeared offspring as I tried to convince them of the technical marvels mankind had achieved when it peaked in my youth.

Though I lost a favorite author, I did gain the outline of what has become a convenient intellectual tool for categorizing folly, namely the Clarke Syndrome, which I define as: "The belief that because something can be done, it will or should be done."

Two delusions, then, figure largely in many product failures—first, the flawed corporate consensus, a sort of organizational genetic inbreeding where groups of highly paid executives commit themselves to chase fanciful, almost fevered dreams based on absolutely nothing at all; and second, the Clarke Syndrome, with its tunnel vision and hydrogen bomb–maker's morality, seizing on anything attractively new and deciding it will rule the future.

Both these phenomena, along with another cameo appearance by the gaseous hydrocarbon butane (which one can almost begin to imagine, exerts some sort of malign force on the world), can plainly be seen in the stillbirth of Premier cigarettes, one of the great product disasters of recent years.

All those who believe "corporate thinking" to be an oxymoron can only sit back and enjoy the saga of Premier, billed by R. J. Reynolds as a breakthrough in technology—a smokeless cigarette—when it was thrust upon the world, quite briefly, in late 1989.

The Premier story begins in the early 1980s, when Reynolds, brooding over the mounting outcry against smoking in general and against secondhand smoke in particular, decided that the answer to all this fuss was to develop a cigarette which would burn with a discrete, internal heat and therefore produce little or no smoke. Wouldn't that be great?

Research started in 1982, and after five years and hundreds of millions of dollars spent developing the new product, Reynolds had its smokeless cigarette, a device of Frankensteinian complexity based on a superheated piece of carbon. Sucking on the cigarette pulled hot air from the glowing carbon through a filter of tobacco and around an aluminum "flavor capsule" that released nicotine and smoke taste, which then passed through a regular filter and into the smiling, satisfied mouth of the consumer.

In theory.

In actuality, there were several major problems, the first being that you couldn't light the cigarette with a match or even with a regular lighter. Either would create "impurities" that would ruin the cigarette's already inferior taste. Not that this made a lot of sense. My theory is that a match didn't burn hotly enough to force flame through the six tiny holes at the business end of a Premier and ignite whatever glowing-ember device made the thing work. The little four-page instruction book affixed to the back of each pack suggested, on its final page, a "good-quality butane lighter like the disposable Scripto Electra XL."

Even if they lighted the cigarettes in the prescribed manner, however, some people who tried Premiers reported that it was hard to draw anything out of them—an experience common enough to be dubbed "the hernia effect" by Reynolds researchers.

Smokers also reported that Premiers tasted bad and smelled worse, one comparing them to "burning plastic," another to a substance that smells very bad indeed and is never tasted at all, if one is lucky.

Then there was the fire hazard. Unlike regular cigarettes, Premiers never burned down, and so it was not readily apparent when a Premier was finished. "You will know your Premier is out when it is no longer warm and you no longer get smoke," suggested the booklet. "Be sure it is out before discarding."

Packs of Premiers also cost more. And to top it off, the cigarette's lone advantage—it didn't have the smoke that causes cancer—couldn't be mentioned by Reynolds, which of course has never publicly recognized that cigarette smoke is dangerous to your health in the first place, a policy stance pernicious enough to make the most agnostic liberal yearn for a vengeful God and His fiery Hell. Reynolds tried to fudge, naturally, claiming the cigarette was "cleaner"— not subtly claiming it either. "Cleaner enjoyment than you may ever have thought possible. We're confident you will appreciate the cleaner taste, the cleaner aroma, the cleaner feel of a new Premier," squawked the little booklet, repeating the word "cleaner" ten times in its four tiny pages. Reynolds hoped, obviously, that smokers would read between the lines and understand "healthier."

Consumers may not have understood what Reynolds was trying to say, but health watchdogs certainly did, and fell upon the brand like ravening beasts. C. Everett Koop, the surgeon general, denounced the cigarette as a "drug delivery system" and the Food and Drug Administration threatened to classify it as such. So self-deluded were the Reynolds team developing Premier—*The Wall Street Journal* called them "wishful"—that they actually hoped health advocates would embrace Premier as a healthful alternative to real cigarettes, an outcome about as likely as gun control advocates endorsing realistic toy guns for kids because they aren't as dangerous as the real thing.

These problems might have caused another company to delay launching the cigarette, perhaps until it could be refined and improved. But Premier was ballyhooed at a press conference (a move some felt was calculated to boost RJR stock prices). After that it was a race to disaster. The cigarettes went on sale in October 1989 in selected cities.

Reynolds officials estimated that it would take a week for motivated consumers to get the hang of smoking Premiers, provided they bought a good butane lighter and read the little instruction book. It was a lot of bother, but Reynolds figured smokers would be concerned enough about their health to make the effort. This was another comical lapse in logic, since smokers are, by definition, a group that cares less about health than does the general public, or why would they smoke? This lesson should have been learned in 1977, when RJR introduced their biggest flop prior to Premier: Real cigarettes, billed as an "all natural" cigarette. "Through sophisticated market research techniques, we have included the consumer and his thoughts and reactions in every step of this product's development," said an RJR executive in a statement that should be in the dictionary under "hubris." "We think Real will be the most successful new brand introduction in the recent history of the cigarette business." The Real brand was withdrawn in 1980, despite massive promotion.

Premier didn't last nearly as long. It was ignored by smokers and attacked by critics who saw Premier as an insidious dodge to weaken the case against cigarettes. The final nail in the Premier coffin was the leveraged buyout of Reynolds, which plunged the company into debt and encouraged the casting off of expensive experiments. Premier—whose tab was by then $325 million and rising—was unceremoniously dumped in February 1990, four months after being introduced, though not without some typically harsh soul-searching by the Reynolds company.

"We do not consider this to be a failure," said Betsy J. Annese, a Reynolds flack, pointing out that for its $325 million the R. J. Reynolds Tobacco Company had learned valuable lessons. Maybe they learned that consumers might be interested in a cigarette that wouldn't kill them, provided it didn't taste like shit and you could light it with a match.

Another example of the Clarke Syndrome in action can be found in the Corfam shoe calamity. Well known to students of business failure, Corfam was a synthetic shoe leather substitute concocted by Du Pont in the 1950s. Their operating theory was that leather, the preferred substance for footwear since Neolithic times, was no good anymore because it wore out.

Corfam certainly didn't wear out. It didn't crack, didn't scar and didn't dry out. Rather, as *Time* magazine noted, it "wore like armor plate." And, like armor plate, Corfam was not particularly comfortable, since it didn't gradually form itself to fit an individual foot the way leather does. It did not break in. Also, like armor, Corfam was hot—it made your feet sweat. And expensive—it was one of the rare cases where an inferior imitation cost more than the original it was supposed to replace. Perhaps Du Pont should have explored the possibility of using Corfam, not for shoes, but for lining the hulls of battleships.

Somehow, the implications of these drawbacks escaped Du Pont during its exhaustive tests of the polymer. Over 20,000 trial pairs of

Corfam shoes were made by two hundred different manufacturers, and test subjects were given special pairs of shoes, with Corfam on one foot and leather on the other, without being told which was which. The substance was introduced in 1964 to great fanfare—in twenty years, Du Pont predicted, one out of four shoes in America would be a Corfam shoe.

But Corfam turned out to be a product without a market. The market for cheap shoes was soon dominated by PVC plastics—a fashion trend that caught Du Pont entirely by surprise. And leather was still preferred for expensive shoes. Then there was the hellbroth of fake leather turned out by competitors—Aztran, Pedura, Porvair and Clarino—competing for the attention of those with a desire for uncomfortable fake-leather shoes.

Corfam shoes did not utterly flop—40 million pairs were sold in 1968—but profits had to be kept low to keep them competitive. By the time Du Pont shrugged its shoulders and gave up in 1971, over $250 million had been lost on Corfam.

Some of the most amusing product failures are foodstuffs, since food companies seem to take a throw-it-against-the-wall-and-see-what-sticks attitude toward developing new products. In 1964 (which by now you should realize was a watershed year for failure), both Kellogg's and Post introduced cornflakes with freeze-dried fruit. Post offered three varieties of fruit: blueberries, peaches, and strawberries; Kellogg's had only bananas. The idea was that when you poured on milk, the dried fruits would rehydrate and, voilà, cereal with fruit! The problem was, by the time the fruit absorbed the milk, the cereal was soggy. And even when the fruit did reanimate, it didn't taste like fresh fruit, which was becoming increasingly available year-round.

A TREASURE-HOUSE OF failed products has been collected by Robert McMath, a business consultant in Ithaca, New York. Called the New Products Showcase and Learning Center, the collection displays discontinued products as a cautionary lesson to manufacturers, who pay large fees to wander through the center and learn from the mistakes of the past. Or at least *try* to learn from the mistakes of the past: Companies as a rule endlessly mimic each other's errors, repeating every blunder short of bringing back thalidomide or radioactive watch faces.

For some reason the press has dubbed McMath's center a "museum," conjuring up images of a Corfam shoe mounted on a pedestal, or a Lucite wall tracing the history of the Betamax. Actually, the showcase is a large, chilly warehouse with a high ceiling and tall industrial shelves displaying jumbles of extinct product containers— some with their contents removed to prevent bug infestation, others inexplicably left full to horribly putrefy with the passing years, the captive foodstuffs punching holes in jar lids and blowing up glass bottles. (Spaghetti sauce seems to be a particularly vicious substance, refusing to be confined for any great period of time.)

The showcase didn't start by focusing on failure—McMath was merely collecting new and intriguing forms of packaging for use in his lecturing and consulting work. But with 90 percent of all new products ultimately failing, his collection soon turned into a morgue for marketing dreams—80,000 containers, he estimates, representing billions of dollars of development expense, all in vain.

McMath himself is a very tall, severe man with a gray beard and the beginnings of a belly. Constantly busy with the demands of the media, or at least liking to appear so, he leaves most fine points of civility to his wife of thirty-five years, Jean, a tall, elegant woman who helps him in the business and is curator of the showcase.

The containers, Jean explains, as McMath strides off purposefully to attend to business, are grouped thematically, under headings such as "clam sauces," "pasta sauces," "soups," "cookies." She is a constant aid to her husband, refreshing his memory when it lags, hauling across town to pick up stray products left at another office, straining to be helpful while staying in the shadows. Robert Mc-Math, who has a hidden reserve of sweetness under all his Scottish austerity, breaks character from time to time to give his wife credit. "Actually, Jean could do this," he says.

In the front of the warehouse, McMath's favorite product flops are grouped for easy access. The high-profile flops are usually the result of some simple flaw in packaging or presentation. For instance, Wine & Dine dinners from Heublein were basically packaged dinners that came with a little bottle of wine. Not a bad idea for consumers who wanted a little wine along with their chicken Madeira dinner but didn't want to crack an entire bottle. Unfortunately, it was cooking wine—spiced and salty—which customers were supposed to pour into the product as they prepared it. Needless to say, people tended to drink the wine accidentally—despite a little graphic of a bottle pouring into a skillet on the box and "Not for Beverage Use" in fancy script on the bottle label—an experience that didn't exactly inspire consumers to buy the dinners again.

Had Heublein called the product "Don't Drink the Wine!," it might have done better. But then again, given the number of people who pour Lemon Pledge on ice cream, maybe not.

Sometimes, simply the source of the item can cause a problem. Gerber, the baby food company, was faced with the dilemma that its customers were always outgrowing Gerber products. So, forgetting its slogan, "Babies are our business . . . our only business!" Gerber created Singles, grown-up dishes like sweet-and-sour pork, beef burgundy and creamed beef, which the company unwisely chose to package in the same little jars used for its mainstay products. McMath says the meals were "perceived as baby food" and the name, which "connotes loneliness," didn't help either.

Similarly, Reddi Wip, forgetting how closely its name was linked to fake whipped cream, introduced Reddi Bacon—precooked bacon in a foil pouch to be dropped into the toaster. But the two products did not sit well together on the plate of the mind, and consumers rejected the newer one. Also, fat from the packet dripped into the toaster and caught fire, a common problem for failed toaster products. The Electric French Fry, a board of fries popped into the toaster, then broken apart for eating, did the same thing. Downyflake Toaster Eggs didn't burn. They were just disgusting.

Many companies try to stretch their names into unusual areas and fail. Dad's Root Beer offered Root Beer–Flavored Milk and found few takers. Pepsi offered flavored versions of its product, Pepsi Raging Razzberry and Pepsi Tropical Chill. Colgate toothpaste tried to leap into the food business with Colgate Kitchen Entrees, though the thinking behind the effort is difficult to imagine ("Toothpaste . . . goes in the mouth . . . and . . . so . . . does . . . food"). Colgate also failed with Bite 'N Brush, a chewable toothpaste in tablet form. Jell-O thought it could extend its line of fruit-flavored gelatin by introducing Jell-O for Salads, with flavors such as mixed vegetable, tomato and celery. It couldn't.

Campbell's has had a lot of trouble finding success in areas other than soup. Its Souper Combo and Souper Supper were both attempts to sell the food that people typically eat along with their soup, but neither worked. Ditto for a line of crackers to go into soup.

Sometimes, Campbell's even managed to fail with soup. Once, the company introduced a line of no-salt soups, changing its familiar red can to a bright blue. The soup failed because without salt it tasted lousy. But the red Campbell's soup can is such an ingrained cultural artifact that changing it to shocking blue couldn't have helped. The result looked unnatural, almost terrifying—the sort of thing Campbell's would use to package a new line of radioactive soups: "Plutonium and Stars," "Cream of Deuterium," "Heavy Broth."

In 1980 Cracker Jack tried the novel approach of selling just the peanuts from its confection, without the popcorn—sort of like Lucky Charms selling packages of just the marshmallow treats. Another attempt, Cracker Jack cereal, went nowhere as well, despite a free surprise inside.

Some products just have bad names. The worst name on any product in McMath's showcase comes, surprisingly, from a major company, Nestea. Its carbonated, lemon-flavored, yellowish tea might have tasted swell, but it was called . . . (Ready? Drum roll, please) . . . Tea Whiz.

Perhaps the most poignant containers in McMath's collection are ones where the sheer desperation of the manufacturer managed somehow to show through. The saddest has to be Tri-Me, a blue laundry detergent concentrate, whose plea apparently went unheard. 7-Up also offered a line of flavored sodas with the wan and hopeful name of Howdy! Then there was Goff's Low Ash cat food ("contains only 1.5 percent ash"), which may have been designed to appeal to those knowledgeable about cat food ingredients, but still seems akin to naming a frankfurter "Few Mouse Hairs." Also, the kitty on the Goff label looks about to burst into tears.

Then there are the also-rans. Almost every successful foodstuff has, at one time or another, spawned imitations that tried to leach off the successful product's name. Near the 7-Up containers at Mc-Math's showcase are such knockoffs as Lucky 7 ("A crystal clear lemon 'n' lime") and Upper 10 ("The *perfect* lemon-lime soda").

Knockoffs have been around almost as long as brand names.

Nabisco's Uneeda biscuit—one of the first successful national brands—was challenged by Iwanta, Uwanta, Ulika Bis-Kit, and I-lika soda crackers, all of which were quashed in court.

To generate speaking engagements and attract new business, Mc-Math needs to keep his name in the media, and while I visit him he spends six hours with a team from Canadian television, picking various products off his shelves and saying something about them. Since there are successful products, too, on the shelves of the showcase, there is always the risk that McMath will be pontificating about dreadful flops while standing before some company's as-yet-to-nose-dive entry. Needless to say, it makes the companies unhappy.

"What are we talking about here?" asks Jean McMath, leaping up and taking control of the setup of a shot. "You're talking about failures—honey, sit over there." Jean pulls various still-viable products off the shelves and moves them out of camera range. "That's brand-new—move that up there," she says, grabbing a jar of Taster's Choice flavored coffee. "Jeez-Louise!" She turns to the cameraman. "Are you seeing this shelf?" Against a backdrop of certified flubs, the interview with McMath continues.

THE TOY BUSINESS is particularly prone to disaster, since children are the objects of special, not to say excessive, concern.

In the late 1970s Ideal Toy Corp. bought a small company's concept for toy figures called Fairies. The toy was a cute little doll with mechanically fluttering wings. "A guy at Ideal had an NIH problem—Not Invented Here," recalled a toy industry insider. "So he had to piss on it, insisting on changing it to Angel Babies. So now they were these chunky little toddlers with halos and wings. They lived on clouds, played harps—very cute."

The toys went into production and were debuted—as most new toys are—in an elaborate display at the New York Toy Fair.

But none of the store buyers at the toy fair would order Angel Babies, bringing up an objection that, during the entire development process, had never occurred to anyone at Ideal. The insider remembered: "The buyers said, 'OK, Angel Babies—they're dead babies, right? Babies that died and now they're in heaven.' Nobody would touch it."

Ideal was also responsible for one of the toy industry's most legendary toy failures. In 1958 the company introduced a 9-inch Christ Child doll, which came packed in its own little manger, with a beatific cardboard Mary and Joseph kneeling on either side.

The toy baby Jesus was in the classic medieval portrait pose, on His back, legs kicking, wrists bent back in a gesture of benediction. He wore a white loincloth, and His blond hair was cut in a Prince Valiant style.

Needless to say, horrified parents refused to buy the doll—they couldn't imagine the Lord attending tea parties with Raggedy Ann, Buster Bear and a sock monkey. Each Ideal employee was given one of the unsold dolls at Christmas, and the rest of the plastic Saviors were buried in a landfill.

For those curious about what prompted Ideal to such an error, the story is that Ben Michtom, Ideal's president at the time, had met with the Pope while on a visit to Italy in 1957 and was so moved he felt the doll to be a good idea, forcing it on dubious underlings.

In general, direct life experience seems to be a bad idea for top toy executives. In the 1960s, a Wham-O bigwig was vacationing in Africa when he noticed fish appearing in a dry lake bed that had filled in after a rainstorm. This led to the creation of Instant Fish, packets of dried fish eggs that would hatch when water was added. But Wham-O marketed the product before they had established a steady supply of that particular breed of African fish. Able to fill only 2 percent of the orders placed, Wham-O was forced to discontinue the fish.

The lessons of Instant Fish were lost on Creative Playthings, which in 1968 introduced the Animal of the Month Club, sending out real live animals such as snails, musk turtles, Mongolian gerbils and newts to its young subscribers. There were two problems. First, like Wham-O with Instant Fish, Creative Playthings had trouble tracking down enough of any specific exotic pet to meet the huge demand. And second, the animals tended to arrive dead, a situation that could have worked had the company advertised them that way —"New from Creative Playthings! Dead Animals at Your Door!"— but was scuttled by the element of surprise.

Getting back to dolls, a failure on a par with baby Jesus was the Baby Joey doll, introduced to capitalize on the publicity surrounding the Christmas 1975 birth of Mike and Gloria Stivik's baby on "All in the Family." The manufacturers made one fatal miscalculation: they gave Baby Joey a penis. Anatomically correct dolls had been standard in Europe for years, but the company underestimated the lunatic puritanism of the American public. There was an outcry about Baby Joey and his penis. Crazed religious fanatics took to breaking the packages open in stores and hacking the penises off. The doll had to be yanked from the market.

The Baby Joey doll—a superior product doomed by momentary social conditions—points to the importance of timing when dealing with new products. A decade later, endowed toys were no big deal.

Many failed products are just ahead of their time. For years, dairymen were frustrated by the public perception that yogurt was for the old and the infirm. Several giant ad agencies labored mightily, but nothing could successfully promote yogurt until the nation slowly, like an ocean liner changing course, turned away from its thick-steak-and-plenty-of-sour-cream-on-that-potato-thanks ways and became more health-conscious. As soon as emaciated joggers started grazing on sprouts and dry grass, yogurt suddenly looked appetizing, and the stage was set for a rise in its popularity.

Being ahead of the times is not nearly so common a problem as being behind the times. The curve arcs upward, reaches a zenith and falls back, and somebody is always caught napping—the lone trombonist marching straight ahead after the band has taken a hard right turn.

This was the case with the Edsel, which everyone knows as the Great American Überfailure without realizing exactly what was it that made the Edsel fail. It wasn't that the car was ugly, at least no uglier than other cars of the 1958 season. And it wasn't the name, necessarily, though that is what gets the blame. (Look at the Lincoln, which is not a name that denotes either sexiness or speed. If anything, the name suggests premature violent death, yet it has lasted over fifty years.) Other long-lived bad car names are the Probe, which women began referring to as the "Speculum," and the Nova, which had trouble in Spanish-speaking countries because *no va* means "won't go" in Spanish.

Rather, automobiles had been getting progressively flashier and gizmo-laden, and just when the Edsel arrived—"more uselessly over-powered, more gadget bedecked, more hung with expensive accessories than any car in its price class," as *Consumer Reports* lamented at the time—people simply got sick of excess. Remember, 1958 was the year that the Volkswagen Beetle first became big in America. Beetle certainly was every bit as bad a name as Edsel, and was further tarred with the stigma of having been conceived by Hitler, which would initially seem to have put the Beetle at a competitive disadvantage to the Edsel until, of course, one examined the politics of Henry Ford.

Before letting the subject go, I should point out that the absolute worst car name was introduced in 1994, the Impact, General Motors' entry into the electric car business. Critics say that GM wants the Impact to fail in order to preserve the company's investment in the internal combustion engine. If this is true, they certainly picked the right name—perhaps only the "Fireball" or the "Electroshock" would have been more suited to their apparent purpose.

The ultimate example of stretching a technology beyond its limits, then having it lopped off by new developments, is the case of RCA's introduction of SelectaVision: the final gasp of Thomas Edison's phonograph, an Irish Elk with grooves, its giant horns caught in a thicket.

SelectaVision was really an amazing, if rococo, device. A tiny diamond stylus tracked through a fine groove wound 27,000 times across a vinyl disc. The stylus vibrated, but instead of creating sound, like a record, it created a moving image. I can't imagine how, but apparently it worked. RCA spent fifteen years and $200 million developing SelectaVision, finally bringing it to market in 1981.

Almost as soon as it hit the stores, SelectaVision was declared an amusing antique. Videotape recorders had been available for seven years, and were gaining in popularity as prices lowered. One Wall Street analyst predicted that 98 percent of those who compared videodisc and videotape would choose videotape. Actually, he was being a bit of an alarmist. In 1983, 250,000 SelectaVisions were sold, compared to 4,000,000 VCRs, which meant that only 94 percent had compared the two and chosen videotape.

RCA lost $580 million on the project but cannot be faulted too much—the early 1980s were a maelstrom of confusing television technologies. Even later than SelectaVision was Matsushita's VHD, a similar system that also bombed. Magnavision and Pioneer's LaserDisc were introduced and managed to survive—but as esoteric devices appreciated by a handful of video connoisseurs. Then there was Betamax, the videocassette format that lingered on for years, dying a protracted death worthy of *Tristan und Isolde*, flopping around on the electronic stage, trying to prop itself up, clutching at the curtains until—finally—it expired.

BUSINESSMEN ARE generally adept at analyzing other businessmen's failures while incapable of recognizing their own. Several good books document the difficulty of coming up with something that will be clutched to the fickle bosom of the great lay public. One favorite is the unpoetically titled *Getting It Right the Second Time* by Michael Gershman. In it, he takes forty-nine products that are now part of the established consumer pantheon and describes how they fizzled when first introduced, or how their difficult births required heroic steps to bring them into the world.

The book is filled with great trivia, such as how Kimberly-Clark was a newsprint and wrapping paper company until World War I ended, leaving it with a huge reserve of Cellucotton, a wood-derived substance it created to replace cotton in medical dressings. Trying to get rid of the stuff, Kimberly-Clark developed two products—thin sheets of Cellucotton, which it dubbed Kleenex, and thick pads, which it dubbed Kotex.

Neither was immediately successful. Kleenex, marketed to up-scale ladies as a way to remove cold cream, went nowhere. And Kotex had even greater problems—so unmentionable was the use of the product that Kimberly-Clark formed a holding company to produce it so its name wouldn't be on the box. Women's magazines refused to run even the most discreetly worded ads, and stores would not display the product, keeping it behind the counter. But women, used to fashioning their own feminine-hygiene pads from rags, were too ashamed to ask for it.

Kimberly-Clark really wanted to get rid of that Cellucotton, however, and they persisted. Responding to helpful customer suggestions, they repositioned Kleenex as something to blow your nose into. And Kotex was packed into plain white packages, so stores could display them without shame and women could buy them without having to speak to anyone—by depositing coins into honor boxes or in vending machines, where the product can be bought to this day.

Other initial failures documented by Gershman include Jell-O (the brand, marketed for two years without success, was sold for $450), light beer and Pepsi-Cola, which, bankrupted three times, was offered for sale to the Coca-Cola Company in 1932. Coke passed on the offer.

The basis of Gershman's book—that many popular products started as flops—underscores the importance of a time frame when discussing failure. If next year Premier cigarettes are reintroduced in some enhanced form and are embraced by the smoking public, now suddenly concerned about puffing themselves into the grave, so much so that all other brands of cigarettes peter out and only Premier is left, then Premier will no longer be a notorious marketing fiasco, but another market leader that got off to a rocky start.

Because products, unlike people, have no absolutely finite life span and can be reincarnated stronger than ever after a seemingly final demise, one must be circumspect in pronouncing certain items ridiculous flops. For instance, laser discs have so far failed to find a mass market but have been preserved by a coterie of videophiles. Now it seems that laser discs will get a new shot at success when high-definition television is rolled out. Videotape just doesn't provide the pixels HDTV needs to produce those heart-stoppingly crisp images, and laser discs will likely ride HDTV to belated popularity.

Another piece of technology worth mentioning, just for its

Mummy-like ability to be shot and stabbed and buried and still keep coming at you, is the video telephone.

I'd be inclined to say that video telephones are a pure example of the Arthur C. Clarke Syndrome in operation. Technically feasible for the past thirty years, they have been introduced with a burst of hoopla every decade or so, only to be resoundingly ignored by an indifferent public.

Dubbed the Picturephone, the first commercial video telephone was introduced in May 1964 (naturally), with a hookup between the Bell System's pancake-shaped pavilion at the New York World's Fair and Disneyland in California. The next month, Bell began service from booths in public buildings in New York, Chicago and Washington, D.C. But given the staggering cost of the service ($27 for a three-minute call between New York and Chicago) and the utter lack of a need for it, the Picturephone never really had a chance.

Again, in the early 1970s, despite no appreciable demand, AT&T again tried to shove the Picturephone down the world's collective throat. Again, a rosy future was confidently predicted: AT&T saw 100,000 units sold or leased by 1975, with Picturephones "widely used by the general public" by the 1980s. In reality, several hundred went into use in the test city, Chicago, and at a few scattered businesses, mostly for interoffice use.

In 1992, AT&T executives, after no doubt brooding in a Stalinist rage at the stupidity of the camera-shy proletariat, resurrected the damn thing yet again. Dubbed the VideoPhone 2500, the new phone transmits color pictures over a tiny screen ($2\frac{1}{2}$ by 2 inches), and calls are charged at the regular rate.

The problem with VideoPhone, besides the ghastly price of $1,000, is that the picture is broadcast at approximately five frames a second, so that it "jerks around like an old home movie," according to one trial user. Since so much information is going over just one line—think of how long it takes for a single-sheet fax to transmit—the picture also lags behind the audio, so that you hear a person speak and then, a few seconds later, the mouth moves choppily, as in a badly dubbed Godzilla flick.

Noise from the telephone line also disrupts the picture, which sometimes degrades into "an impressionist nightmare," the trial user said. Interestingly, AT&T advertisements for video telephones feature not the current, sadly flawed product but some imaginary, perfect large-screen video telephone of the future, with sleek and lovely parents reaching out to touch their children while making connections for the shuttle to Mars.

I would place bets on this latest effort fizzling as well. First, under most circumstances—excluding perhaps grandmothers phoning their progeny in prison—callers have no desire to see the person they are talking to on the phone. And absolutely nobody answering the phone wants to be seen by the person on the other end of the line.

Second, AT&T officials have been quoted as saying that consumer interest in the phones is "huge," "strong" and "intense," bleats of hubris which usually indicate that divine retribution is near. I've never met anybody in my life who owned a video telephone. Nor have I ever heard the subject brought up in conversation. Nor do I ever expect to.

But human nature being what it is, I'd hesitate to pronounce the video telephone an absolute flop, lest it become wildly popular due to some twist in the collective psyche, and my tut-tutting quote be lifted out of context and preserved, along with other fearful reactionary idiocies, in some future collection of dimwitted misreadings of the future. Twenty years from now, when everybody has a personal computer/telephone/television/factotum, it might be nothing to tack a camera the size of a piece of chalk to the thing, and for the extra five bucks, who wouldn't do it? Until then, grimly persistent AT&T overlords will no doubt continue reintroducing video telephones, trying to disguise their essential superfluousness with shrieking arias of millennial propaganda and clunky brand names like "DigiVision Marvelphone."

Aside from investment analysts and tabloid psychics, most people want to hedge their bets when dealing with predictions of future failure. I have to remind myself that I'm the guy who thought car telephones were a fluke. They seemed such an intrusion into the private space of your car. How could you speed down some back road, blasting the radio, drumming your fingers on the steering wheel, bobbing your head and singing along to "Help Me, Rhonda," knowing that any second the phone at your right knee might twitter and your boss, Mr. Smithkins, begin quizzing you about some meaningless bit of interoffice palaver? I thought it impossible. In fact, the first article I ever sold was a reaction to Ameritech's "Every Minute Will Be Productive" ads of the early 1980s. The idea seemed insidious, frightening, the opening bell of a dystopian world where people work twenty-four hours a day—torn from sleep, from sex, even from *driving down the street*, by the inane demands of the workplace. I did my best to paint a cautionary picture of distracted drivers screeching their death rattles into cellular phones as they careened into concrete abutments and slid under the wheels of semi—trailer trucks.

To no avail. Now the inability to occasionally detach oneself from an umbilical cord to the office has become a symbol of status. When I have lunch with my brother, who runs a livery company, he actually lines up his tiny *Star Trek* communicator-size telephone, his two-way radio and his alphanumeric display beeper on the white linen tablecloth, like a surgeon setting out his instruments. I wouldn't be surprised if someday he removed from his briefcase a large dipolar antenna, or perhaps a collapsible 3-foot-diameter satellite dish, explaining he's expecting an important call from a client aboard the space shuttle and has to be ready to receive.

To me, the need to be in constant communication puts a person in the company of school janitors, who must be reached quickly so they can hustle over to the cafeteria where little Billy Peters has just vomited.

There is nothing wrong with being unable to augur new trends in society so long as your shortsightedness is based on sound principles and you don't invest any money. I remember the exact moment when I first encountered Madonna (speaking of consumer products . . .). It was 1984 and I was living in the elegant home of a university professor who, despite years of formal education, had foolishly rented his residence to three young reporters when he went out of town on sabbatical. He had left us connected to cable television, and we spent hours slumped over a sofa picked off somebody's front lawn, transfixed by that recent phenomenon, MTV. As Madonna's *Like a Virgin* video first came on the screen, I did not feel I was in the presence of a talent that would soon metastasize until it covered the earth, like the Glidden paint ad. I did not particularly like the song. Rather, I leaned forward, to better fix my gaze at Madonna's midriff as she floated through the Grand Canal, and had this thought: "I better get a good look at this bimbo, because I'm never going to see her again."

I hope this isn't bragging. I tell the story not to shuck off my share of the world's collective blame for the fact that Madonna isn't taking orders at a Church's Fried Chicken in Michigan right now. Rather, I mean to say that our own personal shortsightedness is what puts us in sympathy with the failures of others. Being able to laugh at the disaster of Premier cigarettes does not necessarily mean that had you or I been in the boardroom at R. J. Reynolds when the fiasco was being carefully planned, we would have pounded our fist on the thick, highly polished cherry table and said, "No, this is folly! If you are going to pursue this course of action, then I'll just give up my high-paying executive position, yank the kids out of private school and ship them off to some Dickensian public institution, sell the wonderful designer house with the step-up octagonal marble bathtub, and go live in one of those prefab townhouse condos thrown up overnight on Sprague Road by the Army Corps of Engineers."

Tragically few people can do that. First, because error is such an intrinsic part of the operation of any business. If employees made a stand at every perceived misstep, then no one would have jobs. Second, because people are craven, and desperate to please. They will therefore endorse any idiocy or atrocity as long as it is presented to them by superiors in an institutional setting.

Third, because it is so hard to predict the future with any confidence. We usually never know if the action we are pushing for is absolutely the right one. We struggle forward, but rarely know ahead of time which decision is the one that saves or damns us.

Michael Gershman lists a few of the hundreds of candy-coated popcorn and peanut confections available at the beginning of this century: Yellow Kid, Honey Corn, Uniot, Goldenrod, Honey Boy, Western Scout, Little Buster, Jolly Time, Razzle Dazzle, Happikrax, Kor-nut, Osmun's Dandy Snack, Shenkberg's Nutty Corn, Five Jacks, Maple Jack, Sammy Jack and Cracker Jack.

Only the last has survived to the present day, not because it tasted better, or had more peanuts, but solely on the basis of the inclusion of a nifty little toy. For most of this century, millions of whistles, compasses, rings, clickers, charms, puzzles, tops, and assorted minuscule prizes have pushed America's appetite toward molasses and popcorn.

I remember one prize in particular. Twenty-five years ago, or so, I bought a box of Cracker Jack that contained a blue plastic deep-sea diver. The toy consisted of a small blue man—less than an inch high —and the blue deep-sea-diving suit that snapped around him. I possessed it for only the time it took to find a deep puddle in the street, make a few dives, and lose him down a crack into the vast netherworld I imagined existing under suburbia. It was a terrible loss.

Since then, Cracker Jack has begun stiffing people on the prizes. Worried—perhaps with some justification—about ruinous choking-death lawsuits, they no longer package anything more solid than a joke booklet or a sticker in their boxes of confection. Though I don't particularly like the product, and resent the crummy prizes, I still buy the stuff once in a while, perhaps out of a vestigial, irrational hope that maybe someday I'll find a neat blue diver inside.

But I don't buy it very often, and I can't see how those paltry stickers and fake tattoos have sufficient appeal to keep people eating enough Cracker Jack to satisfy the company. I hope I do not seem vindictive if I say that Cracker Jack, despite its long past, has an uncertain future. Companies forget what made them great and go under. It will be interesting to see, as the last generation remembering good prizes ages and begins taking all of its nourishment out of catheters, whether sales of Cracker Jack begin to lag and, if that is the case, whether the company throws caution to the wind and starts giving away real little toys again. One would hope so.

TWO

Were the Mountain Smaller

—

Pointless Failure

OPPORTUNITIES FOR adventure do not happen every day. The roof of the John Hancock Building, sixth tallest in the world and third tallest in Chicago, is usually populated by nothing more than a handful of upper-air spiders and the occasional stray migratory bird. But now the uppermost regions of the building were crawling with a squad of workers, refurbishing the two giant communications masts atop the roof—repainting the superstructure and replacing the red beacons for the first time since the landmark, 1455 feet tall including the masts, was built in 1968.

A photographer at the Chicago *Sun-Times*—Robert Davis, a Harley-riding hotshot—had arranged, through persistent negotiation with the Hancock management, permission to photograph the work. As a staff reporter on the paper, I had collaborated with him on a series of offbeat stories—a day at the morgue, the social life of transvestites, an urban tent revival meeting—and he asked me to come along and write something about the painters.

I met Bob outside the Hancock at four o'clock one warm summer morning. Work had to be done in the small hours because the radio and television antennae—jutting from the masts in various odd butterfly, dish, drum and arrow shapes—needed to be shut off.

Otherwise, their signals were so strong they could, in theory, cook a person.

After explaining our mission to a series of sleepy guards and janitors, we found ourselves at the 98th floor, the terminus of the elevators. There we gazed at the array of superannuated electrical equipment—3,000-amp fuses the size of tomato juice cans, floor-to-ceiling transmitter cases, a giant Westinghouse knife switch, 2 feet long. The switch seemed as if it would cut the power to the entire building, if not the city. Pull it, I imagined, and you would hear a loud hum quickly descending down the tonal register into a low moan and dwindling into dark silence. I had Bob take my picture while I pretended to pull the switch.

A foreman met us and we went up two flights of stairs to the 100th floor, where the workers were taking a break, eating home-made brownies and drinking big cups of coffee. They were a friendly, paint-encrusted bunch, without the air of hostile superiority some blue-collar workers assume when encountering the recumbent professions. "You don't think about it, that's the thing, you just do it," said one of the painters, William Mudd. "You start thinking about it, you screw up."

They tossed Bob and me safety belts and told us to feel free to climb as high as we'd like.

That was unexpected. Newspaper reporting is often like being one of those wind-up toy cars—furiously scooting forward, only to pin yourself against the sunroom molding, grinding away your stored energy, getting nowhere. It can take an astounding amount of fina-gling just to get permission to observe some mundane task, impeded as you are by all sorts of unexpected hurdles, regulations, restrictions and controls. There is a chocolate company in Chicago which, when the wind is right, bathes part of the downtown in a blanket of the most delicious-smelling aroma of cocoa. For years, I've wanted to write a story about that aroma, wafting out of the vats of chocolate, delighting and intoxicating passers-by. Only the company won't co-operate. For years, I've called them periodically and asked them to let me visit, just to look at the vats, as a starting point to the story. For years, they've turned me down flat. They never say why.

On the roof of the Hancock, there was no resistance, no insur-ance release forms, no dissembling public relations officers hovering nearby. Instead, the foreman handed us wide leather safety belts, each trailing a webbed cord ending in a carabiner, and pointed us toward the masts. How high could we climb? As high as we wanted to.

Resolutely strapping on the safety belt, I knew at once how high I wanted to climb. While normally content to limit my scope of adventure to trying out an unfamiliar restaurant, now that fortune had dealt me the opportunity, I had no question about exactly how high I wanted to—no, *had to*—climb: to the top. The tippy top.

THAT URGE—call it "tippytoppiness"—is a drive deeply felt in Western cultures. People seem to need to climb to the very pinnacle of things—buildings, hills, mountains, piles of dirt, whatever presents itself.

It is a puzzling sort of impulse, given the time expended, the lives lost, the money spent, trying to satisfy it. Puzzling and zeal-ously absolute. Quite near the top won't do. In the general vicinity of the zenith isn't enough. You have to be on it, at it, right there, the very highest spot. And being the second person on top doesn't really count either. First is what counts.

It is a philosophy that churns out failure, a factory of disap-pointment and defeat, as demonstrated with agonizing clarity by the tortuous thirty-year effort to climb Mount Everest, the tallest moun-tain in the world, a 29,000-foot behemoth of rock and ice lording over the Himalayan range between Nepal and Tibet. The fact that Sir Edmund Hillary and Tenzing Norgay were the first to climb the mountain in 1953 is generally known, though many people forget Tenzing, which is understandable. He was not white, and had a strange name, and it is easy to overlook him. Even his colleagues, the British climbers of 1953, forgot about him, with disastrous results, as will be seen.

Like Tenzing, the dozen or so expeditions before Hillary's that tried to climb Everest but fell short of their goal are almost utterly forgotten by the general public.

This is unfortunate for several reasons. First, the expeditions are in themselves interesting—quixotic, massive crusades gilded with a veneer of pith-helmeted, Great White Hunter, Anglomaniacal enthusiasm which is utterly extinct today in that strip-mined, godforsaken nation of skinheads, soccer hooligans and public dole recipients still anachronistically referred to as Great Britain.

Second, it is these failed expeditions—and not the height of the mountain itself—that really gave the eventual climbing of the summit whatever glory and significance it might possess. They are the tacit rationale behind all the knighthoods, the medals, the speaking tours, the dozens of books on the subject.

Had the first person to cast an eye on Everest simply scampered nimbly to the summit, there wouldn't have been much hoopla or remembrance in the matter. Progressive failure breeds interest, however, the way more and more people play the lottery as it rolls over week by week, even though their minuscule odds of winning are no better. Somewhere in the Pacific is the deepest ocean trench in the world, and an anonymous oceanographer has no doubt visited it in a bathyscaphe or something, but nobody particularly knows or cares because he was not preceded by generations of divers, storing air in seal bladders and weighing themselves down with cannon shot, constructing primitive diving bells out of wine casks, and in general littering the ocean floor with their crushed bodies in a vain effort to touch the bottom of the trench and return.

The entire concept of heroism, of the romance of adventure, is based on the presumption that a lot of people must seek the goal and bungle it before the victor can be allowed to happen by. "Hence the series of jousts, of single combats and of competition for the main prize in tournaments," Elspeth Kennedy wrote in "Failure in Arthurian Romance." "Battles must therefore be lost by lesser characters in order to enhance the stature of the hero."

Or, to flip the logic around, if Disneyland were located at the South Pole and hundreds trekked across the frozen Antarctic to reach it, only to be decapitated on "Space Mountain" or maimed by the vicious, exposed machinery in "It's a Small World," then going to Disneyland would no longer be viewed as a dreary, obligatory descent into cultural fatuousness, but as a rare adventure and a preening mark of manhood.

We should realize that tippytoppiness is particular to our society and not a universal human attribute. The Tibetans and the Nepalese certainly knew the mountain was *there* all those centuries. They called her Chomolungma, which means "Goddess Mother of the World," and believed that gods dwelled at her summit. Yet there is no indication that anyone who lived nearby ever tried to climb the mountain or, for that matter, ever thought of climbing her until the British showed up with sloshing buckets of money early in this century. The closest the locals came to pitting themselves physically against Everest was the occasional construction of rough hermits' shacks, where ascetics would sit, buffeted by the elements, contemplating the throat-clenching majesty of the mountain landscape.

Predictably, this unity with one's surroundings was viewed as cowardice by the British, who first took notice of the mountain, which they lyrically named Peak XV, in 1849, during their survey of India. The two kingdoms sharing the mountain, Tibet and Nepal, were feeling increasing pressure to place themselves under British protection, and the Brits, like a child memorizing the specifications of a bike expected for Christmas, wanted to know exactly what they were going to get.

Accounts of the early expeditions make it clear that the native idea of the mountain being holy, or the thought that climbing it might be a grandiose expenditure of time and effort, could not be grasped by the Victorian psyche. Initially received by the Tibetans as glittering, superior beings, with wondrous devices and incalculable wealth, the British quickly came to be viewed as lunatic rich people locked into a pointless quest—somewhat the way New Yorkers would view a Japanese billionaire who arrived in the city and announced that it was his mission to lick the surface of the Chrysler Building, and that he wanted to hire servants to build scaffolds and hold him up to reach the high parts.

Despite the mountain's belonging to someone else and already having a serviceable name, in 1865 it was given a moniker that rolled off Western tongues a bit more suavely than Chomolungma. The honor fell to Sir George Everest, a London surveyor who had spent his career taking the measurements of India.

The British no doubt would have rushed to the mountain, waving ice axes and lengths of rope and shouting "Pip-pip-pip!" the moment Peak XV was discovered, had they not been possessed by an Anglo-Saxon reverence for authority and order. Fortunately for the extremities of several generations of idle monied young Englishmen, Nepal and Tibet were not exactly c'mon-in-and-make-yourself-at-home types of places. Despite the considerable influence wielded by Britain, permission to make the climb was not forthcoming from the subjugated, nominal rulers of the countries containing Everest. It is perhaps odd that while the British were eager to risk their lives on the side of the mountain, a bureaucratic "no" from countries they dominated was enough to keep them from even making the attempt. No one seems to have thought of just sneaking in (in 1962, with China controlling the area and the borders closed, an American team did just that). The Brits, ever ready to pit themselves against nature, were still respectful of the fig leaf of sovereignty left to nations they hadn't yet rendered into puppethood.

Despite this lack of access, talk about climbing Everest persisted, and the plucky Brits were galvanized into action as they saw the trophy conquests of the world slipping away, seized by other nations. The North Pole had been attained by the Americans—either Peary or Cook, depending on which revisionist historians you believe—in 1909; and the South Pole had been reached by the Norwegians in 1911, a particularly humiliating and tragic blow to British pride. (In the "Bad Timing" chapter we'll see how British explorer Robert Falcon Scott, after battling to be first at the pole, arrived to find Norwegian flags flapping in the killing polar breeze and a note from Roald Amundsen that said, in effect, "Hi! Discovered the Pole for Norway a few weeks back. Sorry I missed you. Have a fun trip home.") Having blown their chance at both poles, the British sought to make it up with Everest, which was dubbed, somewhat pathetically given the circumstances, "the third pole." A reconnaissance of the region around the mountain was scheduled for 1915, but the Great War inconveniently interfered.

With that distraction ending in 1918, the Alpine Club of London and the Royal Geographical Society got serious about conquering Everest. In 1919, the two groups began a concerted effort to lobby, first the Indian secretary of state, and then, after he was persuaded, the Tibetans.

Once the political roadblocks were dispensed with, a Mount

Everest Committee was formed and charged with assembling a team to assault the mountain. Just the names of the members of the Everest Committee give a good indication of the sort of people they were: Sir Francis Younghusband, Mr. Edward Somers-Cocks, Colonel Jacks, Professor Norman Collie, Captain J. P. Farrar and Mr. C. F. Meade. It was an elite group, but not necessarily a wealthy one. They needed to scrounge around for funds, hampered by the fact that few common people cared enough about the glory of conquering Everest—which at that point no one had tried to climb—to dig into their pockets to fund a bunch of inbred sportsmen. A public subscription raised £10, enough to get the expedition to Dover. Eventually some sympathetic rich souls were rounded up, including the King and the Prince of Wales, and they bankrolled the effort.

The committee supervised the first three attempts at Everest, in 1921, 1922 and 1924. Various members of the expeditions left behind highly readable accounts of these attempts, each alternatingly hopeful of success, eloquent in engaging descriptions of colorful locales, and frank in weary disappointment at their failure to reach the summit. "This book is the record of a repulse" is the first sentence in Younghusband's introduction to E. F. Norton's *The Fight for Everest: 1924.* "The repulse has been cruel. Yet the pain has not diminished the determination of man to conquer the mountain: it has increased it."

Each of the first three expeditions included George Leigh Mallory, a universally admired schoolteacher whose fine character and honed sensibilities personified the old-school, heigh-ho quality pervading the expeditions. He shared the genius for understatement pandemic among the climbers. "Mount Everest, as it turned out, did not prove difficult to find," Mallory noted in his account of the 1921 expedition.

The attempts were presented as voyages of discovery rather than pure sport, and as valid science, testing to see how high man could climb in addition to documenting an unknown region. Mallory's wide range of interests and knowledge was seen as vital—accounts of the expeditions take almost as much time to describe flowers and clouds as they do mountaineering. Here is Mallory in a letter home to his wife, Ruth:

> On the Sikkim side a most lovely little primula flourishing from 9,000 to 11,000 feet, with the habit of our English primrose, only somewhat smaller and neater, and of a delicious crimson colour; and Rhododendron falconeri, the big bright red fellow, was flowering freely a bit lower.

Since no Westerner had ever been within 60 miles of Everest, it was decided that the first expedition would just be exploratory—although hope was held out that scaling the summit might be possible once climbers got there. "If they actually found a quite feasible route to the summit, why then, of course, they were not to be prevented from having a try," wrote Younghusband in his delightful, straight-from-the-wing-chair style. "This was one of those vague hopes with which members and leaders and organizers of expeditions buoy themselves up."

They needed buoying. It was an ordeal just getting close to the mountain. After traveling by ship across the Mediterranean Sea, down the Red Sea, across the Indian Ocean, then transecting India from Bombay to Calcutta, they assembled a mini-army of several hundred porters in Darjeeling and set off for the 200-mile slog through Tibet.

The first casualty of Everest climbing, Scottish mountaineer Dr. A. M. Kellas, didn't make it to within 100 miles of Everest, but died while the party was approaching the mountain. (There is sometimes an unintentional, Monty Pythonesque humor to the accounts of death on Everest expeditions. Younghusband sniped that Kellas was "not a man who looked after himself," and rationalized that he "remained cheery and no one considered that there was anything critically serious with him," even though he was so ill he couldn't walk, or even ride a yak, but had to be carried by porters on a litter.)

They spent four months on and around the mountain, viewing it from varying angles, mapping out the best route to the top. That done, they couldn't help attempting to reach the summit while they were in the neighborhood.

The incredible hardship of trying to climb Mount Everest cannot be overstated. With the temperature below zero and whipped lower by fierce winds, a person's extremities can freeze with a few minutes' exposure. Mountaineers face the trade-off between keeping warm and padding their fingers so much they can't grasp at tiny cracks and crevices in stone walls. Avalanches are a constant threat. Oxygen levels are barely sufficient to support life, causing severe headaches and nausea. The lack of humidity ravages throats and, coupled with intense physical exertion, creates an endless thirst, which on early expeditions could only be slaked by the agonizingly slow process of melting snow over tiny portable stoves.

Complaints that would send you or me screaming for the lowlands of India were shrugged off. "Wheeler thought he might be good for some further effort but had lost all feeling in his feet," Mallory wrote at one point.

The first expedition couldn't get close to the summit, and comforting themselves with the thought that this was supposed to be just an exploratory mission anyway, the climbers gave up the attempt at 23,000 feet, a vertical mile below the top. They returned home, where their mission was pronounced "a total success." Immediately, plans were laid for "a real, all-out effort."

Once back in London, climbers and organizers met to discuss what was learned from the mission. W. H. Murray neatly summarized their conclusions with this brief and gloriously unhelpful statement: "It was thought that the mountain could indubitably be climbed were it five thousand feet smaller."

Before the 1922 expedition began, there was a passionate debate over the proposed use of bottled oxygen. On one hand, some physicians and scientists predicted that the mountaineers would suffocate and die once they passed 25,000 feet. On the other, there was concern that using oxygen was somehow unfair—that it would be cheating.

"There was just a suspicion at the back of men's minds that it was not exactly sporting to use it," Younghusband wrote. "It could be argued of course that inhaling oxygen was no more unsporting than taking a nip of brandy or a cup of beef-tea. But there the fact remained that a man who got up without oxygen would be looked upon as having done a finer deed than the man who climbed Everest using oxygen."

Ironically, no one ever questioned the sportingness of using hundreds of porters—called "coolies" at the time—to cart the supplies within spitting distance of the summit. But that's how the mountaineers were. They either ignored the darker races they encountered or viewed them with a blend of ostentatious respect and corner-of-the-mouth condescension, if not loathing. Team leader C. K. Howard-Bury nurtured a "very highly developed sense of hate and contempt for other sorts of people than his own," noted Mallory, who, in keeping with his general lack of human flaws, did not seem to share the disdain felt by his colleagues.

The climbers nicknamed their Sherpas—a mountain race known for their ability to climb cheerfully under the most atrocious conditions—"Tigers" as a tribute to their bravery, but they also viewed their indifference to climbing the mountain except for pay as arising from a communal lack of spirit.

"The faint-hearted people around it fear to approach it," chided Younghusband, perhaps forgetting that even if any local Buddhist had had the inclination to climb the mountain—since gods lived there, the climb would have been tantamount to a Britisher scaling the face of St. Paul's—none enjoyed the wealth and luxury of time required to mount an expedition.

For the mountaineers, exactly why *they* were using their wealth and luxury of time in such dubious fashion was an awkward question they were forever trying to answer—attacking it, like a difficult summit, from various approaches. To the Tibetans they offered a fanciful explanation that may have had a grain of truth in it. There was in England, Gen. C. G. Bruce explained to the lama at Everest's Rongbuk Monastery, a race of men who worshipped mountains, and were now traveling to the highest mountain to pay homage by climbing it.

Pithy, epigrammatic answers seemed preferable for the public back home, from Mallory's classic "Because it is there" to Hillary's noble "It is not the mountain we conquer, but ourselves." Later mountaineers were more verbose. American Woodrow Wilson Sayre spends ten pages of his Everest account offering various jabs at the question. He settles not on the mythic but on the mundane—it's hard sitting behind a desk; you never really feel you get to know the other guys in the office, at least not in the way you do huddled in a two-man tent hanging off the side of a cliff in a gale at 28,000 feet. He also seems to view mountaineering as a human version of the adrenaline rush squirrels supposedly get darting out in front of traffic, with a subtle vein of masochism buried below the surface. "Deep within us I think we know that we need challenge and danger," he wrote. "And the risk and hurt that will sometimes follow."

(The most delicious rationale for mountaineering, however, comes from a successful 1975 Red Chinese expedition. The artlessly titled account of their climb, *Another Ascent of the World's Highest Peak*, presents the expedition as "a triumph of Chairman Mao's proletarian revolutionary line, another creditable achievement of the Great Proletarian Cultural Revolution and the movement to criticize Lin Piao and Confucius," and renders Mallory's "Because it is there" into this awesome bleat of propaganda: "New China promotes mountaineering as a sport to serve proletarian politics, the interests of socialist economic construction and the building of national defense, to help improve the people's health, and to foster such fine qualities in them as wholehearted devotion to the people and the collective, and fearing neither hardship nor death.")

The 1922 expedition ended after a third assault at the summit —a last-ditch effort led by Mallory—ran into an avalanche that swept seven Sherpa porters over an ice cliff to their death. So tortuously intertwined and conflicting were British feelings of fairness, superiority and prejudice that Howard Somervell later bemoaned the fact that none of his countrymen had been killed in the avalanche, too, so as to equitably distribute the ennobling loss between sahib and coolie. "Why, oh why, could not one of us Britishers have shared their fate?" he has himself lamenting as the party worked its way down the mountain.

Slightly embarrassed to be alive, the expedition returned to England.

The Alpine Club decided to skip a year, to give themselves time to plan a new expedition and raise more money. This was done in a way commensurate with the extreme politeness, gentility and good-sportingness characteristic of those early expeditions.

Here is Younghusband on how Mallory came to be involved in

the 1924 quest, phrased in sentiments that, to modern ears, are about as foreign as the chants a Celt would use in worshipping a tree:

> Mallory was a more delicate problem. It was in the highest degree desirable to have him. But was it fair to ask him? If he were invited he could not well refuse. Were the Committee justified in virtually compelling him to go? He was a married man. He had already taken part in two expeditions. In the last he had been in two serious accidents, in one of which seven men had lost their lives. He had already played his part—and played it nobly. Could the Committee, with any fairness, ask him to do more? On the other hand, might he not be deeply offended if he were *not* asked—he who had borne all the cold and burden of the day? Might he not be cruelly affronted if he were passed over? It was a difficult point to decide, and delicate feelers were sent out toward him to ascertain which way his wishes lay. The Committee were satisfied that in his heart he wanted to go. An invitation was offered. And to the joy and relief of the Committee he gladly accepted it.

The 1924 expedition set out in March. It began festively in the Tibetan highlands with a five-course camp dinner that included champagne (though one of the hard lessons learned from the expedition, according to Bentley Beetham, was that "champagne is certainly not worth its weight" on remote climbing expeditions. Beetham recommends port be substituted).

Several assaults on the summit were made by varying pairs of climbers, and one climber almost succeeded. Pushing on after his partner was forced back, coughing up blood, E. F. Norton came within 800 feet of the summit. But he was exhausted and having trouble seeing—he would go snow-blind the next day—and turned back, fearing if he went on alone for the summit, he would never return. That he was able to abandon the summit without "the bitter feeling of disappointment" Norton later passed off as altitude sickness. "The better qualities of ambition and will to conquer seem dulled to nothing, and one turns downhill with but little feelings other than relief that the strain and effort of climbing are finished," he wrote.

A few days later, on June 6, 1924, Mallory and Andrew Irvine, who at twenty-four was the youngest member of the party, strapped on 25-pound oxygen cylinders and left Camp IV for their rendezvous with eternity. They were glimpsed the next day—as a pair of specks at about the same spot where Norton had turned back—but only momentarily before the clouds closed in upon them.

They were never seen again. Ironically, it was only when they failed to return and their exhausted fellow climbers had to miserably search for their bodies, then descend without them, that some passing credence was given to the Tibetian view of the mountain. "What right had we to venture thus far into the holy presence of the Supreme Goddess, or, much more, sling at her our blasphemous challenges?" N. E. Odell had himself thinking as he struggled up from Camp VI in a vain, aborted attempt to look for his friends. "If it were indeed the sacred ground of Chomo-lungma—Goddess Mother of the Mountain Snows—had we violated it, was I now violating it? Had we approached her with due reverence and singleness of heart and purpose?"

Mallory and Irvine were lionized in death. "It was worth dying on the mountain to leave a reputation like that," Bruce said of Irvine. A memorial at St. Paul's was attended by the King and Queen. The Bishop of Chester, addressing God, referred to the pair as "those whose names are written in your Records in letters of gold."

For years it has been an enigma whether the two died before or after reaching the summit. Odell first reported that they were "going strong for the top" when the clouds closed around them, but he later admitted he may have overestimated how close they had been, to soften the harshness of the tragedy.

THE BASE OF the west mast of the John Hancock Building, a hollow metal cylinder about 15 feet wide, was warm, like a boiler room, with copper pipes and conduits paralleling the metal ladder. Every 25 feet or so, the ladder stopped at a spindly metal platform grid where, trying not to look down through the floor to the emptiness below, climbers shift over to the next segment of ladder. It was not a wide, house-paintery sort of ladder, but narrow, perhaps a foot wide, like something out of a submarine. The light was harsh, coming from unshielded bulbs.

Concentrating on pulling myself up rung after rung, and on not either kicking Bob, climbing below me, in the face or letting the guy above me step on my fingers, I really didn't have time to debate the wisdom of going up. There was no pressing reason related to the story to go to the top. I could have interviewed the men while they finished their brownies, thanked them and been back home, in bed, before dawn.

The reason I was going up, I think, was my underlying awareness of the fleetingness of the opportunity. The Ice Cream Truck Reflex —you hear the tinkling bells, realize this is your chance, and reach for change whether you want ice cream or not. If I could pay $25 and climb one of the communications masts of the Hancock any weekend I wanted, I would never consider doing it. It would seem stupid, risky, and I would sneer at all those red-faced postcollegians who had nothing better to do on a Saturday than entertain themselves by climbing a high ladder. There is something repellent about mercenary thrills—bungee jumping and skydiving and white-water rafting. Open to anyone, without a purpose other than gut-punching the adrenal glands, they offend some hidden puritanical chord: an upscale version of heroin.

But you can't pay to climb the towers, and I am attracted to ephemera, sometimes unwisely. Once I was watching a voodoo ceremony in a slum in Port-au-Prince when a noxious concoction of rum, cologne and God-knows-what-else was passed around in the base of a human skull. Now, I had no particular desire to drink the slop, particularly not out of so vile a receptacle, but then again, how often would the opportunity arise? Not too often. And if I refused now, there was slim chance that when I was back home in Chicago, slumped on the couch, my wife would walk by drinking her banana smoothie out of a skull and offer me a sip. If not now, never. I drank.

And finally, deep down, I suppose there was a desire to offset my cringing, muffin-clutching, pear-shaped true nature—by now established as recognized and inviolate—with some dash of legitimate flair and daring atop the Hancock. I actually pictured myself grasping on to that last little peg sticking out of the topmost section of mast, narrowed now to a thin metal pole, swaying more than a quarter mile above the street. Dramatically straining skyward to cup my hand over the top of the huge red beacon while choruses swelled and a ray of sunlight burst through the morning clouds to illuminate my upturned face. Or something very similar. And the beauty was that I wouldn't even have to brag about it to my friends—they could read of my heroics in the newspaper, in a slyly conceited boast disguised as reporting, an ode to my bravery that I knew would be satisfying because I would write it myself.

After climbing up about 100 feet inside the mast, we came to a final landing. There the men who had already replaced some of the beacons had written their names in bold letters, memorializing their work. Above was a square metal hatch, just big enough to let a person through. The workman above me turned a handle and pushed the hatch open, then continued climbing, outside. You could hear the roar of the wind. I followed.

AFTER THE 1924 expedition, the Dalai Lama, concerned over the ill effect these annual infusions of British money were having on the local population, closed the borders of Tibet. In August 1932, he changed his mind, and four more British expeditions were sent, in 1933, 1935, 1936 and 1938. They lacked some of the romance of the earlier attempts—perhaps because the novelty had worn off, perhaps because they didn't get as close to the top, perhaps because they didn't have a legendary figure like George Leigh Mallory disappear into echoing oblivion.

The 1933 expedition was the largest and most elaborate yet, with fourteen English climbers and "a small army" of porters. Their accounts are somewhat less demure than those of the 1920s, and a truer sense of the grotesque discomfort of their chosen endeavor begins to emerge: "Individuals differ very widely in their physical reactions to the effects of high altitudes," wrote 1933 team member Eric Shipton. "Some vomit a great deal, some suffer from blinding headaches, some cannot sleep, while others can hardly keep awake, some gasp and pant even when at rest."

The most noteworthy event of the 1933 attempt was the discovery of an ice ax lying exposed on a glacial slab. The ax must have belonged to either Mallory or Irvine, and its location indicated that they probably had not reached the summit before whatever happened to them happened.

The expedition was buffeted by storms, and eventually driven back by intense cold "like a draught from outer space."

Everest expeditions always caught the public's attention, and the

1933 quest, plus the first aircraft flyby of the mountain, also that year, may have had something to do with drawing to Everest in 1934 perhaps the most unusual climber ever to attempt the summit.

Maurice Wilson, thirty-seven, was a nutritional fanatic who believed that fasting could cleanse the soul and provide unusual powers to the body. He believed that not eating for three weeks would bring some sort of absolute purification and rebirth to divine existence. He further believed that it was his mission in life to bring this philosophy to the world and, finally, that the best way to do this was to use his special powers to single-handedly scamper up the side of Everest.

His first thought was to crash-land a plane high on the mountainside and then proceed to the top. This was no pipe dream. He learned to fly, bought a plane, and got as far as India before his aircraft was seized by authorities.

Undeterred by this setback, Wilson proceeded to Darjeeling, where he hired three Sherpas for the journey to the mountain (even a visionary ascetic Englishman, it seems, needed servants). In April, he presented himself to the lama at the Rongbuk Monastery, near the foot of Everest. Perhaps not too surprisingly, the lama was more impressed with this solitary English climber than he had been with the previous invasive hordes. He gave Wilson his blessing and praised him to later expeditions.

For equipment, Wilson took with him a pocket mirror, to signal his presence on the summit, and a Union Jack to place there. He provisioned himself with a little rice water, estimating it would take him three days to reach the top in his rarefied condition.

Wilson of course never had a chance. Driven back by severe conditions, he established himself at Camp III of the previous year's expedition, 21,000 feet up the East Rongbuk Glacier, and lived off supplies they had left behind. He was quickly deserted by the Sherpas he had hired, and spent several weeks doggedly heading up the mountain each morning, only to be driven back to camp by nightfall.

The 1935 expedition found his preserved body, along with a diary explaining it all. They buried him in a crevasse. This odd incident was almost enough to spike the expedition—the Sherpas considered the body a bad omen and would not go farther until harangued by the sahibs.

This expedition had been formed as a reconnaissance party, permission not coming in time to get the group to the mountain before July—the middle of the monsoon season—when it was assumed an attempt at the summit would be impractical. Like Mallory in 1921, however, the members hoped they might scoot to the top anyway, but found the risk of avalanche to be just too great. Instead they climbed smaller neighboring peaks.

The 1936 expedition was labeled "a bitter deception" by Shipton, and he must have been referring to the weather. Conditions were so severe the party could not occupy its base camp, never mind think of scaling the mountain. No sooner had they evacuated to lower regions than the monsoon struck, early. Heavy snows led to the threat of avalanche, and after Shipton was nearly carried over a 400-foot ice cliff by cascading snow blocks, the expedition was called off without ever having attempted the summit.

In 1938, reacting in part to criticism of the expense and unwieldliness of the big-siege expeditions, and in part to the success of a small Anglo-American mission up 25,645-foot Nanda Devi, the British tried a new approach—an expedition of only seven climbers. (Climbing Everest was such exhausting work that the practice had always been to bring along large groups, under the assumption that some climbers would become ill, exhausted or frostbitten and unable to assault the summit. Support climbers cut steps, beat trails and otherwise assisted those who were going for the top. Expeditions

were also swelled by naturalists, botanists, mess sergeants, radio operators, photographers and, most tellingly, geologists, who collected
samples even though the lone stipulation made by the Dalai Lama in
granting permission to climb was that nothing be taken from the
mountain. Those locals and their quaint beliefs.)

As in the previous missions, none of the climbers got close to
the top, and they, too, turned back in defeat.

During this time French, German and Polish teams reportedly
also tried to climb the summit. But little is known of them other
than the fact that they didn't make it.

World War II gave mountaineering types something else to focus
on. Afterward, the Dalai Lama ignored requests to climb Everest, and
Tibet was seized by the Chinese in 1950, closing the route to Everest from the northeast.

But at the same time, perhaps in reaction to suddenly finding the
Red Chinese on its borders, Nepal decided that permitting foreign
climbers into the country might not be such a bad thing. In 1950 an
American party was allowed to explore the mountain from the
southwestern Nepalese approach, but they did not try to reach the
summit.

Fearing that the Nepalese side was unclimbable (Mallory had
glimpsed it in 1922 and dismissed it as "one of the most awful and
utterly forbidding scenes ever observed by man"), the British dis-
patched their own exploration party to the area in 1951. They
deemed the approach worthwhile, and were preparing an expedition
for 1952 when they were blindsided by the Swiss.

After watching from the wings for three decades, the originators
of Alpine climbing had decided to take a whack at scaling Everest
themselves. A Swiss team put in an application to the Nepalese
ahead of the British, who, caught off guard, tried to wheedle their

way on to the expedition but were forced to cool their heels on the sidelines, with considerable anxiety, while the Swiss took their turn.

To read the Swiss accounts of climbing Mount Everest is to peel away the last veil of polite euphemism and omission drawn by the British and to get a better feel for what climbing the mountain must really be like. In the Swiss narrations, climbers drool into their oxygen apparatus, fear they or their colleagues are going mad, collapse vomiting into the snow. Members of the expedition argue, hate each other, get depressed, embrace, huddle together at night for warmth.

The Sherpas emerge as human beings. Portrayed as noble rocks in British accounts (rocks that occasionally must be goaded forward, usually by the sahib's setting an example and actually *hoisting the load himself*), the Sherpas are treated in the Swiss accounts as individuals who struggle and suffer in a fashion amazingly similar to that of white people:

> Tenzing returned, escorting our three Sherpas, who were all in bad condition. Pasang declared that he wished to die where he was; Phu Tharke zigzagged like a drunken man; Da Namgyal was suffering from migraine and held his head in his hands . . .

The Swiss also manage to extend to the Sherpas genuine respect, perhaps even a little admiration, for attributes the Swiss found superior to their own. Wrote René Dittert:

> They greeted us by taking our outstretched hands in both of theirs and bowing. How vulgar is our European handshake compared with this Tibetan greeting in which trust, respect and friendship are combined. It is not our race that has kept the secret of grace and distinction.

Tenzing Norgay, the famed Sherpa guide later minimized in British accounts, is lauded by the Swiss, who praise his "extraordinary condition" during an expedition plagued by foul weather. It is Tenzing who, when the party is prostrate with exhaustion, manages to heat soup in a crowded tent at night. The next morning, it is Tenzing who cheerily wakes them with chocolate. He pushes on with Raymond Lambert toward the summit after all the other Sherpas have turned back, depriving them of their sleeping bags. They spend an agonizing night huddled together at 27,000 feet in an empty tent. The next day, they fight their way up to 28,215 feet, with Tenzing struggling forward until Lambert decides they must either return or court death (not that Lambert was a softy—he was attempting Everest despite having lost his toes to frostbite in the Alps in 1938).

To put in perspective what getting that close to the summit must be like, think of setting out from New York to Los Angeles with the goal of dipping your foot in the Pacific, getting as far as the base of Santa Monica Pier, and then being forced to turn back.

One problem hobbling the Swiss was their oxygen equipment—breathing through the apparatus was so taxing that they could draw from it only when they weren't moving. Lambert felt that it was the pleasure of standing still, breathing pure oxygen, that sabotaged their resolve to reach the top. "When I stopped I felt magnificent," he wrote. "Everything seems to be going well and at precisely that moment one fails."

As the exhausted Swiss party worked their way down Everest, the weather suddenly cleared and the summit could be seen, serene and calm, as if mocking them.

Meanwhile, in England, John Hunt, an army officer, was assembling a team for the 1953 assault. They were relieved, and perhaps a little daunted, at news of the Swiss failure. "My imagination began to run away with me as I pictured the Swiss, men of iron muscle and nerve, lying crumbled by the buffeting wind, their toes and hands numb," wrote Wilfrid Noyce, a member of the British group. "I looked at my own hands, projecting from my pullover: very ordinary hands, hands that looked cold even with the chill of a London November."

But the Swiss weren't finished yet. Taking advantage of their year grant from the Nepalese, they decided to make an unprecedented second attempt that season in the late fall. The British, naturally, were surprised and aghast at this bit of conduct, which transgressed their unwritten and constantly evolving code of fair play. "To our prejudiced minds it almost seemed unsporting," wrote Hillary. "They'd had a fair go . . . why didn't they give us a chance now?"

But the second Swiss expedition was even more ill-fated than the first. Two porters died of exposure on the march to Everest. Another Sherpa was killed after being hit in the face by an ice block that fell from a serac. Though weather on the early trek up the slope had been ideal, by the time they reached the upper altitudes it was minus 40 degrees Celsius, with gale-force winds. They withdrew.

At the moment the Swiss were turning back, the British team were honing their mountain skills on the Jungfraujoch in Switzerland. Noyce hadn't been happy about their choice of mountains to practice on—he worried they would look like fools if the Swiss scaled the summit of Everest while the British were pottering around on an Alp. "The large Sherpa sacks marked 'British Mount Everest Expedition, 1953' might have been politely mocked if the news of a Swiss success had come through during the visit," he wrote.

Needless to say, they were delighted at the failure of the second Swiss attempt—the news was welcomed with "deep relief and thankfulness," according to Hunt.

The assault was set for the spring of 1953. Like the Swiss, the British planned on using oxygen equipment, a detail that, thirty years after Mallory, was still being sniffed at in some quarters. W. H. Murray, whose *Story of Everest* went to press while the British were climbing toward the summit in 1953, compared using oxygen to "taking drugs" and suggested that conquest of the summit without oxygen would be "a much more satisfying reward."

Another interesting piece of equipment taken on the expedition was a 2-inch mortar with a dozen shells, for dislodging dangerous snow formations. The Indians refused to allow the weapon into their country, fearing it would fall into the hands of insurgents, so the British smuggled it within their eight tons of baggage while passing through India.

The British expedition of 1953 is the most documented mountain adventure in history. No fewer than four members wrote books about it, including Tenzing, who was illiterate. A reporter for the *Daily Mail*, sent to the area to dog the expedition, which had already sold its story exclusively to the *London Times*, wrote a book on *his* exploits (which consisted mainly of trying to get the climbing party to speak to him).

The first assault team—Tom Bourdillon and Charles Evans—pushed as high as the South Peak, 28,700 feet up and 300 feet from the summit. But the final 100 yards was protected by a difficult ridge and a demanding ice wall. Calculating the time it would take to get up, they realized at that point they could make the summit but would not have enough daylight or oxygen left to return. They turned back.

The second assault team consisted of Hillary and Tenzing. After camping the night of May 28 at 27,900 feet ("the thermometer was registering minus 27 degrees C. but it wasn't unpleasantly cold," wrote Hillary, who had to singe his boots over a Primus stove for an hour the next morning to get them supple enough to put on), they got an early start and climbed steadily and strongly, with Tenzing sometimes blazing the trail, Hillary at other times cutting steps for Tenzing to climb. After negotiating a series of difficult cornices, twists, dangerous slopes and a 40-foot vertical crack near the top, into which Hillary had to wedge himself and laboriously climb, the pair suddenly found themselves at the top of Mount Everest.

They shook hands "in good Anglo-Saxon fashion," Hillary noted in his memoir of the climb. "But this was not enough for Tenzing and impulsively he threw his arm around my shoulders and we thumped each other on the back." That bit of unpleasantness out of the way, Hillary took pictures all around—the view was fabulous. He snapped three photos of Tenzing holding his ice ax with four little flags flapping from it. Hillary did not ask the Sherpa to take a picture of him, a fact he perhaps later regretted. "As far as I knew he had never taken a photograph before and the summit of Everest was hardly the place to show him how," wrote Hillary, who did think of Mallory and Irvine and glanced around the summit, looking for a sign they had been there. Tenzing scratched a hole in the summit and placed an offering—some sweets and the stub of a blue pencil. Hillary buried a crucifix. They shared sweet lemonade and a Kendall's Mint Cake, Hillary collected some small stones, and then they turned around and began the long descent back into the world. They had been on the summit for fifteen minutes.

THE HATCH OPENED out onto a reddish orange metal lattice tube that formed the mast for the next 200 feet. The lights of the city spread from horizon to horizon, a dazzling array of amber points, mixed with reds and yellows and blues. I climbed out and Bob began to follow, but taking one sweeping look at the vertiginous panorama, he quickly ducked back inside. I called in after him, and he explained he had to gather himself for a moment.

Immensely pleased with this development, I left Bob behind and continued my climb toward the top. Bob had been the one, the year before, who bolted out of the autopsy room at the Cook County Medical Examiner's Office and into the men's room. Just to splash water on his face, he later explained, though of course I never believed him. I had been ribbing Bob about that for a year, it was getting old, and now I had something new to tweak him with.

The problem with the safety belt was that, every second or third step, it had to be unhooked and reattached to a higher rung. This slowed things down and, not incidentally, required taking a hand off the ladder. Not intending to fall, I let the belt dangle between my legs.

A strong, steady wind blew. I felt as if I were in the rigging of a ship, especially with the great black bulk of Lake Michigan looming off to the east.

I continued to climb. The physical exertion was not extreme—just climbing a ladder that happened to be several hundred feet long. That wasn't the problem. I came upon an area where the workers had roped a tarp to the latticework, to catch dripping paint. It was sticky work trying to maneuver around the flapping tarp—getting caught in the ropes would be a bad thing—and it gave me time to stop and think.

I stopped and thought the following: Perhaps this isn't such a good idea.

I wasn't afraid of falling. Not that falling would have meant plummeting 1,300 feet to the street below—rather, it meant thumping ignobly into an air-conditioning unit on the roof. I'd be dead just the same, but a 200-foot drop to the roof somehow didn't seem that dreadful a proposition compared with the extra several seconds of pinwheeling terror implied by a plunge to the sidewalk.

And I couldn't really imagine falling—as one worker said,

"You'd be surprised at just how tight your grip can be until you get up there."

Actually, it was that tight grip, and the thought of being at the very top, outside of the societal safety net, which really worried me. No fireman would climb up there and pull me down, no helicopter would brave the winds around the building to get close enough to reach me. I'd be on my own. The final 100 feet of the tower had no comforting latticework around it—just lineman's rungs jutting out of a cold metal pole. I could imagine how frightening it would be on that last rung. My fingers tingled. I pictured myself shutting down, clinging there, frozen, howling. I'd become a tourist attraction for a few days, people setting up telescopes on Michigan Avenue and charging a buck for two minutes of watching The Guy on Top of the Hancock. My wife would try to send up sandwiches attached to balloons. A local disc jockey would write a bad song.

Immediately I was comforted by the thought that, hey, of course we'll be back—thorough, painstaking journalists such as Bob and myself don't just visit the masts once and then dash off a feature. This is just a dry run. A reconnaissance. A practice session. Next time, I'll shoot right to the top. It will be easy, familiar.

I gratefully changed direction and started carefully climbing down, making sure that Bob, now recovered and snapping away at the workmen, got a picture of me hanging off the mast at sunrise, the city stretching out below me, a champion.

I never went back.

"THE HERO'S ACHIEVEMENT," Elspeth Kennedy wrote, "at the moment of apparent triumph, is revealed to be flawed. This flaw usually involves a lapse in judgment, a wrong choice of priorities, a lack of awareness."

Kennedy was writing about the Knights of the Round Table, but she might as well have been referring to the British quest to conquer Everest. A thirty-year national struggle to claim a point of pride is hubris in extremis, and it was nice of reality—at the precise moment that the dream was realized—to dilute it in such a satisfactory manner.

And no, it wasn't the oxygen. Despite three decades of debate and tongue-clicking, in triumph nobody seemed to mind the oxygen.

The problem was this. The whole point of climbing Everest had been to show what a man could do—a British man. The fact that he was aided by hundreds of Sherpas and other assorted mountain races didn't matter. They were as invisible as the servants slipping noiselessly through a great estate in Sussex. Tenzing Norgay didn't matter—his role was to help Hillary get to the top. John Hunt later wrote that he had selected Tenzing to be on the summit team as a tribute to all the Sherpas who had aided the British in their quest, but that was wisdom after the fact. The reality was that Tenzing was the porter, the valet, a tool for helping Hillary reach the top. After that, he was to be discarded, like an empty oxygen cylinder.

But not for long.

Returning from the summit, the pair staggered into camp, their thumbs in the air. Nobody asked who had reached the summit first because, in the eyes of the British, only one man had gone.

"Then, in the hurly-burly and bustle of triumph, something occurred that spoiled everything," wrote Yves Malartic in his biography of Tenzing. "Everybody crowded around Hillary; he was congratulated, slapped on the back, his hand was shaken, people laughed in his face—and no one gave a thought to Tenzing who, roped together as usual with his companion, was following the triumphal group of the New Zealander at a distance of some twenty-five feet."

With all the chin music about teamwork and companionship,

the snub wounded Tenzing, who had reached the summit with Hillary and was possibly the first one to set foot on it.

News of the accomplishment was flashed across the world—it reached Britain on the eve of Princess Elizabeth's coronation as Queen. The climbers bore their triumph back to Katmandu, the nearest civilization, where congratulatory telegrams addressed to Hillary were already pouring in. But the triumphal procession was tripped up over its own unexamined assumptions. Though invisible to the British, Tenzing was quite substantial to the people living below—he was their hero, the first man up Everest. This reintegration of Tenzing, a person forming out of the thin air, led to an ugly episode that dogged all attempts at pomp and grandeur.

The Nepalese greeted the returning mountaineers with wild affection—for Tenzing. It is not clear whether he ever claimed to have been the first man atop Everest, or whether they just assumed he had been. But either way, the British and their coveted achievement were swept aside in a single gesture of contempt. This is Noyce's description of the parade in Katmandu:

> At last it came, a state coach invisible under flowers and drawn by four horses with liveried horsemen. As outriders there rode four dark damsels dressed in white. Seated high in the centre of the coach, facing forward, was Tenzing, flower-wreathed and looking bewildered, but at the same time exalted. Below him his wife and daughters. It was some time before we spotted John and Ed, who faced to the rear and sat in a sort of pit below Tenzing. The crowd nearest to the coach was thickest, and we must wait some time before we could join in the procession, which must by now have included every motor vehicle in Nepal. All were full; the chant of "Tenzing Zindabad" rose from every bumping car. That just behind us was the most vociferous, in English for our benefit. "Hail Tenzing, first man to conquer the Everest! Hail Tenzing,

first man to conquer the Everest!" The chant repeated itself, on and on and on. The chanters never grew hoarse.

Noyce, who includes his own poetry in the book, recorded the scene without any editorial comment. At the official ceremony, Tenzing's few hesitant remarks were greeted with thunderous applause, while Hillary almost wasn't allowed to speak. When he was finally permitted to stand at the podium, introduced as "the second man on Everest," Hillary spoke to a hushed crowd and was horrified by the "enormous and active dislike" he felt flowing toward him.

The British reacted angrily. John Hunt denounced Tenzing to the Indian press. "Tenzing was nothing at all, merely a simple aide. He did not possess any technical knowledge of mountaineering; during all of the final assault, Hillary had been in the lead," said Hunt, who, nevertheless, did not dispute the allegation that Tenzing had been first on the summit. Nor did Hillary ever publicly claim to have reached the top first, insisting it didn't matter. In private, he passed this off as modesty. "I don't like to tell them I did," he told Noyce. "It sounds precious, like swanking."

And Tenzing, stung by the aloofness of the British party, began to press his claims, apparently, though it is difficult to sort out what he said from what the local press and population made up for him. When Hillary and Tenzing arrived at Katmandu, cartoons on the walls already showed Tenzing straddling the mountaintop and hoisting a limp Hillary up by a rope. A week later, the *New York Times* printed a news story citing "reports" that Tenzing had been to the summit twice, first by himself, the second time after returning to lead an enfeebled Hillary to the top.

Whatever each was actually saying, the tension was very real. Tenzing avoided a reception at the British embassy and suggested he might turn down newly crowned Queen Elizabeth's award of the

George Medal. Hunt and Hillary were knighted. John Hunt, now Sir John Hunt (and, eventually, Lord Hunt of Llanfair Waterdine), threatened to cancel Tenzing's trip to England to accept the medal unless he retracted his claims. The *Times*, which had bannered the conquest of Everest on its front page, above the coronation, bemoaned what was happening in an editorial beginning, "If anything could have marred the splendid heroism of the conquest of Mount Everest, it would have been an argument as to who got to the top first, a New Zealand bee keeper or a Sherpa guide," and ending with a quote from Kipling, the bard of reluctant imperialism. India was sparring with Nepal over who could lay claim to Tenzing (he was born in Nepal but lived in Darjeeling), and there was a movement percolating to rename the peak "Mount Tenzing."

King Tribhuvan presented Tenzing with the Star of Nepal, that country's highest honor. Hillary and Hunt were given lesser medals.

With events spinning out of control, both sides saw whatever dignity and splendor their accomplishment may have once had slipping away, and compromised. In the office of the president of the Nepalese Council, both Hillary and Tenzing signed a sworn statement never to disclose who had been first to reach the summit.

But the issue would not go away. When later in June the British climbing party, along with Tenzing, his wife and young daughters, arrived in London, newspaper reporters quizzed his family on who was first to the top. "Mme. Tenzing and her daughters had been schooled in discretion," a disappointed *Times* noted. "They flatly refused to talk about the controversy . . ." Though mum on the subject of Everest, Tenzing's two daughters captivated the London media with their charming, naive enthusiasm, such as their reciting the nursery rhyme "Pussycat, Pussycat, where have you been? I've been to London to visit the Queen" on their way into Buckingham Palace.

When the participants sat down to document their versions of the events, each chose a different approach to the controversy. In his book on the climb, *High Adventure*, Hillary describes the final ascent to the summit like this: "A few more whacks of the ice ax, a few very weary steps and we were on the summit of Everest." In his book *The Conquest of Everest*, John Hunt lets Hillary narrate the ascent, and he again is vague. (Before publication Hunt, in some strange attempt at a public display of humility, announced that he was refusing to call his book *The Conquest of Everest*, but preferred the more modest *Ascent of Everest*. Such matters are not always in an author's hands, however, and the bolder title was selected over his objections.) Noyce is mum on the subject. The guy from the *Daily Mail*, who wasn't there and nobody would talk to, is confident that Hillary had been first.

Twenty years later, in his oddly titled reminiscence, *Nothing Venture, Nothing Win*, Hillary is still coy, but strongly implies that Tenzing beat him to the top. "Finally I cut around the back of an extra large hump and then on a tight rope from Tenzing I climbed up a gentle snow ridge to its top. Immediately it was obvious that we had reached our objective," he wrote, not mentioning whether Tenzing held the rope from above or below. He does discuss the controversy, insisting that what was important was the teamwork and not who reached the summit first, adding that he "was stupid to have resented it later," without explaining whether "it" was the controversy or Tenzing's having reached the summit before him.

Two accounts of Tenzing's side provide directly contradictory views of the ascent. Malartic deals with it this way:

> If one takes into account the character of Tenzing, his frankness and his capacity for loyalty, to which all those will attest who have ever known him, one is inclined to believe that if he had been the second to reach the top, he would not have hesitated to admit it.

Actually, he does admit it. In *Tiger of the Snows*, written as an autobiography, Tenzing does give Hillary credit, but in such a pained way as to make one wonder whether he is really trying to set the record straight, or is just tired of the issue and wants magnanimously to bury it:

> It is a question that has been asked so often—that has caused so much talk and doubt and misunderstanding—that I feel, after long thought, that the answer should be given. As will be clear, it is not for my own sake that I give it. Nor is it for Hillary's. It is for the sake of Everest—the prestige of Everest—and for the generations who will come after us. "Why," they will say, "should there be a mystery to this thing? Is there something to be ashamed of? To be hidden? Why can we not know the truth?" . . . Very well: now they will know the truth. Everest is too great, too precious, for anything but the truth.

> A little below the summit Hillary and I stopped. We looked up. Then we went on. The rope that joined us was thirty feet long, but I held most of it in loops in my hand, so there was only about six feet between us. I was not thinking of "first" and "second." I did not say to myself, "There is a golden apple up there. I will push Hillary aside and run for it." We went on slowly, steadily. And then we were there. Hillary stepped on top first. And I stepped up after him.

BACK AT THE NEWSPAPER, I wrote an article about the refurbishing of the Hancock masts. It began: "A hundred and thirty floors above downtown Chicago, the city is utterly quiet. No car horns, no grinding truck gears, no sirens. Only the endless howling of the wind." It seemed like poetry to me.

At the end of the story, there was a detailed description of what it was like to climb to the very top of the masts, fudged from my experience of climbing halfway there. Like Hillary, I never made any false claims. I just sort of smoothed the reality over with a crust of art. But this equivocation gnawed at me, and I wondered when people would start coming up to me, asking whether I had really climbed to the top, the tippy top. What would I say? Could I lie? Could I not?

People did come up, amazed, wanting to know if I had really climbed on the masts. I told them yes, and braced myself for the inevitable follow-up question. But to my acrophobic colleagues, climbing up the masts was incredible enough. Nobody asked whether I had gotten to the tippy top. Nobody seemed to care.

AFTER HILLARY AND TENZING reached the summit—whoever was first—climbers continued to battle up the slopes of Everest.

Oddly enough, the Maurice Wilson philosophy of climbing took hold in certain quarters, under the rubric of "superalpinism." In 1978, the climbing team of Peter Habeler and Reinhold Messner climbed Everest without oxygen. Messner, though not British, claimed they were the first to scale the mountain by "fair means." Still unsatisfied, Messner climbed Everest again, in 1980, this time without oxygen or a climbing partner, and was acclaimed among the several thousand people who care passionately about such things.

Some six hundred people have climbed Everest and the number is constantly growing—sixty-one people reached the summit in 1993 alone, forty of them on a single day, May 10 (climbers, savoring their moment of personal triumph at the summit, heard shouts from below to hurry up, that others were waiting).

As many as one hundred people making the attempt have died,

thirty-four in the past five years—in falls, from exposure, from hypothermia and, in attempts to duplicate Messner and Habeler's 1978 climb, from causes related to oxygen depletion, such as cerebral edema.

For a while, mirroring the atomization of society, climbers attempting Everest sought to be an ever more specific first something atop the mountain—first American, first woman, first person over fifty, first American woman over fifty. Attention also shifted to which route was taken up Everest. Hillary and Tenzing, it turns out, not only cheated with oxygen but took the easy way up. So the more difficult routes had to be conquered.

Stacy Allison, the first American woman up Everest, spent forty-five minutes at the summit photographing herself with the logos of her numerous corporate sponsors. Later, appearing on "The David Letterman Show," she took a stone from her pocket, explaining that it came from the top of Everest, and asked permission to heave it through Dave's famed studio window. "Of course," said Letterman, and she threw the stone, accompanied by the usual breaking-glass sound effect.

Today Everest is climbed so frequently that trash is a problem—the Nepalese government has had to require that expeditions carry out all their garbage, lest the slopes become an utter junkyard of discarded oxygen cylinders and mint cake wrappers.

From a vantage point of forty years, comparing the end result of the dynamic, peakward-yearning philosophy of the British mountaineers to the austere, mountain-fearing mysticism of the Sherpas, one doesn't have to be a devotee of Eastern religions to wonder if perhaps the world might be a more appealing place had Everest been a little higher, the winds a little stronger, the cold more harsh, and the highest mountain in the world remained forever beyond the grasp of the humans living below.

"The mountain appears not to be intended for climbing," noted Mallory in his diary in 1921. He was speaking of the physical challenge, but oddly enough, at least some Western contemporaries also found philosophical obstacles. When the first expedition was being organized, a few London editorialists wondered about the wisdom of making the effort. "Some of the last mystery of the world will pass when the last secret place in it, the naked peak of Everest, shall be trodden by those trespassers," one prescient critic wrote.

In early June 1953, on their way down the mountain toward fame, the British expedition stopped at the Thyangboche Monastery to pay their respects. John Hunt told the elderly abbot that they had just climbed to the summit of Everest. "He was plainly incredulous and nothing would shake his unbelief," wrote Hunt, oblivious that if you thought God was on top of a mountain, you couldn't very well imagine a bunch of haggard, bearded foreigners tramping up to visit Him. "But his natural courtesy forbade him to give expression to this in so many words, and when we left he graciously congratulated us on 'nearly reaching the summit of Chomolungma.'"

THREE

Shiver Like Rhesus Monkeys

—

Institutionalized Failure

T HE KINDERGARTEN had a dollhouse and a collection of blocks, both heavy wooden ones and waxy red cardboard ones, made to resemble bricks. A variety of simple musical instruments—triangles, tambourines, rhythm sticks—were stashed in a big box. There was a large wooden airplane with wheels; you could sit on it and push with your feet. Inside the plane, for some reason, were small wooden bowling pins. There was an old upright piano.

My memories of the first day of kindergarten at Fairwood School are still very clear. Though I had coerced my mother into removing me from nursery school in the middle of the previous year (people were playing with my toys) and had dropped out of dance class (we had to take our socks off), I wasn't nervous or afraid now, the way some others were. A tiny redheaded girl named Jane Bush was crying, and had to be comforted by an immense plastic doll her mother had brought from home. This struck me as bad form.

The only personal detail I can recall about myself on that day is my mother's equipping me with a zippered change purse shaped like a clown's face. I took great pride in it. The nose squeaked.

We sat in groups of four at low, oblong tables. At mine was a very pretty girl named Carrie Shafts, whom I liked immediately and for the next dozen years, though our relationship never progressed beyond that initial point.

Many events of that year stand out. We made milk into butter. We marked the location of our homes on a map with colored pins. We dressed in our costumes all day on Halloween and paraded through the school (mine was a monster man, complete with a flashlight-like device that illuminated a miniature version of the scary mask I was wearing; when my name was called in roll call, I growled). We sat cross-legged and sang songs while our teacher, the sweetly named Mrs. McCloud, played the piano. On a rainy day, we made a big boat out of the blocks.

And, very near that first day, we were given mimeographs of an outline letter "A," surrounded by an apple, an airplane and other "A" words. The mimeograph was a vague purplish blue and smelled wonderful. We took out our flat black box of jumbo crayons, crayons distinguished by their own song, which we often sang ("Red and yellow and green and blue, brown and orange and purple too, all the colors that I know, live up in the rainbow").

Then we began to color the "A" sheet.

I don't remember coloring the subsequent letters, but I do remember launching into that initial "A." It was a propitious event. I didn't know it then, but we were all, up to that point, on equal ground in the eyes of the school. Though differing wildly in our backgrounds, abilities and potentials, we now found ourselves all kneeling at the same starting line. There were no slow learners, no gifted classes. No one had failed. No one had been draped in honor. We received our "A" handouts, held them up to our noses and sniffed their narcotic chemical air, and began to color. And we were never on equal ground again.

THE NATIONAL SPELLING BEE is a contest open to all students who are younger than sixteen and have not passed beyond the eighth grade. It is sponsored by the Scripps-Howard newspaper chain, aided by two hundred newspaper subsponsors nationwide.

Each year, about 9 million schoolchildren enter the bee, drawn by the prospect of scholarships, prizes and trips to Washington, D.C. Out of the nine million kids who enter the bee, only one wins. The rest lose.

The image of so many students being forced through that funnel, where a solitary student emerges at the end, a victor, while the others slink off in defeat, drew me to the bee, making it seem a paradigm for so much that goes on in organized mass education.

The education system, more than anything else, has created the terrifying image of failure that dwells in our inner souls, the dread, paralyzing demon to be avoided at all costs, the burning red F, the stigma, the shame.

A tutor can lead her handful of students through setbacks, detours and blind alleys in their quest for education without needing to unchain the concept of failure—the students may stumble, may botch assignments, but they dust themselves off and move on. Nobody has to fail, at least not in the way they do in public school.

But once you start packing forty kids in a room, things change. With the bright kids pawing the ground and straining to go forward, only so much time can be wasted on dummies before a teacher must shrug her shoulders, fail the stragglers and hope they do better the second time around. It is not a good way to accomplish what school is trying to accomplish.

Ditto for the bee. Not only does just one child out of 9,000,000 win, but the 8,999,999 losers lose in a public and humiliating fashion. As will be seen, it would be hard to think up a way to make failure in the bee more demeaning, particularly at the later stages, short of having a quartet of circus clowns drive deficient spellers from the stage with seltzer bottles and flappy paddles.

My plan was to pick someone who had competed in the nationals the previous year, on the assumption that she had to be good to have gotten that far once and, having whiffed victory, would redouble her efforts this year.

I settled on a twelve-year-old girl named Sruti Nadimpalli, basically because she lived close to Chicago and her last name did not present the phone book problems implicit in finding Gary Lee, the other local speller who had made it to the nationals the year before.

Even as I was leaving a message at the Nadimpalli home, I was nervous about explaining precisely what I had in mind. I couldn't lie and say I wanted to track Sruti's triumphant return to the nationals, culminating in victory this time.

But I couldn't say I wanted to document her second failure on the national stage either, to observe her humiliation and dissect it for my own particular purposes. "Hi! I'm a stranger writing a book on failure, and thought that I'd devote seventy-five pages to your young daughter, provided you give me access to her . . ."

What, then, to tell the mom? In my mind, I had conjured up a wildly protective, fictional mother for Sruti, someone who would share her daughter's bee compulsion. A fearsome image who would probably turn me down cold. And then what?

Even at the moment we were on the phone together, up to the point when Sruti's mother, in her charming, lilting accent, asked "And what is this book about?," I wasn't sure what to say. Naturally, I fudged. I said that the book was about "success and failure," then slowly peeled away the success part.

As always, the reality was more interesting than what I had imagined before the fact. Dr. Nadimpalli didn't need me to soft-pedal at all—she quickly grasped, and even seemed to embrace, the idea of the spelling bee as a failure metaphor, and cheerfully agreed to present my proposal to her daughter. A week later, I was at their home.

The Nadimpallis—both husband and wife are doctors—live in a large, boxy house in Highland Park, one of the affluent northern suburbs of Chicago. Inside, the house is elegantly decorated, with lovely sculptures of Hindu deities and a modern, open kitchen. Dr. Nadimpalli, the mom, met me first, and we spent a few minutes talking on the couch before her husband, daughter and son appeared.

Sruti is a tall girl, pleasant-faced, with round glasses that at times give her a somewhat startled look. She seemed well-spoken but, like most children, was not brimming with pithy phrasings or deep insights, particularly on the subject of spelling.

She said she has been in spelling bees since the fifth grade. She knew every word she had missed in each of the three competitions—"chieftain" in fifth grade, "idiosyncratic" in sixth, "arriccio" in seventh. I didn't know what the last word meant, and neither did she. This lack of concern over the meaning of words would trouble me more and more as I delved into the bee.

Getting to Washington, D.C., had been dramatic for Sruti. "If you saw the videotape of my reaction, when I spelled the word, my voice was shaking," she said. "I threw my head back and said, 'Oh my God!' And I was crying."

But she lost in the nationals, and suffered the added insult of newspapers around the country printing a wirephoto of her onstage, fast asleep in her chair, her mouth open. (In the initial round of the national bee, students must wait over three hours between turns, and battling boredom is a challenge. Imagine a marathon high school earth science class conducted under klieg lights.)

"I was really disappointed last year," she said. "At first I was thinking about not doing it next year, because I knew the pressure would be even greater next year because I went all the way to Washington the previous year, so if I don't get as far, then everybody's going to be really disappointed. That's why I was really nervous."

While Sruti talked, her little brother, Vamsi, sat cross-legged on the floor. A smart-looking nine-year-old, also in glasses, he had had his own spelling bee at Wayne Thomas Elementary that very day, and came in third. I had sympathy for him; his presence in his school's bee told me he was toiling in his older sister's shadow. I thought of my own brother, Sam, who is five years younger than I, but still had a social studies teacher calling him "Neil" in high school. Worse, the teacher laughingly refused to correct the error when it was pointed out to him, and it became such a problem my parents had to go in and convince him to stop.

I left the Nadimpalli house worried. They were very nice. Sruti seemed fairly balanced about the bee—serious, pleasant, not at all the Faulknerian monster of spelling I had hoped for.

EACH DAY, we got another letter to color, and slowly we groped forward, together at first as a pack, then separating ourselves into the brighter kids, who cruised through the Pilgrims, Henry Hudson, cursive, long division and whatever else was served at them, and the less bright, who flailed away in a losing battle to keep up. While we didn't have a lot in common, and our hugely differing levels of ability became clearer day by day, we were still basically kept together as a class, all in the same room, roughly the same thirty people, for the first seven years.

I was a bright kid, perhaps because of my own diligent efforts and deep intrinsic personal worth. Or perhaps because my father was a nuclear physicist who crammed our house with thousands of books and because my mother kept me constantly occupied with activities and read to me every day, all day—that is, when we weren't doing puzzles, or singing, or visiting the firehouse so I could check out my future place of employment.

Despite being bright, or perhaps because of it, I was a discipline problem. After learning about volcanoes, I built a volcano out of snow on a hot radiator in the hall. Gordon Gregg and I held the outer doors closed when kids were trying to come in from recess. I put a cookie on a girl's chair during lunchtime. And this was all just in the first grade.

For each transgression I was punished. For the cookie incident I was banished from the cafeteria for a week, forced to go home every day for lunch. Midway through my exile, my mother visited the school and met with the principal, Mr. Neptune. "Don't you understand, you're not punishing him—he *wants* to have his lunch at home," my mother told the principal. "You're punishing *me!*"

THE FEBRUARY DAY is crisp and bright, with snow on the ground. I walk into the Northwood Junior High School for its spelling bee, the first of three steps feeding contestants to the national bee. Many schools also have individual classroom bees, but this year Northwood doesn't, relying on written tests, much to Sruti's disappointment.

In the front hallway is a small poster. "If you can spell, you can win," it chirps. "The 1993 *Chicago Tribune* Chicagoland Spelling Bee." The poster, done in *Tribune* blue, with bees and honeycombs on it, is intriguing in some way I can't immediately put my finger on, something beyond its breathless "Hey, Kids! Win Prizes!" enthusiasm. My attention centers on the word "Chicagoland," repeated four times on the poster. Not a real word, of course, but a pompous *Tribune* construction, a byproduct of their insulated *Tribune über alles* philosophy that sees no conflict with sponsoring a spelling bee on one hand and manufacturing words of convenience on the other.

Then it hits me. Of course. The *Tribune*. Simplified spelling. They were the guys who decided that the language of Shakespeare, Poe and Whitman was too idiosyncratic and sloppy for so fine a publication as their own ("The World's Greatest Newspaper," no less) and had to be cleaned up in the name of efficiency, a quality the *Tribune* so admired in the Germans.

So beginning in 1934, the *Chicago Tribune* imposed "fantom," "lether," "crum," "tho," "trafic," "dialog," "frate" and seventy-three other simplified words on their readership in the regular news stories and headlines of the paper.

Not that the *Tribune* invented the idea, around since Benjamin Franklin's time. The heyday of simplified spelling was the turn of the century, when it was promoted by people such as Andrew Carnegie and Theodore Roosevelt, who really should have known better. Simplified spelling neatly encapsulated the robber baron paternalism and well-intentioned progressive disregard for the wishes of the general population so common at the time. Needless to say, it was a doomed endeavor. A country that ignores the clean logic of the metric system and, in some quarters, still fights against Daylight Saving Time as the personal handiwork of Satan himself is not going to embrace "thoroly," "thru" and "dropt."

(Still, some people must have been drawn in. One can only mourn for the children of parents who purchased *Nurseri Riemz and Simpl Poemz*, a 1912 volume published by the Simplified Spelling Sosieti and featuring such ditties as "Litl Boi Bluu," "Roc a Bie Baibi" and "Twincl, Twincl, Litl Star.")

The *Tribune* actually came late to the game, when World War II was about to render into painful quaintness such wistful notions of human perfectibility as Esperanto and simplified spelling. The policy was foisted on the *Tribune* by the paper's owner, Col. Robert McCormick, a puffed-up Pooh-Bah if ever there was one, who never let his endless rondo of self-congratulation be tempered by suspicions that his publishing success might have had something to do with his grandfather being one Joseph Medill, founder of the newspaper (and himself a simplified speller. Medill's 1867 monograph "An Easy Method of Spelling the English Language" contains sentences such as: "Lerning tu spel and red the Inglish langwaj iz the grat elementary task ov the pupol").

In 1955, with McCormick buried in his classical Greek sepulchre not quite five months, the *Tribune* could begin the task of freeing itself of simplified spelling. "Teachers were having trouble with it," explained editor W. Donald Maxwell. "They'd tell a child a way to spell a word and he'd bring in a *Tribune* to prove the teacher wrong." An editorial on August 21, 1955, revealed that the crusade had ended a few days before. "To our surprise, not one reader, as far as we are aware, noticed the change," the *Tribune* sighed. "We did not receive a single letter or telephone call on the subject." Still, the newspaper clung to certain spellings—"tho," "thru," "thoro," "cigaret"—which, from the lofty height of Tribune Tower, "appear to have won widespread acceptance." It was the late 1970s before the *Tribune* finally let go of the dream.

THE NORTHWOOD JUNIOR HIGH teachers are excited about the spelling bee. Mrs. Lenore Mornini predicts it will come down to a battle between Sruti and Jonathan Niehof, a new student from Canada.

The bee is held inside the school's immaculate auditorium, with clean, unslashed red-and-white padding on the walls and a "Huskies Rule!" sign decorated with a painted basketball. The noise level ratchets up as each grade enters and fills the seven rungs of bleachers pulled out from the cinderblock wall. The girls are both orderly and demonstrative, throwing chummy arms around each other as they head for their seats, laughing loudly, sucking on their necklaces. The boys linger on the way to the bleachers, looking for trouble—one approaches the judges' table and does a riff of impudence, as if declining a special form of sassy verb. "Hey, are you a judge?" he asks. "Are you all judges? Can I be a judge?" A teacher grabs him by the wrist and drags him away.

Soon the bleachers are filled and students begin sitting cross-legged on the floor. Dr. Charles Smith, the assistant principal, invites any participant who needs to use the bathroom to do so, and three students sprint for the johns. Sruti is not among them. She sits calmly at the far-left chair in an arc of sixteen chairs, facing the bleachers. She purses her lips and gazes placidly at her schoolmates.

Neil Codell, the young principal, is a friendly, small and handsome man with oiled hair, like a basketball coach's. His eyes are dark and alert, scanning the room, ready to spot mischief. After his school has settled down, he delivers a brief speech, which, filled as it is with nuance and conjuring up the atmosphere of a school better than some novels, deserves to be conveyed in its entirety:

> "We want to welcome all of you today to observe and enjoy this year's 1992/1993 school spelling bee. In the spirit of competition and participation, you as students know what our expectations are. If we find that you cannot live up to our expectations as an audience member, you will find yourself removed from today's assembly and a parent will be called. I need not say more. Our expectations are very significant in terms of your display when you are out in public like this. Please remember we do not want you cheering wildly, or at all, for any individual students. It is a

competition that is schoolwide; we appreciate that each home-room—excuse me, each classroom—is represented. However, the spirit of competition means that we are cheering for *everyone* here, so there is no clear-cut preference for anybody. Please understand that."

Codell introduces the contestants. It is immediately obvious that despite his instructions, there are indeed clear-cut preferences among the students for certain classmates. The wildest enthusiasm is for the new kid from Canada, whose name is greeted with a chant—"Nie-HOF! Nie-HOF! Nie-HOF!" Sruti also gets her share of applause. Turning the contest over to Dr. Smith, Codell utters this dark warning: "Remember, your noise influence could cause a candidate to make a mistake."

Dr. Smith explains some rule changes, and then they get started. The quest for the championship begins with Danny Entin, from Mrs. Weinstein's class. He looks at Dr. Smith expectantly.

"Okay, Danny, we'll be going in order," Dr. Smith says. "Just a reminder to all of the contestants. If you do not understand the way I say it, or what I said, ask me to repeat it. First word: 'salute.' "

Danny spells "S-O-L-I-T."

"Sorry, Danny," Dr. Smith says. The students murmur, and Danny goes to sit down, not visibly distressed.

Sruti's first word is "ambush." She spells it quickly, with a matter-of-fact, almost bored expression. Over the next ten rounds, she spells her words—"punish," "difficult," "profile," "objective," "temperate," "passenger," "subscribe," "podium," "palace" and "un-interrupted"—with almost the same languor. The only hint of drama comes in Round 6 when, in spelling "temperate," she has the upward shift of a question in her voice on the second "e," which, coupled with the fact that I have already spelled the word wrong in my notes, makes me momentarily fear she has missed it.

Contestants can ask for the definition of a word, for its nation of origin, and whether the root is a specific root they have in mind—whether the root of "humanitarian" is "human." In Round 11, Christina Fidel asks for the definition of her word, "existential," and I lean forward slightly in anticipation. I've always wanted to know—the best conception I have involves Sartre wanting to puke whenever he sees an oak tree, and that can't be right. But I get no closer to the truth. "A state or fact of being of existence of existentialism," the teacher reads, none too helpfully, stumbling three times over the last word.

Mrs. Mornini was right. By Round 12, only Jon Niehof and Sruti are left. They spell "probability" and "outrageous," respectively. In Round 13, Jon's Canadian accent makes his "g" and "e" sound like "j" and "a" when spelling "generosity," but he inserts an unambiguous "u" and blows it. The students howl.

Since Sruti has come after Jon in order during the rounds, she must spell two words correctly now to win. She misses the first, "irreducible." There is a huge cheer from the Niehof supporters. Sruti's fans groan. Jon slumps and touches his hand to his chest.

"Another squeaker," says a teacher, noting there are six minutes left before the end of the period. Getting spelling bees in on time is a high priority.

The two students duel through Rounds 14, 15, 16 and 17, Sruti spelling "compromise," "memorabilia," "similarity" and "inferential," the last spelled so quickly it makes my fingers tingle.

In Round 18, Jon misses "relinquish." Hope keeps the Niehofophiles quiet after Sruti spells "melancholy," but then she knocks off "authentic" for the victory and there is a loud

"Awwwwww . . ." from Jon's supporters, while Sruti gets cheers from her partisans.

As the students begin rising to go, Codell makes another little speech, this one also freighted with implication:

> "Congratulations to all the contestants. And we now know that next year we will finally have a new champ. But this year, three years straight, Sruti Nadimpalli, defending her crown . . ."

His voice is lost in the screams of the departing students. I ponder the "finally" in his statement, which seems to speak volumes, making me wonder whether Codell would say the same thing of a departing star athlete: *"Finally* the MVP award will go to somebody else next year . . ."

I figure I should go over to Sruti, lingering with her knot of friends, and say something. But the effort fizzles. I offer congratulations; she looks at me blankly. With no idea what else to say, I blurt out "I'll call you" and walk away, shaking my head over this banal adultism.

In the hall, dense with children, a teacher scolds one of her charges: "You're entitled to your opinion, but you should congratulate her anyway . . ." I burst out the front doors into the winter air, where yellow buses are lined up and the kids, dressed like skiers, are on their way home, the older ones with their coats open, defying the cold.

I CAN'T REMEMBER ever getting an F, ever, in my entire academic career, which means either I never got one or I somehow suppressed the fact. I think I would remember—the spelling test in second grade when I blanked out on the spelling of "of" and ended up spelling it "ove" is still a crisp memory.

But people did get them. I remember seeing F's on classmates' papers and feeling a mixture of pity and revulsion. The pity might be a later interpretation. Sympathy is not a particularly common emotion in public schools, and I could have laid it over the scene, like a gel, to soften the beastliness of our undiluted contempt for the dullards in class.

The system was set up for a certain middle approach, and those who strayed too far ahead could be cut off as ruthlessly as those who fell behind. I was always getting entangled in the swoop of my imagination and tripped up by my outside reading, floundering into nasty encounters such as the Bushy Tail Episode.

In third grade, we had a workbook quiz whose purpose was to instill within us the difference between the concepts of "possible" and "impossible." We were given a list of statements and asked to check whether they were possible or not. One statement was "A pig with a bushy tail." I checked "possible," and it was marked wrong.

This surprised and offended me. The next day, I brought in my *Golden Book of Biology* from home and showed Mrs. Nemeth the section about salamander body parts being grafted onto each other. If the leg of a big salamander could be grafted onto the body of a small salamander, I argued, wasn't it *possible* for, say, a bushy fox's tail to be grafted onto a pig?

I think she hated me after that.

THREE WEEKS AFTER the bee at Northwood, I am back in another affluent suburb—this time Deerfield, where the Lake County Spelling Bee is being held this evening at South Park Elementary School.

Students are met in the teacher's lounge by Mrs. Denise Nielsen-

Hall, the very large, Hershey's Kiss–shaped principal of the school, who checks their names off a register and hands out name tags, and white cards with numbers on them to be hung around the neck with a string of red yarn, as well as fancy little flower arrangements.

"It makes it a little festive," she explains, referring to the boutonnieres and corsages, each of which has a little bee alighting on the flowers. The bees, she adds, are ordered especially for her by a florist.

Despite this enthusiastic flourish, Mrs. Nielsen-Hall is no spelling bee booster. "They're public and traumatic and I don't like them very much," she says, then tells this story:

> "I had a bee at a school district where I was principal. There were maybe twenty kids in the bee. We got down to the last four children. One of the little girls, I gave her a word, and she misspelled it. She became so frantic she ran from the stage into the audience, into her parents arms . . . We continued then, and I gave the next word. She turned around and, in front of two hundred people, screamed at me: 'That word is easier than the word you gave me!' It was terrible."

At the moment she ends the story, as if cued by the word "terrible," a girl comes up to the table, and the principal's demeanor shifts.

"Hi, are you a contestant?" Mrs. Nielsen-Hall says brightly. "And what's your name—Kelly Talbot?—okay, Kelly Talbot, you are number eighteen—that's a good number! Kelly, you need to put that around your neck and put your name tag on and then you can throw your coat on the table . . ."

The bee is held in the gym. I note that the trappings of officialdom are already beginning to creep into the bee process. In addition

to the stark numbered card hung around each neck, there is a program—colored the pastel orange particular to children's aspirin and
school publications. The program mentions the *Chicago Tribune* three
times and Scripps-Howard, the sponsor of the national bee, five
times.

Affixed to the blue pleated curtain at the back of the gym is an
array of large yellow paper bees, charmingly crude, in a range of
different sizes and shapes, colored in a bold, scribbling style that
suggests kindergarten. I carefully count, several times, until I am
certain there are forty-six primitive bees.

"I'd like to W-E-L-C-O-M-E all of you to South Park School,"
begins Mrs. Nielsen-Hall, to general laughter. During my months
examining the bee, I can never quite appreciate the appeal of this
pervasive bee pun. Most of the newspaper headlines about the bee
use some form of it, tired and clichéd though it is (plays on the word
"bee," or some hive reference, coming in a distant second). A fuller
exploration of this phenomenon I will leave to my future scholarly
monograph, "Bee Buzzing with L-A-U-G-H-T-E-R: Modal Attempts at Humor in Orthographic Contests."

Mrs. Nielsen-Hall also tells the students, "You're all winners,
because you're here tonight," a concept parroted again and again by
bee officials at higher levels, and one completely at cross-purposes
with what the bee is actually doing—that is, weeding out the losers
and creating increasingly smaller sets of winners who move on to lose
at higher levels.

I wonder about the necessity of the lie. Children are smart, and
they will realize that, Mrs. Nielsen-Hall's good intentions notwithstanding, they are not all winners. They will not all win and move up
to the state championship. What they have done—and what I think
Mrs. Nielsen-Hall means to say—is win to get here, thus having
accomplished something notable whether they move on or not. Too

bad she can't just come out and say something like: "By the time tonight is over, most of you will have lost—we can only have one winner here tonight—but just because you have lost, do not feel like a loser, because by struggling to get here you will have attained a private victory." It seems a much healthier sentiment. At least it would be more honest. With kids, adults feel the need to sugarcoat.

As the bee process unfolds, one is always confronted with some previously unimagined marvel, and tonight it is in the form of Mr. Bill Cloud, introduced as "a professional spelling bee pronouncer."

An older, ruddy-faced man, Mr. Cloud begins an earnest explanation of every aspect of the bee rules. He introduces his wife, Madge, who is also a pronouncer and will share his duties. His thorough sincerity is very comforting—he is obviously not a man who is taking this lightly. But he is also like an emissary from the adult world of mortgages, lawsuits and witness stands, where a single slurred syllable can take on huge significance. His instructions, delivered in a mellifluous, calm, bell-clear voice, are designed to prevent common bee crises, the frissons of which are still felt, as a distant echo.

"I cannot tell you how many unexpected things can occur," he says philosophically. "Think about what could occur, in accents and so on. It has happened as far as Madge and I have been able to tell. Sometimes a videotape is played over for an hour while three judges try to decide what actually was said. It can get complicated. Most of the time it is not, but it can get quite complicated."

The thirty-six contestants have a choice of high or low microphones to compensate for their greatly differing heights. There is a practice round. The second speller, Sunnie Levin, holds a lucky troll. The word she is given is "nozzle." She asks Mr. Cloud to repeat the word, and he does, in an achingly precise way: "Noz-zle."

"Nozzle?" Sunnie asks, then spells: "N-O- . . . Z-Z . . . L . . . E."

"That is correct," says Mr. Cloud, turning to address the audience. "You will notice that when she said 'nozzle' in a questioning way, I did not say 'yes,' " he says. "So Mrs. Cloud and I will never say 'yes,' we will only repeat the word. Of course, the reason is we might not be thinking of the same word the contestant said. So we'll never verify when you say it, we'll always just repeat the word if you wish us to repeat it."

Five of the thirty-six contestants miss words in the practice round. Sruti, who is No. 27, is given "politician," and nails it.

Then the real bee begins. Round I is a killer. George Holdcroft, who wears glasses, adds an "e" to "ransom," takes his certificate, and is out before seven o'clock. The program states that all contestants are required to remain until the entire contest is completed, but that rule is simply ignored. John Evans, a dignified, husky-voiced, heavy boy with a buzz haircut, misses "worthwhile." He has a vacant, perhaps stunned, expression as he slowly walks down the center aisle, and I follow him, wanting to ask him something, to probe his emotional state. But I can't do it—from afar, I watch John and his family quietly put on their coats and leave. No point in holding a mirror to their misery; it's all too clear. I return to the gym.

Matthew Briddell misspells "dullard," and goes to sit by his mom. She rubs his back comfortingly. "It's okay," she says. Together they examine the certificate carefully, as if it were a work of great detail and interest.

The bee falls into a pattern. The cycle begins with Mr. Cloud's rhythmic introduction, "Your word is . . . ," followed by the suspense of the student's spelling and the relief of a muffled "That is correct" from the judges' table. Sometimes, the judge says that a spelling is incorrect, and Mr. Cloud eulogizes, "The correct spelling is . . ." At higher levels, the process will not be nearly so kind.

To my surprise, no child reacts violently to defeat. Rather, each conveys some small message of disappointment or sadness. Winifred Alves gives a slight nervous smile when she misses "resistible." Patrick Putnam misspells "pleurisy," and does sort of a rolling turn away from the microphone, leading with his head, as if being shot. Jill Gluszik's openmouthed reaction to the word "deficiency" shows she doesn't know it. She doesn't.

Though spelling correctly, No. 24—Robert Zwirner—stands out for the startling look on his face. It is a tight frown, shaped like an upside down U—a cartoon character's frown. He sits clasping his hands on the sides of his chair, his face sharp, the corners of his mouth drawn intently down, as if he might cry any moment. It is a disturbing expression.

At a break, I go to seek out the Clouds. They are high school English teachers from the suburbs of Chicago. They've taken many courses in linguistics and phonetics and the history of language. They get paid for their work this evening—$200 for the pair. Over time, Mr. Cloud says, he has observed that the winners are usually those who worked the hardest. "The people who win tend to study with their parents an hour a day for years," he says. He also imparts a bit of insider cut-throat spelling bee strategy—sometimes, he says, a speller will ask the derivation of a word just to see which part of the dictionary it is in, whether Mr. Cloud turns to the front for "f," for instance, or more toward the back for "ph."

George Holdcroft's mom comes up, sort of laughing. "My poor guy," she says. "He studied all those words. He knew all the advanced words and everything. He was the one who spelled 'ransom' wrong. He goes, 'Oh, I knew ransom. R-A-N-S-O-M.' He was so nervous. He was the first one out . . ."

Mr. Cloud is used to this. "Ohhh, that's too bad," he coos sympathetically. "What grade is he in? Fifth grade? Oh, he'll be back."

"I felt so awful," Mrs. Holdcroft continues. "I thought, At least he misspelled a really easy word. If he misspelled a hard word, he would have thought, I didn't study enough."

Unable to contain myself, I ask her how her son felt to be the first one out. "Awful, probably," she says dismissively, as if it's a dumb question, which it probably is. "But he was sitting there, he could spell all the other words." Then Mrs. Holdcroft reveals her true purpose—would a list of the words used in the bee be available? Mr. Cloud tells her no.

Back at my chair, in the moments before the bee resumes, I strike up a conversation with the father sitting to my right. "I remember standing up there," he says. "If you get the word right, you're a hero. If you don't, you're a dummy."

By Round 4, most of the contestants have been eliminated and the audience is greatly attrited.

Robert, the kid in the frown mask, is given "succotash," which he pronounces crisply and begins spelling confidently, "C-U—" He stops cold. He knows. He shakes his head, disbelieving. You cannot correct yourself at the bee. The end of the word is spelled quickly, in a crushed whisper: ". . . C-C-O-T-A-S-H."

Mr. Cloud has pity on him. "The correct spelling is—by the way, you knew that, didn't you?" he says. "The correct spelling is S-U-C-C-O-T-A-S-H. Sometimes you can tell they know it, but are thinking of the next letter. Your word is . . ."

The bee proceeds, but on Robert's face an amazing thing happens. He smiles for the first time that night, a big, bright smile, his expression transforming back into that of a child as he takes his seat in the audience.

By Round 6, there are eleven students. These are the diehards. Round 6 is the first one to pass without a single student missing. A baby in the audience breaks out in a full-throated cry as Sruti is given the word "latticework." She spells it, her articulation of the "w" a gem of pronunciation, over the baby's screams, which stop the moment she spells the final "k."

Four contestants are left by Round 12. No. 22, Bob Berman, a chubby little boy in a blue-and-white-striped shirt, buttoned at the wrists but untucked at the waist, is shaping up to be Sruti's toughest competition. He stands very straight, almost at attention, shoulders square, head level, his little fists on his hips, and methodically spells "encroachment." In the next round, he spells "lanolated." He is a rock.

There is a break before Round 16. The students return to find a much tougher world. A spelling bee is, first and foremost, a show, and should it drag on, the organizers are quick to bring out the heavy artillery to slay the stragglers. Sruti starts the round carefully spelling "armigerous," but "kaolinize" hangs in the air in front of Jordanna Grant like a palpable menace. She asks for a definition, and is told that it is "to convert a feldspar mineral into a fine white clay." That doesn't help much; she doesn't get close. Foluso Williams misses "exaration"—"an act or a product of writing"—and looking glum, is out.

Two are left, Bob and Sruti. There is a pause as the really tough words are slipped out of their lead-lined case (or so I imagine). The silent atmosphere of expectation is thankfully broken, however, as Mr. Cloud, the pronouncer, stumbles on the first monster word.

"Your word is 'decumbuctchured' . . ." he says, obviously mangling the word, and there is general laughter. "Decumbiture," he says precisely, and, when asked, gives the definition as "the time of taking to one's bed because of sickness."

Bob works out the word, squeezing his eyes shut. "D-E- . . . C-U-M-B- . . . I-T-U-R-E," he spells, and the judge's "That is correct" has an emphatic hint of wonder in it. There are gasps and oohs and applause from the audience. Bob looks around, beaming, as if he can't believe it himself.

Mr. Cloud again stumbles, over "cruciferous," drawing more hilarity, and Sruti knocks it down with a minimum of fuss. Bob is given "nictitant"—"adapted for winking"—but adds an initial "k" and is out. Sruti must spell one more word—"scurrilous." It is too easy. She spells it, receives a long, hearty applause, and the bee is over.

There is a quick ceremony distributing fame. The runner-up gets a trophy and, in a clever stroke, his school building gets an identical one marking the accomplishment "so it will be long remembered" there.

IN ELEMENTARY SCHOOL, my primary concern was not good grades but being late for class. I never was, and worried about protecting my streak in the last couple of years. In junior high, good grades became a mania. I remember groveling before Mr. Garman—a cagey old seventh-grade English teacher who had charmed me by explaining that the word "dashboard" came from a panel used to block mud from sprinting horses—to change my justly deserved B to an A. I prevailed through sheer desperation, but I still remember his sneer of disgust as he agreed to change the grade, if only to shut me up.

It wasn't that I had some tyrant at home waiting to cane me if my grades slipped. I did well enough that my parents didn't mind the occasional B or C. What spurred me on—and I assume other people—was the point average. With the 4-point A, it correlated nicely to a batting average in baseball, and if you were a 3.2, you thought about pulling it up to a 3.5; a 3.5, to a 3.75; and so on.

In this fashion, grades became an end in themselves, divorced from any idea of learning or education or anything. In high school, an A in an honors course counted for a heady 5 points, and I became loathe to take nonhonors courses, not because of the lessened challenge—sometimes nonhonors classes were harder, if only because you had to rub elbows with the hoi polloi—but because their low-octane A's would pull down my grade point average.

Toward this end, I became perhaps the only student in the history of Berea High School to take the same class twice while getting an A both times. It was Bonnie Brown's Honors Advanced Placement Literature class. When I signed up a second time, she complained to the principal that a student couldn't take a class that had already been successfully completed. I argued that since the focus of the class alternated, one year European literature, one year American literature, it was an entirely different body of material and thus a different class. The principal shrugged and let me take Miss Brown's class again.

I think she hated me after that.

TWO SPELLERS ARE sent to the nationals from the greater Chicago area: one from the city, one from the suburbs.

The suburban championship is held on a grayish spring day in an auditorium on the seventh floor of the Tribune Tower, a gothic horror show of a building, festooned with arches, flying buttresses, peaked cornices, fleurs-de-lis and vaulted doorways.

With an hour to go before the bee, there is time to wander around the seventh floor's dark wood–paneled hallways. A mother is amazed that all spelling lists have to be checked at the door, like guns in a Western saloon. "So what's the idea with this?" she says to her son, who is eating a big cookie. "They think I'm going to cheat for you? That I could sign the right spellings to you?" She wiggles her fingers in imitation of some complicated sign code. The lady doth protest too much, methinks.

Sruti's mother is in the cookie room having a cup of coffee. We chat pleasantly—Sruti is nervous, as always, her mother tells me—until Sruti shows up and levels a meaningful look at her mother. "Did it pop again?" Dr. Nadimpalli asks, and goes off to fix a pre-bee crisis—a defective skirt zipper. A particularly awkward and embarrassing situation, but I hold out hope that the skirt predicament will actually help, by distracting Sruti from the pending bee so she won't be as nervous. I am confident she is going to win.

In a side office I discover our friend Mr. Bill Cloud, lounging with other bee officials. We strike up a conversation, and Mr. Cloud asks me what this book that I'm writing is about. I have barely uttered a sentence when a red-faced, portly man who turns out to be Casey Banas, education writer from the *Tribune* and one of the judges, butts in. "You're going to say spelling bees are a failure?!?!" he sputters angrily, his fists doubled, as if he were about to leap up and punch me. I quickly calm him, pointing out that what I really hope to do is see how kids cope with failing in the bee, and so on. Then I beat a hasty retreat, marveling that a man with such a stevedore temperament can cover anything, never mind education.

Settling down in my aisle seat, I have time to scope out the room, which is richly appointed with *Tribune* lucre. Twenty-one stylish brass chairs with green cushions are set up and ready before a brown velvet curtain at the front of the room.

Right behind me, two people are talking, and as I tune into their conversation, one is complaining bitterly. "Look how close we are to the front row," she says in a flat, nasal voice, obviously referring to the distance between the audience and the contestants' chairs. "I don't like this. We're too close to people."

"You're just going to have to block us out," says an older woman, apparently her mother. "Look over people's heads."

I turn in my chair to casually scan the room and, while doing so, slyly examine the contestant behind me. She is No. 19, Janelle Jensen, who, like the intensely frowning boy in the Lake County bee, has a disconcerting adult look to her; in this case, a pinchedness, a sour tension, set off by her hooded eyes and her secretary's outfit—white blouse, blue skirt, hoop earrings, high heels. She could pass for being forty years old. This is not comic exaggeration. She could process your new driver's license at the Department of Motor Vehicles and you wouldn't think twice about it.

The contestants take their chairs at the front of the room. Maureen Martino, from the *Tribune* public relations department, trots out the standard bee philosophy of universal victory. "Whoever wins the championship, we all go home winners," she says. "Just remember that." Then she warns parents not to mouth words, even silently to themselves, lest their children—winners all—be disqualified.

With everyone in their places up front except for Sruti, I begin to genuinely worry. Just then Sruti shows up, finally, tottering a bit but regaining herself. A big sweater hides the balky zipper. She takes her seat with the other spellers, facing us.

Mr. Cloud looks more like a banker than a teacher—nice loafers, a charcoal suit. He paces as he gives his introductory speech.

"Good luck to all of you," Mr. Cloud says in conclusion, then turns to the audience. "They really are all winners, and by the way, so are you, you parents and teachers."

There is a practice round. The first round starts with fairly easy words, such as "daughter," "verify" and "brilliance." Sruti spells "dainty."

Janelle Jensen, the girl from the DMV, spells "maimed" with a crisp efficiency.

Round 1 passes with no one missing. "Madge, would you go get us a hotel room—this is going to take a couple of weeks," Mr. Cloud jokes between rounds.

The first person out is No. 8, Shawna Hammons, from downstate. She misses "conveyance" and, showing no emotion, sits down in the front row.

I have just decided that Janelle Jensen will be Sruti's toughest opponent when Janelle is blindsided in Round 2 by "wunderkind." She obviously doesn't know the word—she asks for it to be repeated, then for the definition and for it to be used in a sentence. She is grasping at straws, buying time. But she puts an "e" where the "i" should be. Wearing that same sour look she began with, she goes back to sit by her mom.

The competition proceeds, with students dropping out in every round, none in any dramatic way. Byron Barnes's mom hurries in, late, and sits down between me and her husband. Whatever kept her, it was not indifference—her eyes are riveted to her son. When he spells, she purses her lips tight, clamps her right hand across her chest, and rocks nervously. In Round 3, he is given "pompadour." He stands very still, his large hands jutting out of sleeves that may be a little short. He asks for the definition, for the sentence, for the word origin. He thinks, then spells the word, correctly. He smiles broadly. His mother lets out her breath. Byron has inherited his mother's nerves. In between turns at the mike, he makes gentle, silent clapping motions with his hands, as if to dry them off.

Sruti has only three distinct gestures I can detect. At ease, she slumps in her chair severely, as if about to slip to the floor. Nervous, she fools with a bracelet. And while spelling, she locks herself down by clasping her right hand around her left wrist.

In the next three rounds, Sruti spells "telegenic," "dowager" and "lambently" (which she pronounces more clearly than Mr. Cloud).

Before Round 5, there is a break, and afterward Sruti again scoots in at the last second, but not before causing a bit of panic for her neighbor, Jessica Delfert, a girl who constantly cocks her head to the side while thinking. "Oh my God, I don't know where Sruti is," she chirps, head tilted, gazing toward the door. Sruti has a habit of chatting with the girl next to her, and usually, by the end of the bee, the girls are friends.

Fifteen people are left at the beginning of Round 5.

Sruti spells "perennate." Jacob Gordon-Schlosberg, who has a haughty, bored expression and a tone to match, snaps out "repechage" as if he had a train to catch.

Sruti spells "feracious." In Round 7, Byron Barnes goes out on "dodecuplet." He has sort of a hazy, faraway smile as he takes his seat next to his parents. Sruti spells "smorgasbord." Jacob spells "idiosyncratically," and nods at the "That is correct" as if to say, "Damn right that is correct, lady."

Nine are left at Round 8. Sruti spells "tatami." There is a pause before Jacob is given his word, and he rolls his eyes impatiently. He is punished with "contrariety." He grasps for the definition and the sentence. He takes a shot, and is out. I think, "Not so cocky *now*, are we, Jacob?"

The bee grinds on. Sruti spells "prejudicial." She spells "cointise." She spells "vizierial." She spells "phosphoresce." She spells "adjuvant." She spells "pterodactyl," while Jessica Delfert looks at her with something akin to wonder, her head tipped to one side, her mouth agape. Sruti spells "cronyism."

It goes slowly. Six are still left at Round 15, and nobody goes out. Sruti spells "specie." She spells "jurimetrician."

Before Round 17, there is a short break. The *Tribune* guy, Casey

Banas, stands up, hitches his pants around his gut, and grunts dismissively, "All girls left."

The extra chairs are stacked and removed. Sruti is last of the six contestants. She gets "obstetrician"—which should be cake for the daughter of two doctors, but she asks for a definition anyway. Spelling it, she allows herself a "whew" in the mike, and laughs. Nerves.

She spells "unaccommodating."

The six hold out, round after round. Sruti spells "repetend." She spells "cottagey." She spells "palustrine." She spells "psychrometer." She spells "pignorate."

The Clouds may need that hotel room yet.

Before Round 23, Mrs. Cloud visits the judges. I anticipate a fusillade of lethal words, and am not disappointed. Contestants spell "suspirious," "caladium," "paranee," "bilander." Finally, Jessica Delfert goes out on "enfilade." She sits down next to her mom and cries. Sruti spells "lyncine," "kishke," "bartizan," "paseo."

Then in 27 it happens. Four are left. The competitors spell "halieutics," "champignon," "caisson." Sruti gets "desinence." She stammeringly asks the word to be used in a sentence, then takes a stab at it. "I'm sorry, that is incorrect," says Mrs. Cloud. Sruti, glumly playing with her bracelet, goes back to her seat, in the front row, and puts her head on her mother's shoulder. She, too, starts to weep, her mother comforting her.

I am almost surprised that, with Sruti out, the bee continues. With three left, there is a round-robin effect, with one girl always at the mike, one girl always standing waiting to go, and the third sitting down.

There is a three-minute break before Round 36. Mr. Cloud announces that 265 words have been given.

In Round 36, Leah Petrusiak, a red-haired Catholic school girl who wears bumblebee earrings and delivers her spellings in a monotone, is faced with "transcendental." In the state bee for the third time, Leah asks for the word to be repeated, for a definition, for the word to be used in a sentence. She asks for the word origin, for it to be repeated again, and yet again.

She spells the word, apparently without the "c," yet it is deemed correct. A murmur breaks out in the audience and the judges quickly ask for the tape to be played back. A moment later the exchange booms in perfect clarity from expensive *Tribune* speakers. Leah sits with her hands at the sides of her face, agonizing. The "c" is clearly dropped. Mr. Cloud asks for the tape to be played yet again. The phrase "torturing her" is heard from the audience. Finally, Mrs. Cloud says, "I'm sorry, that's incorrect," then gives the correct spelling, stressing the "c."

In Round 38, Cheryl Oliver misses "bastion." Jo Marie Sison, a girl I hadn't really noticed before, spells "metamorphosis" and "jingoistic" and is the champion.

Maureen Martino is back. She hands out certificates to the contestants, who have stayed around this time, and leaves the audience with this thought: "You're all going home winners, just remember that. On behalf of the *Chicago Tribune*, I'd like to thank you for supporting the Chicagoland *Tribune* Spelling Bee."

Casey Banas has taken Jo Marie into a corner and is interviewing her. I consider drifting nearby and listening in; but afraid of Banas, I decide against it. As suburban champion, Jo Marie will be consigned to a single paragraph at the end of Banas's story on the city champion, Sophoan Khoeun. Normally, it would be considered a conflict of interest for a journalist to write about the annual picnic of a church he belongs to, so Banas's dual role as judge and journalist is ample proof that the *Tribune* views the bee as an utter nonevent.

Sruti is still crying when the bee ends, so I thank her parents for letting me tag along, quiz a few of the losers, then beat it out of there.

At this point, I'm ready to let the entire matter drop. My contestant didn't make it. The bee was not the baroque horror I had hoped for—nothing detestable, just a sad process, a formality, a strange adult ritual that magnifies the natural disappointments and frustrations of childhood, all toward a dubious end. Good spelling is a handy skill, but as a professional writer, I know that 99 percent of good spelling is keeping a dictionary handy and using it when you are in any doubt. If I am a little shaky on the second vowel in "separate" (as I am, from time to time), I don't squint my eyes and try to dredge the proper spelling out of some inner core. I look it up in a dictionary.

IN COLLEGE I met my match. Basic Writing was taught by an old geezer, George Heitz, who would retire at the end of the year. Our first assignment was to write an article about our preparations for the first class. I wrote a solipsistic thing involving, I believe, my gazing out at the beads of rain on a window.

The next class, Heitz stood at the front of the room, holding our papers loosely in his hand. His tone was subdued, sorrowful. "In my many years of teaching," he said, "I don't believe I have ever read a group of articles as inadequate as these . . ."

At this point, I sincerely expected him to continue, "except for this one, this gem of perfection," and then read my paper to the class, pausing to shake his head in wonder and wipe tears from his eyes.

Instead, I got a C-minus, the paper an explosion of red pen marks. I still have it somewhere, and would pull it out and reread it if I could stand the thought that I share the same corporeal essence as the person who wrote it.

Through diligent effort, I was able to pull my grade up in Heitz's class to, I believe, a B by the end of the semester. I was very proud of that B.

ON THE PLANE to Washington, D.C. Tuesday morning, the day before the 66th Annual Scripps-Howard National Spelling Bee begins, I find myself sitting next to Holly Pittner, of Sheboygan, Wisconsin, and her daughter, Sarah, ten. Forgetting that the bee contestants have already been in Washington for two days, attending pre-bee functions, I strike up a conversation with Mrs. Pittner, hoping they might be on their way to the bee, which I have decided to attend, despite misgivings.

It turns out they are going to the Odyssey of the Mind, which Mrs. Pittner describes as "a creative, problem-solving competition," to be held at the University of Maryland at College Park. I have never heard of it, but apparently it is a big deal, with 5,000 kids coming from all over the world to compete in both long-term and spontaneous problem-solving events. Sarah, who wears glasses and a purple jumper, is part of a team charged with dreaming up new types of dinosaurs and constructing them out of papier-mâché, then putting on a sketch featuring their creations. The dinosaurs, carefully confined to crates, have already been shipped to Maryland.

"They're not going there to win, they're going there for the experience," Mrs. Pittner assures me.

I tell her that I will try to make it out to the U of M to see the competition if things slow down at the bee, which I imagine they might.

The afternoon before the bee, the Presidential Ballroom at the

Capital Hilton is all set up and ready to go, arrayed with beigish pink chairs. It has an eerie, empty stillness—I'm the only one there —and I can scope out the lay of the battlefield. The 235 spellers will sit in four long rows, stretched across the entire length of the ballroom and elevated on risers. Immediately before them is a dais, where the judges and pronouncer will no doubt sit. In the rest of the ballroom, facing them, are long tables, covered in white linen, where the members of the press will sit. Water pitchers and glasses are ready to go. In an ancillary, smaller room, set perpendicular to the main room, like the base of a T, is where the parents will be exiled, cut off by a square proscenium arch. Four big televisions are set up to bring the action to the bulk of the parents, who won't be able to see much of anything from where they are sequestered. Come early, I think.

Outside the ballroom are bulletin boards. Most have newspaper clippings, hyping the present bee and ballyhooing bees of the past. There are many examples of the previously mentioned bee pun syndrome—"Carlisle's Cheng Wins in C-L-A-N-G-O-R-O-U-S Style" and "Buzzword Is Delinquent for Spelling Bee Champion." On another board, an odd sort of Kiddie Classified has been established, mostly siblings dragged along to the bee, now becalmed in their rooms and searching for distraction. "10-year-old girl who is sister of a speller needs a friend—staying in room #987. Call after 9 a.m. and before 8 p.m.," reads one. Another: "Almost 8-year-old sister of bee speller looking for playmate. If you are too, please contact room 896. From Ellie." A third: "Speller wants to meet spellers from *Florida.* Come or call. Room #868. Ask for Emily! Anyone Welcome!" The similarity to lonely hearts personals is a little unnerving.

In the press room, I find three Scripps-Howard staffers—college kids, in spelling bee T-shirts. They are hanging out, having fun; and introducing myself, I join them. "You have to meet Mr. Bee," says

Ellen Morrison, a DePauw University senior, taking me up to a 3-foot-high wood-and-wire bee figure. Mr. Bee has a pleasing, 1950s, Reddy Kilowatt feel, and I suggest they would sell more bee T-shirts if they put his picture on them rather than the present drab sextet of stylized words (a multicolored "spectrum," "staccato" written over musical bars, a striped "zebroid," and so on).

We have a wide-ranging conversation about the bee. The volunteers are surprisingly loose with negative information. Joel Pipkin, a recent graduate from Midwestern State University, suggests that the bee is a good way for junior high kids to pick each other up—he has seen contestants holding hands. Just joking, of course, he quickly adds. Ha-ha-ha. They tell me about nervous kids falling off the stage, and about the Comfort Room, a chamber off the ballroom where the failed contestants are immediately led to compose themselves after missing their words.

"You won't be allowed in, because the kids will be upset," says Shannon Harris, another DePauw student.

"And because you're a journalist," adds Ellen Morrison, who seems to have a thing against journalists, so much so that I ask why. She explains that a few days earlier the *Washington Post* ran a scathing article about the bee, and so everybody on the bee staff is skittish around reporters. I thank her for this information.

They are so forthcoming with damning details about the bee that I find myself laboriously explaining the journalistic process to them. I say something like: "You understand that I'm a writer. I'm talking to you because I'm writing a book, which will be published and the general public will then read." Normally this speech is reserved for people I suspect of having limited mental capacity, given in the hope of helping them comprehend what is going on and reducing the chances of their being surprised to see their words in print later on.

The next morning, I get to the bee a half hour early, thinking I must sit with the parents since I haven't been accredited as a reporter. The first person I run into is Ellen Morrison, barely recognizable in her peach publicist's suit and done-up hair. She flaps over to me, a flurry of concern, worried that I will quote her candid comments of the day before "out of context."

The concept of being quoted out of context was invented, I believe, by people who blurt out ill-advised statements and then regret them later. True out-of-context distortion—someone saying "It's not as if I'm a thing of evil," and being quoted as bragging "I'm a thing of evil"—is rare to the point of being unknown.

On the other hand, highlighting controversial statements over the more mundane is the basis of reporting. That's what news is. If I interview a kindly old kindergarten teacher who spends forty-five minutes telling me how much she loves the kids, and bakes them cookies shaped in the letters of their names, and then suddenly adds, "Of course, what I'd really like to do is to strip the little buggers naked and torture them to death with a potato peeler," her previous sentiments suddenly diminish in value. Perhaps, from her perspective, it is unfair to seize on a single sentence and obsess over it, ignoring, for the most part, her loftier expressions. But from the perspective of everybody else, I don't have much choice.

I try to reassure Morrison that, Janet Maslin notwithstanding, most journalists are not out to pointlessly skewer innocent subjects. We don't have to. The beauty part of the profession is that the guilty almost always find a way to impale themselves, with little or no assistance necessary.

As if to prove my point, Morrison takes me into the Comfort Room, which I have asked to see beforehand, since as a journalist I will not be allowed to enter once the bee begins.

She gives me a quick tour of the narrow, elegant little room. Her

COMPLETE & UTTER FAILURE 117

narration, in the best and most in-context transcription I can make off my tape, is as follows, beginning with her pointing out a few objects in the room:

> "Mr. Bee. Food. Dictionary. Parents are allowed back here. No journalists are allowed back here. We'll have some upset kids back here. Usually we have a curtain across the middle so the ones that are crying usually go hide behind it in the corner and shiver like rhesus monkeys, you know: wooo, ooo, ooo."

I inquire about the punching bags she has mentioned earlier as a Comfort Room feature, to dissipate excess zeal built up in children participating in the educational event.

"We normally have punching bags, but last year the punching bag we always used deflated—someone punched it too hard—so I'm not sure if they're going to replace it this year," she says.

At this point, she decides that we have lingered, and signals the interview is over by snapping, "Enough? Enough?" In the hallway, she gives me permission to sit near the stage on the ballroom steps and again expresses concern about what I'm going to write. I tell her my darkest intentions are to compare the bee to the Odyssey of the Mind. That gets Morrison's blood going. "Well, we're proud of our bee, and we think it will measure up—we can take on anyone!" she says, the last part in a triumphant, emphatic whisper. Immediately, she has second thoughts about what she has just said. "Don't quote me! Don't quote me!" she urges. I tell her that it wasn't such a bad thing to say. We discuss the possibility that a vindictive Scripps-Howard will track her down and "get" her, and I reassure Morrison that by the time this book is published, she will have hopefully moved beyond the grasp of that organization and into somebody else's employ. She agrees, and we part company.

Eight A.M. and action is heating up in the ballroom. The parents' section is packed, with the only empty seats offering a distant, blocked view of the stage. How early, I wonder, does one have to stake out seats to get the front row of the parents' section, the best place for them to watch the spellers?

The answer is 5:45 A.M.

"This is our twenty-fifth year and we try to get the front row for our family every year," says Harry Bartlett in a soothing elderly Texas twang. "Most times we do."

Bartlett is the production director of the *Amarillo News Globe*, an 85,000-circulation daily. The *News Globe* runs a bee for 14,000 students, taken from a forty-four-county region including western Oklahoma, eastern New Mexico, northern Texas and southern Kansas. Bartlett and his wife, Jeane, take their vacation to squire the newspaper's speller to the bee, and get up early to stake a claim for themselves and their speller's family.

"We do it as a public service, actually," says Bartlett. "There are promotional advantages to it."

Surveying the commotion in the Presidential Ballroom, with its glitzy, inelegantly modern chandeliers—the central one a sort of inverted ziggurat—and its big rectangular mirrors, leaves me somehow deadened. There isn't a feeling like the one moments before a sporting event, where a sense of excitement builds, or the mounting anticipation before some difficult sort of performance—a ballet, an ice-skating competition. The closest thing I can compare it to is the execution of some large, obligatory public ceremony. A flag raising, if it took two days, involved a thousand people, and there was no flag.

At 8:12 A.M., the parents' section is filled to overflowing, and a family snatches chairs from the nearby breakfast room. "Just follow me," the dad commands, and his wife and dependents, each clutching a chair, scoot guiltily across the hall.

The 235 spellers are onstage, in their neat rows, calves led to the slaughter. None seem particularly tense—you don't get this far without mastering serious emotional control. There are opening statements. The tame concept of "winner" has been abandoned to the lesser bees in favor of the more regal "champion."

"No matter what happens today and tomorrow, each is already a champion," a bee official tells the assemblage. This constant reinterpretation of the meaning of victory, coupled with the utter disregard for the definition of the words being spelled, except as orthographic aids, reinforces my growing view of the bee as a near-Orwellian mockery of the idea that words convey meaning. It is like a contest where people hold books at arm's length and try to guess their weight.

Today's pronouncer, Dr. Alex J. Cameron, has a forbidding wall-eyed look to him, but his opening remarks are both soothing and intelligent. "I suppose the real purpose of my standing here for a few minutes is to begin to let the spellers get used to the sound of my voice," he begins in a clear, though not exaggerated, manner. "They will eventually hear entirely too much of that sound."

He explains how the English language is peculiarly constructed to make spelling both possible and challenging, and how American society developed in such a way to bring about so unusual a phenomenon as the tradition of local spelling bees. "They come out of grassroots beginnings, mostly small communities," he says. "I have begun to suspect that for the nineteenth century, the lower-middle-class, upwardly mobile, ambitious Americans saw the bee as a kind of ritual of asserting their access to education and, through that, their access to the American Dream."

Cameron doesn't mention it, but what was true for the nineteenth century is also true for the end of the twentieth. The bee retains the appeal it had as a symbol of the American Dream. A full quarter of the contestants come from ethnic immigrant families—Chinese, Koreans, Thais, Cambodians, Hispanics and subcontinental Indians. They are the same crowd that excel at schools across the country, their families having instilled in them the fierce drive to succeed and the love of education so often faded in those who have been here long enough to take education for granted.

During Cameron's talk, No. 16, James Gephart, from Scales Mound, Illinois, jogs off the stage with a dyspeptic look on his face. Cameron finishes with a more thoughtful version of the you're-all-winners speech, recounting the awesome math of the culling process performed by the bee:

> "A few short months ago, there were ten million of you. Somewhere along the line that number got cut down to the relatively few people that showed up at your regional bees. The regional bees contained less than one percent of that original nine or ten million people. By the time you get down to this stage, that percentage is down to much, much smaller than I would care to figure out. Much smaller than has any statistical meaning. So when we look at the person who will go out first and we think about the person who will survive until the end, with that tiny little bit of difference in percentages, the difference in spelling skill is also so tiny that we never see much difference.
>
> "You've already proved what you're going to prove, you've won, you've moved all the way to the top, and from this point on, who is second, who is twenty-sixth, who is two-hundredth, well, it's part of the game you are going to play while you show off for your parents." (Here there is grateful laughter.) "But other than that, I don't think we want you thinking in terms of anything in particular being at stake. You've done your winning, you've finished all we asked you to do. From this point on, our point here is

to have a little fun. As soon as breakfast settles down at least, have a little fun."

As if in answer, James Gephart is back, looking a little flushed and vastly relieved.

Shortly before 9 A.M., the bee commences, with an appropriately dramatic flourish.

"Are we ready on the tapes? Are we ready on the records desk? Dr. Cameron, are you ready?" says a bee official. "All right, then, will speller number one, April Donahower, representing the *Intelligencer Journal* from Lancaster, Pennsylvania, please step to the microphone."

With a little hesitation, April spells her word, "bulimic." The word is actually something of an anomaly, because most of the words in the first round are of the sort never encountered by speakers of the English language—"thanatophidia," "abiogenist," "strongylid," "pemphigoid," "toolach," "sacalait," "nastaliq." These are the words that get cut when dictionaries are abridged, and they take their toll. A full quarter of the group—sixty-three contestants—are knocked out in the first round.

The speller right after April Donahower is the first to go. No. 2, a small girl from Maryland named Jennifer Sri, mangles "chalaza." She gives a brave smile and, hands straight at her sides, walks the fifty feet between the microphones and the door, where she is greeted by a bee staffer whose job it is to smile, shake her hand, throw a sisterly arm over her shoulder, and lead her to the Comfort Room. It is 9:02 A.M., the first day.

The bee quickly sinks into routine. The kids exhibit great self-control, and there is little about the words they are given to hold interest. The great majority of the bee words could almost never be used under any circumstance imaginable. No. 113 spells "unweariable," an awkward construction that any editor worth his salt would red-pencil in a second. But again, I am looking at the words as units of meaning, while here they are intended only as orthographic bullets to thin the herd.

At this level, an unnecessary cruelty has crept into the process. There is no droning of "That is correct" when students spell a word properly, only the sharp ping of a library bell when they don't. Thus, after the spelling of a word, there is an awful, pregnant moment when students don't know whether to go sit back down or head for the Comfort Room. They walk away in a hesitant, looking-over-the-shoulder fashion, as if waiting to be shot in the back. Sometimes the bell takes forever to ring.

There is only so much of this a person can take at one time. After a few dozen contestants, I head out into the hall and track down Jennifer Sri, the first girl eliminated, and try to find out how her early defeat—two minutes into the bee—has affected her. Like most kids, she is guarded and candid at the same time. "I kinda knew I spelled it wrong because it didn't sound right," she says. "I didn't really feel anything. I just kind of felt really bad. I studied hard. I studied that word, I remembered that word. I just didn't spell it right."

Without exception, the spellers all seem to gauge their defeats by whether they knew the word and had studied it, or whether the word was utterly unfamiliar, the latter case being much easier to live with.

Passing by the Comfort Room, the entrance to which is shielded by a blue curtain, I sometimes hear the sound of compressive, air-sucking sobs. It occurs to me that not only does the Comfort Room protect the overwrought contestants from the prying eyes of the media, but it keeps the media from the contestants and thus eliminates embarrassing footage of hysterical children from the evening news.

Most of the contestants who miss their words seem almost

unaffected, but a few react more dramatically. Peter May drops the middle "s" in "subfuscous" and utters a grievous "No!" a split second before the bell. The crowd groans with him. No. 180, Hannah Choi, from Athens, Pennsylvania, looks about to cry after misspelling "percnosome" and, as an added indignity, almost trips as she hurries off the stage, her face just folding into tears as she reaches the glad hand of the bee greeter.

"I had studied so hard," she says a few minutes later, waiting to be interviewed on television. "I thought it was spelled with a 'u.' I didn't want to disappoint everybody." And her eyes brim with tears again. I walk away, wanting to cry myself—long after the bee is over, I'll realize that I saw many more children cry than I made note of; it was just too affecting.

Having realized the limited utility of just sitting there, watching the progression of spellers, I take to wandering the wide hall alongside the ballroom, watching the television crews interview the losers after they exit the Comfort Room. The best over the two days, by far, is a spunky kid who I believe is Andrew Pennington, from Vernon, Texas. He has the combed-to-the-side Brylcreem haircut of a young Lyndon Johnson, as well as the thirty-sixth President's buoyant confidence. Asked if he is disappointed about being eliminated from the bee, he says, "Heck, I've got a new puppy waiting at home for me!"

From time to time I encounter one of the college volunteers. Ellen Morrison is smiling at somebody's baby, happy in a carrier. "We're grooming him for a future bee," she says casually. Then she realizes she is talking to a journalist and her mood swings into wild alarm. "No! No, we're not!" she blubbers, then, as if making an official statement: "We do not groom babies for spelling bees."

There is a break at 10:30 A.M. I go to chat with Dr. Cameron, who is generally open, though concerned about being misquoted—

he was among those who felt they got burned by the *Post*. I ask him why people like to take shots at the bee, and he says that although newspapers running their own bees know how "tricky" they are, and rarely criticize them, "once in a while someone who's a total stranger" encounters the bee and slams it because, like the Miss America Pageant, it is "too clean-cut."

Trying to follow up on that line of thinking, I preface a question with the fact that I have been shown the Comfort Room, and Dr. Cameron cuts me off by demanding, "Who did that?" I change the subject to something less threatening. Cameron says that his crisp pronunciation of the bee words is no spontaneous act: he practices pronouncing the words for "a good many weeks," to make sure his performance is on the mark.

By 11 A.M. the early spellers, who have now waited onstage for almost three hours, are starting to sink into ennui. No. 10, Rachel Lott, is resting her head heavily on her hands. She is a tall, mature girl from Arkansas; the small boy next to her, No. 11, seems a quarter her size, and taken together, they resemble a ventriloquist's act. No. 1, April Donahower, is slumped against the railing. No. 29, Alexis Dalsfoist, has his eyes closed and is stretched out, almost lying on his chair. I look at him a long time, trying to see if he is actually asleep. He seems to be.

The first round ends—172 spellers are left—and lunchtime blessedly arrives. Ellen Morrison has told me that they won't be able to provide me with the *Washington Post* article that has whipped the bee cadres into such a froth. Nobody has any copies. So, during the lunch break, I step over to the Post Building, half a block away, and —smiling at the wan attempt to keep it from me—put down my dollar for the most recent issue of the Sunday magazine.

No wonder the bee people have been traumatized into babbling self-confession. The *Post* has nailed the bee to its bumper and then gone for a drive in an article called "Killer Bees" by W. Hampton Sides. Just the graphic alone is enough to send chills down Scripps-Howardian spines—a tiny child, in a red-striped shirt, clutching the bars of a cage made from the legs of a scary, giant bee, which is turning to menace the boy, or perhaps gloat, with rows of razor teeth.

Sides rallies everyone from Mark Twain to Philip Roth to his cause. (Twain's quote is a pearl. "I don't see any use in spelling a word right, and never did," he told a Hartford spelling bee in 1875. "We might as well make all clothes alike and cook all dishes alike. Sameness is tiresome. Variety is pleasing.")

I happily note that Sides, too, finds the Scripps-Howard group a bit, ah, *sensitive.* "The staffers . . . are likely to go ballistic if you suggest that the bee is, at least in part, a promotional gimmick for the Scripps-Howard newspaper chain," he writes, before explaining how the bee is exactly that.

Sides focuses on the essential illogic of the bee. It's not a test of spelling, since most of the words are freak constructions never encountered by anybody outside of the most narrow technical subspecialties. Rather, Scripps-Howard puts people through all the trouble and effort to name a spelling bee champion in order to have a spelling bee champion named. It is an end in itself, a tautology.

A booklet published by the East Texas Spelling Bee, which I find abandoned on a table in the always-empty pressroom, puts it this way: "Recognition of the achievements of the champion is the main purpose of a spelling bee." (The booklet also calls the bee the *Houston Chronicle*'s "most extensive public service effort," which makes one wonder if perhaps they would do better to scrap the bee and open a soup kitchen.) In the *Post* article, Dr. Cameron says: "Frankly, I'm not interested in finding out who the best speller is; I'm interested in finding a winner." (Cameron probably wrapped that statement in a fuzzy blue blanket of cheery, positive buzz phrases about the bee, and felt violated when the blanket was stripped away and discarded.)

Much to my horror, Sides even uncovers the *Tribune*/simplified spelling angle, which I thought was a genius juxtaposition of my own. Luckily, he dispatches the entire subject in a paragraph, without revealing the nuggets I have mined from the *Tribune*'s autoerotic corporate memory.

Having been outside in the exterior world, under a lovely blue sky, I find going back for the afternoon session of the bee almost impossible, particularly after reading Sides's article.

Walking into the room, I feel an almost existential horror. The beads of moisture condensed on the cold, metallic sides of the water pitchers. The stark numbered signs, held by blue string. The children, inert, poised, waiting, staring thoughtless into the distance, pounded into a fugue state by boredom. The trained-dog media, most following their local champion, some reporters keeping score, writing down the spelling of each word as if they were going to compile it, as if the bee didn't already have two people doing that, documenting each misspelled letter for posterity.

I struggle to find some sort of meaning, some utility, in this vast expenditure of effort. A child could learn to play the violin, and well, in the studying time it takes to get to the national bee. The best I can come up with is that the contestants are preparing themselves to be grilled by Senate subcommittees. All the lights; the somber officials; the give-and-take of pro forma questioning; the lob of the word; the return of the correct answer.

But this is whimsy. What the spelling bee really means is that kids are always duped by the adult world. Society's values—its fetishes, passions, fears and hatreds—are imprinted upon children, like wet clay accepting the design of seashells, both beautiful and plain.

Some flack at Scripps-Howard half a century ago decided to wed their corporate name to this sort of high-toned, skewed and pedantic endeavor, and the end result was this curse, handed down through generations by the unthinking to poor children who, desperate to excel at *something,* have the misfortune to try to excel at so nugatory an enterprise as this. They might as well be reciting the digits of pi, for all the good knowing how to spell "cispontine" or "accrescent" or "mugient" is ever going to do them.

I find myself getting up every ten minutes to walk through the halls outside the ballroom. I run into bee flack Shannon Harris, who greets my observation that the bee has sunk into tedium by chirping; "It never drags; it's spelling!" I look at her with an astonished gaze—Dante viewing the damned on his journey through the rings of Hell. A reporter meets lots of people in a state of debasement—coke-addict moms and their deformed children, crusty drunks strapped to boards in emergency wards, slobbering hookers wearing strap T-shirts as dresses—but none do I sympathize with less than the ambitious college grad who has sold her soul for a bad job.

Thursday morning I am a little slow getting down to the bee. On the local news, kids over at the Odyssey of the Mind are stacking iron barbell plates atop a little 18-gram balsa wood derrick they have constructed. The kids are focused, very carefully setting the plates down so as not to add any drop force. They are wearing big colorful T-shirts and look very much like children as I remember them. I resolve to head over to the Odyssey at lunchtime.

Downstairs, the atmosphere of the bee has been supercharged by the magic presence of the Cable News Network. In the hall is a table loaded with equipment, mounds of black, snakelike connections, tiny, intriguing monitors, joysticks and fade levers, around which no fewer than five people are always clustered, talking into headsets and flipping switches. The TVs in the hall and by the parents are no longer tied to the single amateur bee camera, but are now receiving the official CNN feed, which means that there is a secondary shot of the loser walking toward the Comfort Room. Dazzled and energized by the presence of CNN, the Scripps-Howard flacks have regained their professional equilibrium. None notice me for the rest of the bee.

Inside, CNN has set up nineteen blinding sunlike lights, ringing the ballroom. They are so bright that at least one speller onstage puts on sunglasses, as do several members of the audience. For a while, I amuse myself fantasizing just how intrusive CNN would have to become before anyone dared complain. I picture them setting up fog machines, giant fans, oscillators, Van de Graff generators, draping the stage in reflective cloth, spraying water—all while the students bravely fight their way to the microphones, and Cameron, dripping, blinded, his fingers in his ears, struggles to pronounce the words.

The Chicago city winner, Sophoan Khoeun, who escaped the Khmer Rouge terror in Cambodia with his family in 1984, misspells "barbarism" and is out. He looks puzzled as he walks offstage.

On the bulletin board is a much more acceptable *Post* article, from June 7, 1974. "Spelling to Bee the Best," written by Don Shirley, who is identified as "a school and district spelling bee winner in Arizona in 1963. He was defeated in the state championships on the word 'brigadier.'" But even Shirley has a few shots to take. "Spelling bees are indeed cute, but they're also a bit dumb," he writes, summing up the purpose of the bee as "The show must go on."

No. 26, Jo Marie Sison, the suburban champ who beat Sruti, goes out on "genuflect."

Shortly after 11 A.M., I notice a face in the audience that I recognize. I can't quite place the freckled teenager with the retroussé nose, but careful study of my bee materials reveals she is Amanda Goad, fourteen, last year's bee winner. Bee rules forbid the winner from competing again, but she is back anyway, along with her mother, a duplicate of her, but a generation older. They wince simultaneously as No. 14 blows "exhilarate," and sadly shake their heads. Both have pads of paper and pencils—Amanda is working out the words before the spellers, testing herself—and this, coupled with their air of wise serenity, gives them the look of a pair of racetrack touts handicapping the trifecta for the sixth race at Arlington International.

With the bee going strong, I get in a cab. The University of Maryland at College Park is disorienting in its immensity. Vast green lawns, like seas, surrounding Brobdingnagian buildings. Headquartered in the ultramodern pressbox of Maryland's spanking new stadium, the Odyssey of the Mind PR staff has none of the self-loathing anxiety of the bee people: Hi, here's a press kit. Here's a map. Here's where the events are. Have a nice day, and help yourself to the buffet before you hit campus. I can't even recall what they looked like.

The competition itself is an unusual blend of the specific and the amorphous. The first activity I come across is the one I saw on TV—students stacking weights on a little balsa derrick. But what the TV didn't explain was that, as part of the competition, they must also produce a play to explain why the weights are being stacked. I watch a group of nine-year-olds in colorful Egyptian garb shimmying to the Bangles' catchy tune "Walk Like an Egyptian." The girls are some sort of royalty; the lone boy, stacking the iron weights on the structure, is dressed as a slave. The structure eventually cracks, which has some sort of bearing on the performance. "Now can we get to be princesses?" asks one girl. "Of course," another replies.

A team from Tampa, Florida, arrives, fretting because their balsa structure is two tenths of a gram overweight—one student explains that changes in humidity can add weight to the derrick. They first try delicately shaving slivers of wood from the structure, then go off to borrow a makeshift drying device another team has assembled out of a hair dryer and a garbage bag.

The derrick, one of their coaches explains, has taken about four hours to assemble, and represents the optimum design from a dozen test derricks constructed.

The coach, Carlotta Reeves, shows off one of the little hand towels, with outline maps of the United States, the Odyssey kids use to display their pins—swapping state pins is of huge interest to participants at the Odyssey. "It kind of takes some of the pressure off," says Reeves, "because they get uptight doing [the Odyssey]."

Indeed they do. The bee does not have a lock on pressure. Despite the creativity and imagination of the Odyssey events, kids still worry about them. "I find it very nerve-wracking. You're really nervous," says Jalyn Johnson, eleven. "You worry about what's going to happen."

On the sidewalk, a ten-year-old girl dressed in a black leotard cries as her mother tries to comfort her. "I don't care," the girl says. "Nothing will make me happy."

The big difference between the Odyssey and the bee is that, at the Odyssey, kids are getting upset over a variety of complex tasks—presenting a parody of Hemingway's *Old Man and the Sea*; operating unusual vehicles of their own design; solving spontaneous word problems. At the bee, kids are getting upset over spelling.

A woman stops and compliments the butterfly wings being set up by Bryce Loveland, twelve, and Melissa Steinman, fourteen. "Those are really pretty," she says.

"See," Bryce tells Melissa, "we're going to win now."

The two are part of a group from Ashland, Oregon, and I tag along with them. Their long-term challenge, "Pit Stop," is to construct a vehicle powered by a mechanical jack. Just what constitutes a "mechanical jack" has been open to question, with teams using everything from an auto jack to, in the Oregon team's case, a block-and-tackle system.

"Once we figured out how to build it, it was easy," says Bryce. "It's a simple device. Very simple. But nobody else has it."

The vehicle has to complete circuits of a course, make stops, go in reverse and, at some point, transform into something more splendid, part of its journey taking place in "full glory," whatever that may be. The two kids go into the basement of the armory where the competition is being held, through a hallway cluttered with massive mechanical devices, into a room their group has commandeered.

The kids agree that winning is not particularly crucial at this level. "It's like the Olympics," says Bryce. "Just getting to it is great." They have none of the crushed-down quality of the bee children. Asked what, if not winning, is important to accomplish at the Odyssey, Bryce says, "Here it's so important that we get on TV . . . and get scholarships and massive stuff and are celebrities for the rest of our lives." In two days at the bee, none of the children I interview display anything resembling humor.

The Ashland group's coach, Jim Shames, says the Odyssey is "wonderful" and "the best educational thing I've seen.

"Collective, creative thinking," he continues. "They learn how to respect each other's ideas. They learn how to take the ordinary and go beyond it to the extraordinary in terms of their thinking. And they learn to accomplish something."

Their vehicle is made from a scavenged bicycle body, with wheels laced with red and green foil streamers. The entire thing is covered with green tie-dyed cloth, which hides the person working the block and tackle, and is supposed to resemble a caterpillar. During its circuit, the vehicle will turn into a butterfly.

They work at, ummm, debugging the vehicle.

"How are we going to solve the problem of that wing not flapping well?" says Shames, who is not supposed to tell the group how to do things. "Jonah, you had an idea . . ."

The dowel system used to flap the wings is fine-tuned. The small kid who provides the head of the caterpillar is perched on one end of the vehicle and enrobed in green. An antennae hat is placed on his head. And, eventually, the vehicle makes a tentative trip a few feet across the room.

We troop upstairs to watch the other vehicles competing. The armory is a lovely facility with tall mullioned windows. Judges ring a roped-off area where a vehicle is going through its paces, and people sit in bleachers, watching. A blond boy, wearing a laurel crown and a shirt of paper leaves, is working the lever of a rolling contraption, circling a quartet of girls who twirl and dance, joyously if not always in unison.

Their vehicle is also a caterpillar, and at one point the boy hops out and adds big pink-and-blue wings, to the sound of light jazz, as three girls slowly pinwheel around the fourth, who has hidden herself under a sheet.

A cardboard moon and sun are passed by, slowly. The hidden girl emerges as a butterfly and they dance again. A girl in green who is a gymnast does flips and somersaults to strains from the *Nutcracker Suite.*

The Oregon kids study this intently. "We're all concerned," says Simon Parker-Shames, fourteen, the coach's son. "They did almost exactly what we did."

"Their wings don't flap," adds Jonah McBride, also fourteen, trying to put a positive spin on the situation.

The spectacle has left me a little flabbergasted at the quality of pure, childish joy—a quality I assumed had been wiped out by Nintendo and preadolescent sex and Judy Blume. It was as if you stopped by an inner-city park and found that a bunch of street kids had rigged up a maypole and were skipping around it, singing "A Tisket, a Tasket."

The dancing group are all children of officers at Maxwell Air Force Base. When they finish, I seek out the boy, Aaron Zink, eleven, certain he was forced kicking and screaming into that leaf shirt.

How did they arrive at all the dancing? I want to know. Did the girls push for it? Was there a compromise? No, Aaron says, dancing was always going to be part of it. He is utterly serene, and deems the Odyssey "interesting. You learn a lot."

I watch more competitions. A jalopy turns into a motorcycle in a Mr. Rogers–inspired playlet (Mr. Rogers's calm is threatened by a mushroom cloud through his window and, significantly, a menacing gigantic bee). The next play has a barnyard motif, with creatures mocking a giant duckling that is, indeed, very ugly. The barnyard animals—including a pig in a pink flannel jumpsuit, its nose held on with elastic—use electric screwdrivers to effect the duckling's transformation, with the paper-bag brown duck sides cleverly flipping over to become white swan wings.

The way the competition works is that students are given points, both on planned and on spontaneous projects. In the case of the vehicle, points are assigned on technical matters, such as the performance of the vehicle, as well as on the aesthetics of the play. Thirteen judges watch, grading in various areas—creativity, execution, technical requirements—but they have none of the false solemnity of the bee judges. To signal the Mr. Rogers team that they are ready for their entry to begin, the red-shirted judges chant, in unison, "Welcome to *our* neighborhood, Mr. Rogers!"

"What we do is we pick off their style for something to come back at them," says judge Dorothy Courtney afterward. "Just to say 'Judges, are you ready?' is really boring."

"It calms them down a little bit, too," says another judge, Jim Bell. "Because they see these people out there, they get intimidated. It says we're human."

"They want to win and everything," says Courtney. "But frankly, not everyone's going to. We make them feel good about it, and if something breaks down, that we're there for them. We're not pouncing tigers."

"This is probably *the* event, but even if they lose here, the camaraderie, the friends they make, the swapping they do—no one leaves feeling like they lost, really," says Bell.

Since I spend only about three hours at the Odyssey, I'm uncertain exactly how objectionable I would find the touchy-feelyness of the event were I to spend several days there. It does seem like a competition transplanted from Sweden—there is something decidedly un-American about the Odyssey, in the sense that professional boxing is American. No pinging bells of defeat here—in fact, no indication that a particular team has fallen short until the very end of the week, Saturday night, when no fewer than fifteen "world champion" teams are named at a big closing rally.

With midafternoon creeping up, I realize I have to get back to the bee, lest it end in some crashing Götterdämmerung finale and I miss it.

Again, it takes a concentration of will to reenter the stark, brightly lit Presidential Ballroom. The contestants—only a handful are left—are a glum, limp-looking lot on a giant stage, now far too big for their numbers. The interplay—the flinging of the horrid, recondite word and then the tremulous spelling or not spelling of it —seems even more medieval, unnatural and repellent.

The most telling comment comes from Bartlett, the old guy from Amarillo. I ask him what changes he has noticed over twenty-five years of attending the bee, and he says there is a problem with kids acting up and challenging the rigid conformity of the event. "Occasionally, there'll be a showboat, someone who really hams it up," he says. "They're not that good a speller; they play to the press; a little aggravating sometimes. At first they didn't say much about it, [but there are] so many contestants right now they have to crack down and run a tighter ship."

Having not seen a child so much as wink at his parents from the stage in the two days I've been at the bee (not that they could see them, particularly after CNN set up its lights), I can't imagine what Bartlett is talking about. Perhaps while I was over at the Odyssey, a small child tried to read a statement about freedom in China and was dragged bodily off the stage by security guards. But somehow I doubt it.

It is the eighth round. Nineteen kids remain. 4:17 P.M.

One by one they go. The pretty redhead from Arkansas, No. 10, who I figured would win—heck, it's Arkansas's year, and besides, she has that sort of 1950s, confident career-girl look to her—gets "dystopia," which Cameron defines as "an imaginary place which is depressingly wretched and whose people live a fearful existence." I wait for the self-conscious twitter from the audience, but it never comes. She misses the word.

The crowd seems to be pulling for No. 45, Wendy Guey, a tiny child in a red headband. There is something ridiculous and awful in seeing her stand at the short mike, angled down as far as it will go, while Dr. Cameron intones "persiflage" and she spells it in her toddler's voice.

Kids are knocked out with "shandry," with "bathyscaphe." A

student desperately grapples for a fingerhold on "censer"—asking for alternate pronunciations, definitions, anything. A full three minutes crawl by, much of it dead silence, between the time Cameron utters the word and the time she spells it "censur."

No. 138, David Urban, of Amarillo, the kid whose family was saved primo seats by the *News Globe,* is given the word "desiccation." He asks, "Does it come from the Latin word *desiccatus,* meaning 'dry'?" I expect the crowd to cheer—for me, this seems the intellectual highpoint of the bee—but people are too exhausted and don't notice. He spells it right.

Soon seven are left. At this point, officials pause the bee, getting ready to go into the final minutes. The rules are reviewed, and the families and sponsoring newspaper escorts are asked to come up and wait at the far right of the hundred-foot-long stage. A bee official informs everyone "exactly what will happen at the moment a champion is crowned," and I wonder if perhaps a real crown will be involved. A big gold–and–red velvet one, like in the margarine ads, I hope.

Round 10 begins. Geoff Hooper, fourteen, a lanky Tennesseean with braces and wire-rim glasses, spells "empyrean." No. 45, the very small girl with whom the crowd is enamored, spells "longanimity," the last seven letters very rapidly, to cheers and applause.

She misses her next word—"meiosis"—and goes out to huge acclaim. Five of her bee friends, who had been sprawled on the floor in front of me, get up and go to look after her.

With three spellers left, at the start of Round 12, the pressure starts to really build. Geoff spells "pharisaical." David spells "contumelious." Yuni Kim, No. 229, can't spell "solipsism" quickly enough —she obviously knows it.

Round 13 passes. In Round 14, Yuni Kim fearfully spells "apotheosize" and misses it, to protracted applause, which drowns out Cameron's attempts to spell it correctly.

In Round 15, Geoff is given "enchilada," to groans and laughter from the audience, but not before he asks, smiling, for the definition, to more laughter.

David gets "renascent" and misses it.

Geoff needs one more word, and Dr. Cameron gives him "kami-kaze." Loud groans break out in the audience. He spells it, hands in pockets, so laconically that, when he gets it right and a loud, lengthy cheer goes up, he doesn't even stand completely straight.

The room dissolves into activity. Someone sets up in front of Geoff three fat velvet ropes on short poles, like at a movie theater. He is handed an old-fashioned loving cup trophy. A stool is produced for him to sit on. No crown. About two dozen reporters and cameramen crowd in front of him to shout the standard questions.

I have been watching the second-place speller, David Urban, to see what happens to him, but he is swept away in the commotion. The first question addressed to Geoff is about the pair of easy words he got at the end—he admits it was a "big contrast between the words that were asked before." I think of Edmund Hillary and the frequent mitigation of victory.

The other questions are less probing: How much time does he spend studying? How did he learn the words? Who was his coach? What's he going to do with the prize money?

I step onto the stage, 50 feet from the where Geoff is being questioned, and turn to survey the audience, trying to gain some elevation, some perspective, to properly capture the moment and understand it more clearly. Suddenly, Ellen Morrison materializes out of nowhere, standing uncomfortably close to me. "No reporters on the stage," she intones in such a serious, emphatic way that for a moment I think she is joking.

On impulse, I decide not to give ground—let them come and arrest me. Take me to bee jail. I gesture to the knot of reporters, some of whom have climbed onstage, gathered around the winner. "Get them off the stage first," I say. But as I do, I see Shannon Harris having the same conversation with the reporters closer to the fat velvet ropes, and it takes the fight out of me. I move off, humiliated, my blood up. Once I am on the floor, I look up at Ellen Morrison and try to think of something pithy and memorable to say.

"No reporters onstage," she repeats again, a final time, smiling maliciously: *Ha-ha-ha! I'm onstage and you're not.*

I move into the audience, where I again run into Amanda Goad and her mother. As people file out, we talk about the bee. Both mother and daughter have the sort of weary, concealed knowledge that gives the impression they could tell you a lot, if they wanted to. Mrs. Goad tells me a bit about the 1991 bee—the year before Amanda won—an "incredibly painful" marathon bee that would not end because of a twist in the rules, since corrected.

They introduce me to Linda Tarrant, a Hunt, Texas, woman being sued by Scripps-Howard for a program she devised that takes their "Words of the Champions" list and pairs it with pronunciations and definitions. Scripps-Howard is claiming that their list of difficult words can be copyrighted and that she is ripping them off.

A fourth woman, who won't give her name but whom I dub Mrs. Robinson because she has that astronaut wife's hairdo and the emaciated, kohl-eyed look of a woman smoking four packs a day and going politely crazy, slides up and begins to make a variety of dark, conspiratorial observations—"the other side of these contests." She condemns the Odyssey of the Mind as "a private thing, a money-maker . . . The parents in all of those cases have to do fund-raising to get the kids where they are going . . . When you get down to it, I always feel as though children ought to have the opportunity to compete without having to provide lots of dollars."

The bee, as well, is a moneymaker—she says—all those side events, the $45 tours of the Smithsonian. But the Odyssey merits her particular concern. "It's wonderful inasmuch as there is problem solving, but it has a high emphasis on the theatrical," she whispers, as if nothing more need be said. The coup de grâce is that the Odyssey founders are "living well on the East Coast." The criticism doesn't hold much water with me—it's like somebody attacking the reliability of the Encyclopaedia Britannica by pointing out that the company makes a profit.

The next morning, with my black garment bag over my shoulder and my leather portfolio bulging with bee materials and microcassettes, I stop by the Presidential Ballroom on my way out of the hotel. Workmen are busy tearing down the stage, setting up the room for another event. On impulse, I step across the hall to the Comfort Room. It is empty now, returned to its quiet Colonial elegance. Except, left on a table, the gaudy blue-and-orange box for a punching bag—a World Wrestling Federation Ultimate Warrior Inflatable Bop Bag, to be precise. So they got a new one, I think, regretting that I didn't ask the kids whether they had bopped the bag, and why. Some must have bopped the bag.

Satisfied, I head downstairs to catch a cab to the train station. In the lobby, I run into Mrs. Robinson. "You have to wonder when he is given words like 'enchilada' and 'kamikaze,' " she says, meaningfully, in the tone people reserve for discussing the Illuminati and grassy knolls. "Did the pronouncer use a set list; if not, what are we doing?"

She may have a point, but I'm not biting. First, the complaint that bees end on an easy word has a logical flaw—contestants tend to miss the really hard words, so of course the final winning word often will be an easy one.

And second, I don't care. The scary thing about being in a world of people zealously interested in a single thing is their intensity—the pure mania in Mrs. Robinson's eyes as, like a character in Sophocles, she appears from behind a pillar to utter her warnings and auguries. She is just pointing out that the winner is, wouldn't you know, wink, wink, *sponsored by a Scripps-Howard newspaper,* when I apologize that I have a train to catch, and grab a cab for Union Station. I make the express to New York City with two minutes to spare.

THE LAST DAY of my participation in any sort of organized educational institution came on June 19, 1982, when I graduated from Northwestern University, nearly seventeen years after that first day of kindergarten at Fairwood School. The college had issued us the standard black robes and mortarboards, and I was so impressed with mine that I wore it the entire day, even during the break between commencement and convocation ceremonies, when I strode into the Pali Kai Lounge, a cheesy bar on Davis Street I frequented at the time, and let the barflies buy me drinks.

To an impartial observer, I must have seemed like a character from Eugene O'Neill—the young idiot in a bar spouting socialist philosophies and railing at the world. Only I didn't even have misplaced, pent-up anger to spout at the world. I sat happily at the bamboo bar and soaked up the booze, confident that the spheres were in order. Properly fortified, I toddled off to get my diploma. On the way to the auditorium, I broke into a run, holding onto my mortarboard, rejoicing in the feel of my academic gowns flowing around me in the wind. I thought myself a wonderful creature, blessed by education, separated by an enormous gulf from the pedestrian workers tossing me a gape as I flew by. I thought the world was about to be jolted by something new and fresh and fantastic, and that the difficulties of life which face most people would dissolve in deference to me. I thought wrong.

FOUR

Myths of Telephone History

Bad Timing

I N THE BEST PHOTOGRAPH that I have of her, Esther is sitting on a beat-up old brown easy chair that had been plucked out of somebody's trash several days earlier by friends of mine and deposited on my front lawn, set up like a living room with a lamp and a garbage sofa, both as a prank and to provide seating for my eighteenth birthday party.

Even without cheating, and retrieving the photo from whatever dusty box or bottom drawer in which it slumbers, I can accurately describe Esther as she is pictured there: She is smiling, her head turned to the side, that sort of half-suppressed smile which brings all the muscles of the face tautly into play. Her shortish tan hair is in fine wisps around her face, and her mouth is slightly open, as if saying "Awww." Her eyes are bright, fierce, clear, and she is looking at the photographer—me—with a kind of gleeful wickedness. She is seventeen and on top of the world. You could eat her up.

For the next five years, when I doodled faces in the margins of notebooks at college and on yellow pads at boring meetings, they would be, for the most part, that face, that photo. I made the eyes huge, like the eyes of a Sumerian statue, but it was supposed to be Esther.

I didn't really know her at all, not that summer anyway. She was at my party only because I was dating her best friend, Sue. In the intricate feeding chain at our high school, Esther was several orders of complexity higher than I: a manta ray to my segmented worm. Normally I would never have been able to socialize with her. But Sue was someone closer to my own phylum—say, a jellyfish—and she served as a bridge between Esther's and my vastly divergent stations.

Two summers later, however, Sue had gone on to greener pastures, and Esther and I spent some time hanging out together, riding our bicycles through the Metropark, visiting the Cuyahoga County Fair. Climbing the tree in my backyard to drink a bottle of wine.

It sounds very romantic, and would have been, had there been any romance. But there wasn't, at least not by my rather narrow definition of it at the time. Esther had broken up with her track-star boyfriend, and probably viewed me as a sort of neutered companion with whom to harmlessly pass the summer until his inevitable return. That happened to me a lot at the time, so much so that I had a name for it—the Eunuch Friend Syndrome.

There was one moment, however, when something almost happened, or, should I say, when I thought something almost happened. I certainly had been expecting something—just being with her plunged me into a sort of giddy, rarefied state where I was beginning to suspect, or perhaps just hope, that anything was possible.

We were doing what we usually did, lazing on reclining lawn chairs in my backyard, absorbing the sun, drinking wine, when I was somehow able to maneuver her inside the house—I don't remember exactly how; maybe the wine had something to do with it. No one was home. My little brother, Sam, was off playing somewhere with his buzzing cloud of friends. My parents were gone, having absented themselves for the summer to Jackson Hole, Wyoming, a rare bit of "Tennis anyone?" stage-clearing I was immensely grateful for at the time.

Once inside, I found myself easing her down onto the thick white Swiss down comforter covering the single ranch oak bed in my father's den. I can see her face—the face in the photo, the face in the margins of all those notebooks—framed against the white comforter.

I was about to kiss her.

The noise an aluminum screen door makes when a racing child blasts through it should probably be written as "BLAM!" In my mind, it was an explosion, a shotgun retort echoing and reverberating through the house. Sam was back, calling out my name, wanting something. I pulled away. Esther escaped from the bed—and the moment was gone. She ended up marrying some guy she met at college and living in Texas, where I understand she is very happy. I got married, too, and am extraordinarily happy myself, at least in that regard.

But I still keep the photograph.

TIMING IS THE most important thing, Hesiod said, more than 2,500 years ago. Not that it is a particularly profound thought. It may appear wise to say that timing is crucial in romance, or in politics, or in war. But there is no need to be so reductive. Timing is important in *everything*.

Just look at bad timing, one of the more difficult failures to contemplate simply because it illustrates the limits of our control over the world. The idea of bad timing is a solemn recognition of the perilous intersection between our fragile tissue of human hopes and desires and the sharp-edged, unforgiving reality of life itself.

While any sound person will attempt to judge if conditions are right for a certain activity—Is the boss in a good mood? Does it look like rain? Is Sam safely playing outside?—the possibility remains that something will suddenly go wrong, that despite precautions, bad timing, like the creature in *Alien*, will burst out of nowhere and change everything.

In my day-to-day living, the potential for bad timing usually dawns on me only in relation to the flight number of an airplane I'm about to get on. Not the thought of flying itself, or airplanes in general, but the actual numeral designation of the particular flight I happen to hold a ticket for. Just the announcement "Passengers on Flight 633 will begin boarding in five minutes . . ." is enough to conjure up in my mind one of those primary-colored, crisp, eye-catching *Newsweek* graphics: "The Brief Tragic Journey of Flight 633," with a progression of smooth and cute little airplanes dutifully following a broad 3-D vector arrow on a corkscrew pattern, ending in a jagged red, orange and yellow crown of explosion.

Bad timing is easy to see on the disastrous, day-to-day level. In the litany of life's tragedies—baby buggies carelessly pushed into the paths of careening trucks, geese sucked into engine intakes, myopic overnight guests mistaking Mercurochrome for mouthwash—anything that happens not because of some inherent flaw or sin, but innocently, because of a wicked confluence of circumstances, can be written off to bad timing. The meteor falls through the roof and kills him—what's a person to do? Actually, the concept can be a very liberating thing. Part of the definition of bad timing is that the problem is not your own fault; blame can be deflected to the gods, to fate, to my little brother, Sam. This is important when deciding if a failure is truly the result of bad timing. Hitler's invasion of the Soviet Union is often written off to bad timing—that first winter happened to have been very cold, the army bogged down, and the invasion failed. But that is an oversimplification. Yes, it was a tremendously cold winter. Yes, the tanks froze. But Hitler was stupid. It always gets cold in Russia in the winter. Maybe not that cold, but pretty damn cold. And had the Russians greeted the invasion with a raise of the glass and a wink, the way the French did, then the Germans would have been in Moscow by Christmas, and timing or the weather—bad, good or indifferent—would never have entered into it.

While clear on the personal level, true bad timing is harder to find on the historical stage. There are so many factors at work. Sure, timing enters into everything, but to what degree? Just how weak and dicey is human control over the march of events? Does history show that 50,000 Americans died in Vietnam because John F. Kennedy didn't lean forward to adjust his sock while the motorcade passed through Dealey Plaza? Or is it a step down the road to madness to think in this direction? Maybe Kennedy would have killed 100,000 Americans in Vietnam, given the chance, assuming he didn't first wage nuclear war on China over Quemoy and Matsu.

Despite the difficulty in applying the concept of bad timing to the historical, it is worthwhile to try, if only to shatter the flawed concept, instilled at an early age and tending to linger on throughout life, that history is comprised of a neat succession of box dioramas and key figures. The cast of great men and geniuses, lurching out of the fog of public education to grab you by the lapels and babble their brief biographies, is almost always a gross impoverishment of what actually happened.

History is much more complex than the pap they feed you in school. Think of it as an onion. The outer, tough brown surface is the outline narrative we are all familiar with—what Voltaire called "the lie agreed upon."

To get to the inner, fragrantly human layers of the onion, where missteps and bungling and treachery and bad timing lie, you sometimes have to peel. It takes time and thought, and most people don't bother—they have a hard enough time keeping the famous figures and buzzwords straight—but it is an exercise that, nevertheless, should be tried at least once.

Consider the telephone.

Alexander Graham Bell invented the telephone. We learn this in grade school. He was a teacher of the deaf, with a big beard, and he invented the telephone. After he invented it, the first words spoken over the telephone were "Mr. Watson, come here, I want you." Everyone knows this.

The date was March 10, 1876. The reason Bell needed Watson was because he had spilled sulfuric acid on his clothes. The acid was being used to alter an electric current in response to shifting sound waves, the central element in the telephone Bell was using, a telephone he did not invent, but which was described the month before in an application registered at the U.S. Patent Office in Washington, D.C., by Chicago inventor Elisha Gray.

And now we begin to peel.

Gray, an electrician who founded the Western Electric Company, is one of those shadow figures of history, a person whose life comes into focus only when the light of failure is shone on the pages of the past. His telephone invention could have—perhaps should have—placed him among the pantheon of immortal American inventors: Fulton, Morse, Edison, Gray.

Certainly Gray appeared to be the right man to invent the telephone. He had eleven patents to his name, all for improvements in the telegraph, and his Western Electric Company had the backing of the powerful Western Union, the biggest company in America. His people saw the telephone coming. In a *New York Times* article of July 10, 1874, detailing Gray's "musical telegraph," a device conveying tones over wires in the fashion of an electric organ, a Western Union official predicted that "in time the operators will transmit the sound of their own voice over the wires."

They did, and quickly too. Within five years people would be paying to talk over a phone Gray had designed, but not over a phone that had Gray's name on it or put cash into Gray's pocket. Gray suffered a single slip, a stroke of bad timing, on his march to glory, and it was enough to sidetrack him into oblivion and ridicule. He is remembered today chiefly for his moment of lateness, a cameo appearance in what is, at first glance, one of the more astounding coincidences of history.

On February 14, 1876, Gardiner Hubbard, Alexander Graham Bell's silent business partner, visited the U.S. Patent Office in Washington, D.C., and filed a patent application for "Improvements in Telegraphy," Bell's modest term for a transmitter/receiver that could send a voice over electrical wires—a telephone.

Approximately two hours later, an attorney named William D. Baldwin visited the same office and filed a caveat for Gray, describing a device for "transmitting vocal sounds or conversations telegraphically" (a caveat was an announcement of a pending patent application). The filing fee was $10.

The Patent Office had a policy for handling two conflicting claims. On February 19, it issued what was called an interference, meaning that both applications were frozen for ninety days to give the examiners time to weigh the merits of the various claims.

The two devices were quite similar. Bell's used a membrane that, when vibrated by sound waves, moved a strip of iron through the field of an electromagnet, converting the sound into an undulating electric current. Gray's was a little more elegant. Vibration of the membrane changed the depth of immersion of a rod in acidified water, varying the current (most people don't realize that it was not the element receiving or broadcasting the voice which was the radically new part of the telephone, but the smoothly varying electric current, as opposed to the simple on/off of the telegraph circuit).

Neither man had actually conveyed speech through his device. Gray hadn't built his; Bell had, but his assistant Thomas Watson had only been able to make out "tones" from it. But in keeping with the standard procedure of their time—and ours—each had bolted off to the Patent Office to try to secure the right to make great gobs of money off his invention as soon as the idea had been conceived.

How did these two men—one in Boston, one in Chicago—end up inventing similar devices with identical purposes and presenting them to be patented on the same day?

Remember, neither Gray nor Bell was a solitary genius wrenching his brilliant creation from his unique intellect. It didn't work like that. The telephone was a by-product, gradually extracted from the telegraph. Neither Bell nor Gray had set out to bring the art of disembodied conversation to an eagerly awaiting world. Party lines, call-forwarding, telemarketing and Rock Hudson/Doris Day movies were well beyond imagining. In fact, there was no perceivable public desire to speak to people who were far away. The public was still pinching itself in wonder over the miracle of the telegraph, invented just thirty-two years earlier.

That was the problem with the telegraph—it was too popular. People wanted to send too many messages over the fragile web of wires crisscrossing the country, since a line could handle only one message at a time. Message requests were routinely backing up. There were delays.

What was needed was a way to send many messages at the same time through any one wire. Toward this end, Bell and Gray and other inventors realized that Morse messages could be keyed to varying pitches, then the entire chord of tones sent simultaneously along one wire and unsorted on the other end. (To one layman, unable to grasp how numerous messages could be sent over a single wire, Bell exploded, "There is only one air!"—i.e., many sounds simultaneously travel through the agency of a single atmosphere.)

Gray won this initial, lesser race. The year before the telephone photo finish, Gray patented a "multiple harmonic telegraph," getting his application in just two days before Bell.

Once a range of tones was being sent through a wire, it was a short hop to think about sending the complex tones and timbres of the human voice. The telephone began to loom on the horizon as the next big thing, and again, many people were trying to create one —there would be six hundred lawsuits filed challenging Bell's rights to the telephone. Newly established in Menlo Park, New Jersey, Thomas Edison, just to name the most prestigious, was hard at work on a telephone and would have beaten both Bell and Gray—he later claimed—had he not been hampered by his deafness. As it was, his carbon receiver was vastly better than either Gray's or Bell's, and was eventually incorporated into the standard telephone.

When more information is considered, the coincidence of Bell's and Gray's devices colliding at the U.S. Patent Office seems less and less startling, more like two runners crossing the finish line at the same time than a bizarre twist of fate (though there is a natural reluctance to let go of that pleasing *New Yorker*-cartoon image of coincidence—the two inventors, sitting very straight in the waiting room of the patent bureau, eyeing each other darkly, their wild and complex, yet identical, inventions perched on their laps).

As soon as the interference was announced by the Patent Office, Bell hotfooted it to Washington to try to smooth things over in person. Gray stayed in Chicago—perhaps a fatal error.

Bell found himself in conference with Zenas F. Wilber, the patent examiner. And this is the core of the onion—what passed between Bell and Wilber has been the subject of great speculation and debate. Bell later admitted that he asked Wilber about the nature of the conflict, and Wilber pointed to a line in Bell's patent application suggesting the possible use of liquid to vary the current. Even this is suspect, as the line is handwritten in the margin of the original application. Bell claimed that he forgot to include it in the text. But suspicion lingers—perhaps unjustly—since Wilber was a deaf-mute, well acquainted with Bell and, just maybe, sympathetic to his cause. They could have added the line on the spot, conjuring up the truism "Behind every great fortune is a great crime." Wilber later admitted that he also mistakenly showed Gray's application to Bell, which, if not a great crime, was certainly a breach of ethics.

By the time patent No. 174465 was granted to Bell, on March 7, he had constructed a working phone—based not on the iron-bar model described and pictured in his newly issued patent, but on Gray's liquid model, at best only alluded to in Bell's application in the handwritten addendum. This was the telephone Bell used in calling Watson, the telephone he displayed at the Centennial Exposition in Philadelphia that summer to an awestruck audience, including Elisha Gray, who, not realizing that Bell was using his device, slunk off in defeat.

Poor Gray! While continuing to press his claims, dripping with tortured Victorian dignity, in publications and in letters to Bell, he was also part of a lawsuit that sealed the Patent Office's decision: Western Union settled all Gray's claims against Bell in 1879, signing away its telephone rights in exchange for Bell's promise to stay out of the telegraph business, a monumental blunder on the part of Western Union. The company couldn't imagine the phone business ever assuming the scope of telegraphy. The Bell Telephone Company reneged on its end of the deal anyway.

Gray ended up a professor of electricity at Oberlin College in Ohio. He continued to win patents for his electrical devices, including over a dozen for improvements to the telephone. While some authors like to portray him as struggling in poverty late in life, taking in boarders to make ends meet, the reality was less dramatic. He was well enough off, in 1880, to pledge $50,000 solid-gold dollars to Oberlin. In January 1901, Gray collapsed and died on the street in Newtonville, Massachusetts. In his obituary, the *New York Times* predicted that while Bell had reaped the financial rewards of the telephone, it would be Gray whom posterity would bedeck with laurels as the inventor of the world-changing instrument. "In the opinion of many who have calmly weighed all the evidence on this subject, [Gray] is likely to receive full justice at the hands of future historians by being immortalized as the inventor of the speaking telephone," the newspaper postulated.

The newspaper was wrong. Gray's name virtually vanished, thanks in part to the Bell Telephone Company, which campaigned vigorously against Gray and his reputation.

The first edition of an 1878 book, *The Speaking Telephone, Talking Phonograph and Other Novelties*, by George B. Prescott, contains an account of Gray's contribution to the telephonic field. Upon the book's publication, Bell hired Prescott, and subsequent editions of the book omit mention of Gray entirely. According to an Oberlin biographer of Gray's, the company "bought up and destroyed all copies of the first edition that they could secure. Hence the rarity of this book."

Even as a young lass, there was something sinister about Ma Bell.

The campaign continued for decades after Gray was safely in his grave. In a 1933 issue of the *Bell Telephone Quarterly*, an odd and characteristically heavy-handed corporate philippic, "Myths of Telephone History," debunks various straw-man legends regarding the telephone—Bell giving away company stock for a dollar, Bell refusing to have a telephone in his home—before rolling up its sleeves and getting to the real task at hand: an elaborate keelhauling of Gray, introducing him with a grimly ornate and protracted meteorological metaphor that deserves reprinting:

> Myths are strange affairs. They are like clouds floating across the sky, none of them, even the highest, really very far from the ground. Like the myths in this article, they are quite different—heavy or light—some ephemeral and amusing, some grotesque, hardly to be taken seriously, some sinister. And they all speedily or slowly melt in the blue sky or pass on over the earth out of sight, are gone and forgotten. One more may be recounted here, the strangest of all, a dark cloud bearing tragic unhappiness in its piled-up masses and muttering with the distant echoes of a storm. It is the myth of Elisha Gray.

Gray is portrayed as a pathetic figure, "considerably older than Bell," with "no lightness in his nature that would enable him to throw off disappointment and take defeat easily." Though he is credited with his harmonic telegraph and with founding Western Electric (which by that point had been absorbed by the ubiquitous Bell System), Gray's belief that he had invented the telephone is seen as nothing more than a "sad, tragic" delusion.

Nevertheless, the author concludes, "time is healing the wounds," demonstrating this state of bonhomie by boasting that open-minded AT&T "impartially welcomes any material pertaining to his claim" for inclusion in the archives of its Elisha Gray Collection.

In other words, if you've got evidence supporting our arch-nemesis Gray, give it to us and we'll keep it in a safe place.

Perhaps it is old-fashioned of me to continue to fear and hate The Phone Company, now that the Beast has been decimated. But no matter how diversified It becomes, It will always appear to me as an insidious, shadow power—the nefarious TPC seen in the 1967 cult flick *The President's Analyst*. In searching for Gray's grave in Chicago's historic Rosehill Cemetery, in order to set some flowers on it on the anniversary of his Patent Office fiasco, and in the hope that the headstone would turn out to be sculpted in the form of a giant telephone, or something, I found only a snowy gap where the grave was supposed to be, according to the cemetery map. I searched for more than an hour, pacing around the crunching snow, wondering whether the body had been disinterred and spirited away for some hideous purpose by AT&T operatives, who, in my mind at least, seem capable of anything. Giving up, I set the flowers down on the snowy gap where the grave should have been, feeling this sort of tribute was in a sense fitting.

HISTORY IS, of course, an argument, and while I was marshaling the facts to parade in Elisha Gray's Carnival of Bad Timing, I couldn't help but notice that something else was at work as well.

It is true that Gray could have as easily been the father of the telephone as Bell. Had the patent commissioner given Gray the rights to the invention, Gray would have slipped comfortably into the role of conniving plutocrat and Bell—worthy soul, teacher of the deaf—would have assumed the mantle of odd nobility so often worn by fortune's victims. And the bad timing of the patent application seems to have been the deciding factor.

But it may not have been. After assessing the reams of information—letters written in Gray's jittery, haphazard script; scholarly reexaminations of the scientific merits of each; contemporary accounts of the dispute ("PROOF from Alexander Graham Bell's Own Mouth, That He Never Contemplated a Speaking Telephone in His

1876 Patent" begins one screed)—a dark something else, buried in
the background, begins to emerge.

The reality was, Gray had the jump on Bell. He could have filed
earlier. But in truth, he doubted the commercial viability of the
telephone and was reluctant to waste his time on it when there was
money to be made from telegraphy. Bell dragged his feet, too, but he
liked money and plunged ahead just in time to beat Gray.

"The whole thing is mine," he wrote to his father, two weeks
after filing his patent application, while Gray was still doddering. "I
am sure of fame, fortune, and success."

WHEN DEALING WITH bad timing, it is important to press on and
look for the Buried Something Else. For years, I interpreted my
romantic failure with Esther as a simple case of bad timing. If only
Sam's little band of friends had continued doing what they were
doing—bouncing a ball against a wall, running full tilt through the
neighborhood, waggling their tongues and screaming, or whatever it
was they did to pass the summer days—for a little longer, why, who
knows what could have happened? It could have been bliss.

Only recently, after maturity began settling over me like a fine
silt, did it occur to me that timing, bad or otherwise, really had
nothing to do with it. Sam could have been refueled with a can of
Mountain Dew, grabbed by the shoulders, spun around, and blasted
back into orbit. If Esther had wanted to, we could have. We had the
whole summer.

The fact is, I now see clearly, Sam did us both a favor—uncon-
scious awareness of this must have kept me from ever getting mad at
him. Esther, he extracted gracefully from what for her had to have
been a delicate situation. And me, he spared the searing memory of
Esther bracing the heel of her hand against my sternum and point-

edly explaining that while I was a nice guy, she just didn't view me *that way*, and she wanted to go home right now.

Thus saved, I was able to flatter myself for years that the merest flicker of circumstance, and not a Van Allen belt of personal deficiencies, had been at work that day. The truth would have been hard to take at the time. It's sort of hard to take now. But the idea of bad timing shielded me until I reached a point where I could almost smile at the whole thing.

THE MOST UNAMBIGUOUS cases of bad timing are those people brushed aside by what English pundit Clive James has called "the Fonck Factor." René Fonck was a French aviator pushing hard in the mid-1920s to be the first person to fly from New York to Paris nonstop, thus claiming a $25,000 prize offered by businessman Raymond Orteig.

James defines the epithet he coined as a circumstance in which someone is cast aside by developments beyond personal control, although—as with most cases of bad timing—Fonck did have a hand in his own failure. A former World War I ace, Captain Fonck was confident the prize was his. He convinced aviation pioneer Igor Sikorsky to provide a S-35 triple-engine airplane—the most advanced plane at the time and, at $105,000, also the most expensive. Since such an epic flight deserved a certain degree of magnificence, the interior of the plane was beautified by an interior decorator, who added panels of Spanish leather and mahogany walls so that it resembled "a tastefully furnished drawing room." Fonck ignored Sikorsky's pleas that the aircraft first be thoroughly stress-tested. With a takeoff weight of 28,000 pounds due to the extra fuel, 10,000 pounds past its design maximum, a stress test might have been a good idea. To make matters worse, the plane was loaded down with all sorts of optimistic tokens, from a bouquet of orchids for the French President's wife to a full-course celebration dinner for six, prepared at a New York hotel and packed in vacuum containers so it would still be hot when consumed at the Crillon in Paris. Moments before the departure from Roosevelt Field, on the cold, gray dawn of September 21, 1926, Fonck was handed yet another gift from a well-wisher. He "lifted it in his hand to test the weight, and with a rueful look placed it aboard the already overloaded plane," according to the *New York Times* report the next day.

Literally burdened with the expectations of success, the plane never became airborne. Its landing gear collapsed during take-off, and the plane cartwheeled into a gully at the end of the field and burst into flames. The plane's mechanic and radio operator were killed. Fonck and his navigator survived. Later, Fonck summed up the crash by uttering this wrenching expression of Gallic grief, "It is the fortune of the air," and immediately vowed to make the attempt again.

Alas for the gallant Fonck, the following spring, on May 20–21, 1927, a 25-year-old former airmail pilot named Charles Lindbergh, flying a stripped-down single-engine plane (pilots preferred those two- and three-engine planes in case one of the engines died in the middle of the Atlantic; Lindbergh was thinking of saving fuel), alone without a crew, crossed the Atlantic in 33 hours, 30 minutes. At times holding his eyes open with his thumbs, or hanging his head out the window to be revived by the icy air, Lindbergh also reported that he kept himself awake by repeating "There's no alternative but death and failure" over and over again.

Lindbergh got the fame and fortune. Fonck got, well, Foncked.

The Fonck Factor, I believe, is what explains those periodic lawsuits where unknown composers claim that one musical superstar or another has ripped off their melodies. Imagine the frustration:

years of noodling on your Casio in the basement; hundreds of dollars spent putting together demo tapes and press packets; the struggle to work up a sense of moment when dropping them into the mail for the long, open-ended wait for responses that never come. Then one fine day, thinking of something else, the hapless schmo turns on the radio and—FONCK!—there's Billy Joel singing a song that sounds very much like the schmo's own "Love Is in the Air Tonight My Dear Irene."

It is much easier, emotionally, to concoct an elaborate chain of possibility, even if it involves Billy Joel lurking outside in the shrubbery, standing on Christie Brinkley's shoulders to press his ear against the window, than to admit that the beloved little song with its three chord changes and jingly bridge could somehow have been thought up, independently, by somebody else, if not a whole bunch of somebody elses.

The saddest Foncked character in history, for me, is Robert Falcon Scott, the polar explorer alluded to in the second chapter. Determined to claim for England the glory of being first at the South Pole, Scott and his men found themselves racing a Norwegian team headed by Roald Amundsen, mushing along an alternate route, aiming to grab the kudos for Norway. Scott's team reached their goal on January 17, 1912, after a hellacious 169-kilometer trek. One account of the expedition is titled *The Worst Journey in the World.*

The night before the pole was reached, Scott wrote in his diary: "It ought to be a certain thing now, and the only appalling possibility the sight of the Norwegian flag forestalling ours."

Bingo. They came upon the tracks of the Norwegians, still visible after three weeks, then a flag—not Norwegian, but an ominous black bunting. And finally, an abandoned camp—sleeping bags, reinskin trousers, broken instruments, Norwegian flags flying and, most gallingly, a letter from Amundsen to King Haakon VII, together with a request that Scott be good enough to deliver the mail when he got back.

"The Norwegian have forestalled us and are first at the Pole," Scott wrote in his diary. "It is a terrible disappointment, and I am very sorry for my loyal companions . . . it will be a wearisome return."

More than wearisome, it was a torturous ordeal that left Scott and his four men dead, 15 miles short of their supply depot, in the middle of March. The men's physical condition had rapidly deteriorated in their race northward in brutally cold conditions. (Again, as with Everest, there was that weird Monty Pythonesque humor attached to the decline. When one of his men's frostbitten fingers started suppurating and his blackish, "rotten-looking" nose seemed liable to drop off, Scott was puzzled to find this state of affairs having a negative impact on the man's good humor. "To my surprise, he shows signs of losing heart over it," wrote Scott. "He hasn't been cheerful . . .")

Ironically, the awful death of Scott and his men (recorded in great detail, up to the bitter end, in their diaries) made them more heroic than they would have been had they reached the pole first. Only, of course, they weren't around to enjoy their fame.

Once again, the concept of bad timing is a screen, obscuring the real reasons for failure. Generous historians conclude that Scott and his men, sapped by disappointment at brushing so close to victory, only to have it snapped up by mere Norwegians, were too dispirited to finish the rigorous return trip. A more honest historian, at the risk of slandering the dead, might gingerly make the point that Scott was foolish—he started his trek 60 miles farther away than Amundsen, and he spurned sled dogs for unproven ponies, which fatally slowed the expedition.

—

BAD TIMING IS a comfort when the Buried Something Else is even worse. In cases of people being killed by random gunfire, for instance, the media almost always trots out some version of the victim's being "in the wrong place at the wrong time," even if that wrong place is a front doorstep and the wrong time is noon. To focus on the bad timing—she had just stepped into the store to buy baby food when the shooting started—is more comforting to the public than the reality that many victims are always in "the wrong place." They live there, in a part of the city where people are constantly shot at random and killed for no reason at all. Tragedy is just a matter of waiting until the wrong time comes along.

Or to take a less grave example. In the summer of 1962, Vaughn Meader was an obscure young comedian who did an uncanny impersonation of John F. Kennedy. He got a shot on the "Talent Scouts" television show, which led to an appearance on "The Ed Sullivan Show" in the fall—and instant fame.

His debut record album, *The First Family*, a parody of the Kennedy White House, was mild to the point of being apologetic. "Things are being suggested and said here about some of the great people of our time, and perhaps the very fact that they are able to laugh with us and enjoy this album is in part what makes them the great people they are," read a disclaimer on the back cover. "No one has more respect for the high offices and the people suggested here than do those of us who had a hand in putting this together."

Nevertheless, the album was a hit, selling over 6 million copies to a nation enraptured with all things Kennedy. Meader's career was made.

For less than a year.

Then came November 22, 1963, and Kennedy jokes were no

longer in good taste. *The First Family* was yanked from record stores. Meader, who was no fool, publicly announced he would never again impersonate Kennedy—as if he had much of a choice—and then went into seclusion for two months.

In early 1964, he reemerged with a new act, devoid of any Kennedy references. No dice. Nobody would touch Meader, who, at the age of twenty-six, was washed up. "I seemed to be like a living reminder of that tragedy," said Meader, twenty-five years later. "It was over."

Meader himself, however, had to contend with the rest of his own life, which meandered from living in a log cabin as part of a San Francisco commune in the late 1960s to stabs at a career as a country and western singer and composer. He married twice and divorced twice, became an alcoholic, and occasionally managed pathetic attempts to resuscitate his career as a comic, imitating first Jimmy Carter and then, briefly and unenthusiastically, Ted Kennedy.

"I'm not crazy about doing it," he said of his impersonation of the younger Kennedy. "Nobody will ever know I can do anything else."

Which brings us to the Buried Something Else hidden by that November day in Dallas. Meader really couldn't do anything else. He wasn't particularly funny.

I say this having listened to his second album, *Have Some Nuts!!!*— recorded in November 1963 (one assumes before the assassination). Even factoring in the passage of time and the loss of topicality, the album is painfully bad, almost unlistenable. (Comedy becomes dated, but funny comedy remains humorous. You can still listen to and enjoy Allan Sherman's "Pop Hates the Beatles" or Tom Lehrer's "Hubert Where Are You?"—both topical and both recorded around that time. Perhaps musical comedy holds up better.)

So while the world might trace the source of Meader's decline to the assassination, it actually might have been, in his case, a kindness. Had Kennedy lived to see the end of a second term, Meader's career might have vanished anyway. After all, Nixon made it to the '90s, but the career of Nixon imitator David Frye didn't.

Show business, of course, is particularly fraught with bad timing. For more than a decade, I've pondered an episode that intrigued me because I slightly knew the participants and because it seemed to show the horrible caprice of timing for those who are chasing a particular, elusive success.

In the early 1980s, there was a comedic troupe called the Practical Theater, a group of actors dwelling on the periphery of Northwestern University. They put on a string of hilarious shows in the tiny, forty-two-seat theater they had dubbed the John Lennon Auditorium, on Chicago's northernmost fringe, and over time they began to develop a reputation and a devoted following. I remember going to see one of their revues—I think it was *The Brothers Bubba*—then returning the next week to see it again.

The star of the troupe was a long-haired wild man named Rush Pearson, who did an amazing stomping, drooling impersonation of Godzilla. He was one of those guys who is both impressive and a little frightening, so strongly is he held in the grip of his particular muse. Rush survived on the hospitality of friends, rotating among their homes in Evanston, living for a while in his van, and in the John Lennon Auditorium itself. (After one show, we were standing around smoking dope, talking, and he told me that he lived in the theater. I said something like "Completely devoted, eh?" and he said, "No, I live *in* the theater," showing me a narrow spotlight crawl space, without enough room to stand up, where he had built a nest of bedding and old clothes.)

In the summer of 1982, Dick Ebersol, then the producer of NBC-TV's "Saturday Night Live," was brought to see the Practicals, as they were called, by actor Tim Kazurinsky. Ebersol was impressed, and summoned the performers to New York City for an audition. Rush Pearson wasn't among them—he had taken time off from the troupe to perform a mud-eating routine at a Renaissance fair in upstate New York. Efforts were made to track him down, but to no avail.

The way the story got back to me, all the Practical Theater members walked into their auditions with Ebersol and started to explain that the person he really wanted to audition was Rush, until Ebersol put up his hands and said, "I don't want to hear any more about this guy."

Ebersol ended up hiring four of the Practicals—Gary Kroeger, Brad Hall, Julia Louis-Dreyfus and, as a writer, Paul Barrosse. All went on to successful careers in entertainment, with Louis-Dreyfus becoming particularly famous on "Seinfeld."

And Rush Pearson? By the time he heard of the tryouts, it was too late. He still works Renaissance fairs, where he eats mud for a living.

Of course, had Rush been there, he might have been deemed too wild for "Saturday Night Live," which was going through a particularly lame period at the time. He might have been denied fame by another stroke of ill luck, or he might have been destined to make his living eating mud. Barrosse, who was another long-hair and had a style similar to Rush's, didn't last a year on the show, and none of the other Practicals were there after two years.

Rush today is philosophical about the whole thing. "There are a million and one things you don't know," he says. "I'd have loved the money. But who knows? I could have turned into a coke addict. Or I could have been the spark that had those guys become a powerful force on the show, instead of fodder. It's hard to say."

Searching for the Buried Something Else in the story, one has to ask why Pearson wasn't in the show that Ebersol saw. It turns out, the Practical Theater had just moved into Second City's new experimental space, and Pearson disapproved of connecting the group with its more famous rival. "I thought going into [Second City founder] Bernie Sahlins's backyard was a mistake," remembers Rush. "He's giving us this space; he's going to take from us . . . I said, 'Tell you what, have a good time with this show.' "

So maybe Pearson, the drooling wild man, was never going to make the sort of practical compromises that usually need to be made to find commercial success.

But the thought of bad timing is seductive. In my mind, I can't help but contemplate that tiny fulcrum of circumstance that may have sent Julia Louis-Dreyfus to stardom and consigned Rush Pearson to collecting dollar bills from a grinning crowd of people who will pay to see him eat wet dirt. The fulcrum might be more illusion than reality, but it is a powerful illusion nevertheless.

IS THERE ALWAYS a Buried Something Else? Do great endeavors ever fail solely on timing alone? Most assuredly, particularly projects of long gestation such as RCA's SelectaVision, which, as we saw in the products chapter, was a perfectly fine and innovative method of watching movies at home, but just happened to lope onto the market a few years after the arrival of videocassettes.

Publishers of books, which generally take at least a year or two to finish, are filled with tales of worthy volumes sinking because of unforseen developments in the world. A prime example is Peter Wyden's *Wall: The Inside Story of Divided Berlin.* Now Wyden was no slouch—he's an expert on Germany, author of many readable volumes on aspects of the subject. And *Wall* was a good book—solid, well-researched, well-written, topical.

A little too topical, as it turned out. The book was published in October 1989 and was well received for a few weeks. Then, in November, the Berlin Wall fell, the world reordered itself, and Wyden's book dropped from view.

Ask Wyden today whether bad timing hurt the book and he lets out a long half-laugh, half-groan. "Oh man oh man oh man oh man . . ." he says. "There is no question, the book was swamped by events." To his credit, Wyden, watching the television coverage of the laughing, dancing celebrants knocking holes in the Berlin Wall with sledgehammers, did not think, Jesus, there goes the book. "Come on," he says. "We're all human beings first. I was thrilled to bits, thrilled practically to tears. Frankly, if anything, I thought it would help the book . . ."

FIVE

It Can't Be Done

—

The Lure of the Impossible

M Y DRIVER'S LICENSE says that I am 5 feet 10 inches tall, though I tell people that I am 5 feet 9, and my wife knows that I am really 5 feet 8¾.

That's average height, almost, for an American male of this particular time period. Not an ideal height for sports, except perhaps croquet, particularly combined with the fact that I am an endomorph—wide hips, narrow shoulders, big head.

Still, when I was sixteen years old, I spent a year on my high school track team. Since I couldn't run very fast at all (oh yes, another endomorphic trait: short, thick legs), I joined the shot-put team.

A high school shot is an orb of iron that weighs 12 pounds, or 6 percent of my body weight at the time. Standing in a 7-foot circle, the putter tucks the shot under his chin and, by either twirling or shuffling across the circle without stepping out, pitches the shot as far as strength permits.

My strength permitted me to put the shot about 22 feet, if I recall. Just in case this figure impresses anybody, let me add that Mark Stoyanoff, the star of the team, could on a good day pitch the shot 49 feet. Which meant that I could take the shot, throw it, go to where it landed, pick it up, throw it farther, and Stoyanoff could, in one fling, beat my two throws combined.

I stayed on the team the entire season. It was fun. We had uniforms. We traveled on buses to meets, along with our "timers," a cheerleader-like squad of girls, including Esther, who kept time at meets. That was a bonus. The guys seemed to accept me, in the main. (Though I treasure a certain expression on Earl Lambert's face —sort of an open-mouthed, head-shaking, dark look of befuddlement. I caught his gaze. "What are you doing here?" he said, genuinely confused. I had no answer.)

And unlike many events, there was no struggle to see who would compete in the weekend meets. Everyone on the shot-put team, no matter how unskilled, got his chance to throw. A throw took a few seconds. What else was there to do while waiting for the cross-country runners to show up? The good guys went first. Then the mediocre guys. Then me.

In the movie version of this story, I'd have maniacally built myself up, with the help of a janitor from Bhutan who had once been Mr. Universe but had been forced to quit. In the course of the season, I'd gain strength while learning some secret Bhutanese shot-put technique. He'd feel better about himself, too, and bullies might factor into the plot somewhere. With Stoyanoff nursing a sore arm on the day of The Big Meet, I'd win the event, sending our team over the top to victory with one epic fling of the shot, a soaring arc that would take about a minute and a half of screen time to land, what with the various angles and slo-mo dissolves and flashes of crowd reaction (my father, shouting and exhilarated; my mother, thrusting her fist in the air, making woofing sounds; Esther, both hands pressed over her mouth, eyes wide), and would give the movie its title: *The Iron Rainbow.*

It didn't work like that. I knew that my doughish arm was never going to throw the shot any appreciable distance, no matter what I did, and that even if I were wrong, even if it had been possible to somehow transform that flaccid arm into a catapult of steel, the intestinal fortitude necessary, the singularity of purpose required to accomplish such a feat, was utterly lacking in my soul. The goal wasn't worth it, to me. I liked tucking the shot under my chin. I enjoyed the little shuffle step you took when throwing the shot. That was enough, because I had learned an important secret: I didn't have to throw the shot very far. I didn't have to win. The guys who banged their heads against the lockers, weeping because they came in second, were misguided, if not stupid. This knowledge changed my life. A few years earlier, I could never have endured the daily practices, could never have publicly flung my weak lob each weekend, plopping the shot into the dirt yards short of the mark, knowing that the Stoyanoffs and the Lamberts where shrugging their shoulders, if not sniggering behind their hands. But I had realized that I could do things I was no good at, things that were impossible for me ever to be good at, fail miserably as a matter of routine, and have fun in the process.

HERE IS A simple little mathematical puzzle. Draw a group of three boxes. Now, directly under it, draw another group of three boxes. It should look like this:

☐   ☐   ☐

☐   ☐   ☐

The challenge is to draw lines connecting each of the boxes on the top row with each of the three boxes on the bottom row without any of the lines crossing.

You may want to redraw the boxes on a piece of paper so as to not mess the page up. This isn't *Highlights*. Nothing is worse than finding a nice book scribbled all over by some anonymous boob.

So draw your boxes, and try it for a while.

Give up? Good, because it's impossible. No matter how you loop the lines, you reach a point where one of the lower boxes is cut off from one of the upper boxes by the lines already drawn.

The game made a good way to pass the time in high school. Even after I figured out that the puzzle couldn't be solved, I still would give it a try every once in a while—beginning aggressively with short, direct lines, quickly shifting into wide, looping lines—to occupy myself and to see whether the laws of the universe had changed. They hadn't.

This seems to me a natural human response, like making a wish on a coin tossed into a fountain, or Democratic Presidents trying to solve ancient afflictions like poverty by fine-tuning federal policy. The fact that something is impossible doesn't always discourage people from trying to do it anyway.

It is that impulse, rather than the puzzle itself, that I find interesting today. So much failure comes from it, as well as, incredibly, an occasional success. The motivation drawing people to the impossible is usually not indifference to failure. Rather, they suspect, in their secret hearts, that they have the special qualifications it takes to make the impossible possible.

Sometimes they do. The concept of impossibility is like a heavy gold frame surrounding reality. Most people exist within the frame and believe in its solidity. And it is pretty solid. Still, disbelievers on the margins push at the frame. Usually nothing happens. But every now and then, the frame moves.

Up until ninety years ago, it was impossible for man to fly in a heavier-than-air craft. A lot of people thought it would remain forever impossible. A few thought it was possible, and two of them, Orville and Wilbur Wright, were the first to pull it off. Suddenly, man could fly. The heavy gold frame shifted.

Usually an impossibility is banished with much less finality than a contraption of wood, wire and cloth lifting off the ground. For three centuries, mathematicians labored at proving Fermat's famous Last Theorem: that $x^n + y^n = z^n$ has no solutions for any number n greater than 2, assuming x, y and z are nonzero integers. Most came to feel such a proof was impossible. Then Andrew Wiles, a Princeton mathematician, slipped in his attempted proof at the end of a three-day lecture at Cambridge University in June 1993.

The initial response was joy, with perhaps a little sadness from mathematicians that their profession's Everest had been scaled. Those who weren't mathematicians didn't have a say, not unless they were going to try to fathom Wiles's two-hundred-page proof. But as the proof was digested by the mathematical community, questions were raised, the loudest coming, surprisingly, from the self-described genius author of *Parade* magazine's dopey "Ask Marilyn" column, Marilyn vos Savant, who sped a book-length critique of Wiles's solution into print (*The World's Most Famous Math Problem*, published an astounding five months after Wiles's seminar at Cambridge). Vos Savant marshaled a list of complaints about Wiles's proof, the stickiest being that his use of non-Euclidian geometry was not a valid way to prove the theorem (somewhat like solving the box puzzle by arcing a line or two above the page, into the third dimension).

The debate over Fermat underlines the need, when talking about what is impossible, to establish just what framework of physical reality we are using. Just as certain technical wonders, such as a phone implanted in the hollow behind your ear, are impossible *now* but not necessarily into eternity, so other impossibilities—creating matter from nothing, transmuting lead into gold, finding pi to its last digit—are impossible *given our present understanding of how things work.*

In other words, yeah, national health care could work, provided government as we know it—the low-level, not-my-table shovel leaning of the federal bureaucracy, coupled with the gimme-mine Boss Tweedism of elected officials—somehow reorders itself into a benign dynamism not seen since Jefferson. Communism could work, too—just not when populated with human beings in their present state of flawed development.

This is an important distinction, one Isaac Asimov draws in a perky little 1968 essay, "Impossible, That's All!"—written in response to his daughter's assertion "Nothing is impossible," uttered when she was told that nothing can go faster than the speed of light.

Asimov framed the problem as a matter of working within systems of understanding. It is impossible to divide by zero in mathematics, he points out, only according to the idea of math that we have created. "Division by zero isn't impossible in the sense that it can't be done in the manipulation of symbols," he writes. "It's impossible in the sense that it breaks the rules of the game."

The frequency with which the rules do get violated, and need to be changed, must be born in mind. Just look at the most ordinary appliances of today, and realize they were the gee-whiz futurism of years past. Fifty years ago a radio came in a wood cabinet and made for a substantial piece of furniture; today you can wear a better radio clipped to your lapel.

I was reading "Dick Tracy" recently and noticed that he is now inserting pea-sized CD-ROM discs into his wrist computer. At first it struck me as ludicrous—discs that small—until I realized that the wrist radio must have seemed equally wild and improbable back in the 1930s. Pea-sized CD discs could be just around the corner; maybe now is a good time to invest in tweezers.

Or maybe not. There is danger in being too open-minded. Usually the frame does not move. One doesn't want to be among the great mass of the credulous, scanning the skies for wonders, swallowing crystals, eager to believe anything, certain that we could flap our wings and fly if only the government would let us. As the patriarch of the status quo, impossibility has an inertia, and its tendency is to continue.

While most people realize this in their upper lobes, deep down in the subconscious there are doubts that come bubbling to the surface in unguarded moments.

In trying to figure out exactly why the little box puzzle cannot be solved, I started by checking into the history of the Königsberg Bridge Problem, a puzzle gnawing at residents of the old Prussian city, cut in half by the Pregel River, breaking into two branches around the island of Kneiphof. The city had seven bridges, crossing the various branches of the Pregel and—well, perhaps another picture is in order. It looked like this:

Residents of Königsberg would occasionally try to cross all seven bridges connecting the island with the various banks on a single walk, without crossing any bridge twice. They knew they couldn't do it, but they didn't know why, not until the great Swiss mathematician Leonhard Euler stopped by and figured it out. (His explanation involves counting edges and nodes and is a bit thick to lay out here. But it's in almost any math book, if you really want to know.)

Looking at a map of the Königsberg bridges in Dominic Olivastro's *Ancient Puzzles*, I lazily drew my finger over a little route, surprising myself by crossing all the bridges without crossing any twice. Sitting up (the most satisfying place to read is a couch, so one may nap at will), I ran through the bridges again. The same success. Excited hopes began to form in my heart. I had done it! I had found a new way! The answer stared the doltish masses in the face for centuries, but they had missed it, and I, with my special gifts. . . .

Oh. Then I realized it—on the third journey of finger over bridges. I had crossed one bridge twice. Oh well. Guess I didn't solve the impossible problem after all.

I AM NOT particularly ashamed to reveal this minor display of dimwitted ego, because it is common to most people and they don't even know it. They think that, in their hands, hard realities soften and become malleable. Look at fear of flying. Airplanes are far, far safer than automobiles, but many fear to get on one, while the worst drivers happily plop behind the wheel and lurch into traffic, threatening us all with sudden fiery death. Why? Because they believe their ego supersedes reality. Passengers on planes must put their fates in the hands of trained professional pilots, whom the passengers don't trust to be as skilled as they themselves are in controlling a car. In a car, you know, trust and love the driver so long as you are driving.

Gambling is an even better example of the clash between ego and possibility. All forms of gambling are sucker's bets, to varying degrees. That is, if you play long enough, the inevitable outcome is that your money departs from you and flows into the coffers of the casino, or lottery, or bingo hall. That's the way the system is set up.

Skill has little or no impact on the games—you don't see casino chess, do you? Yet people, generally feeling wrapped in a protective cloud of specialness, go into gambling experiences suspecting that they are going to win, despite the varying but always greater odds that they will not. In this way the casino business took in $30 billion last year, every dollar put down by people anticipating the joy of winning. Some of that money the casinos paid out in jackpots, true, but a great amount stayed in the pockets of the gambling establishments.

Not that I am against gambling. I sometimes gamble when the opportunity arises, first primly setting aside an amount I expect to lose. I can't see taking any other approach to it, though this outlook does not make for assiduous play. Generally I do lose the amount set aside. I remember once playing vingt-et-un in the Caribbean under the gaze of a drunken Frenchwoman. After blowing the $75 set aside to be lost—and at $5 a chip, it took all of a minute or two—I got up to leave. The woman delivered her comment. "You pleh like an eediot," she said, Gallic disgust flitting about her face. "I wouldn't pleh et ze same teble as yew."

THE REDEEMING PART of my brief flirtation with solving the Königsberg Bridge Problem is that I did not leap off the sofa and call the newspapers after my second go-through of the map. The annals of the impossible are filled with tales of those who convince themselves, incorrectly, that they have achieved some miracle and then go out and announce it to the world.

The history of Fermat's Last Theorem has several episodes of learned mathematicians humiliating themselves by presenting proofs that weren't. Gabriel Lamé was standing in front of the French Academy of Sciences, outlining his proof, when, in mid-lecture, his colleagues began to rise to point out the weak parts and embarrassing errors, which Lamé had overlooked in his initial burst of zeal. The German mathematician Carl Louis Ferdinand von Lindemann spent five years working out a proof, publishing his paper in 1907. A chorus of happy colleagues quickly pointed out a basic error *at the beginning* of the proof. Whether Wiles will join this group is still an open question.

This sort of triumph of enthusiasm over reason pops up in the most surprising places. Half of all public figures, it sometimes seems, spend their private moments spinning talismans, or scattering chicken bones, or studying the entrails of ducks. Usually they have the good sense to be ashamed and keep their activities private. Occasionally, their romance with the occult is revealed to the world—call it the Shirley MacLaine Syndrome (with its more dangerous corollary, the Nancy Reagan Phenomenon, the former representing benign belief in the occult, such as among aging dancers, and the latter a more worrisome gullibility, such as the first couple gazing into a crystal ball while holding hands with Madame Glazinga).

Readers familiar with Michael Crichton's *Travels* (a book that makes Arthur C. Clarke's *Report on Planet Three* seem as earthbound as *Walden*) will remember their surprise at Crichton's sudden slide into the paranormal. The first half of the book unfolds without a hint of the preternatural, a rather thought-provoking autobiographical tale of a young man's journey through Harvard Medical School and almost accidental pop fiction stardom. Then the narrative suddenly shifts into Crichton's search for never-never land, as the best-selling author travels the globe to bend spoons via telekinesis and moon at the feet of swamis.

Crichton's problem—endemic to those who believe they have accomplished the impossible without having in fact accomplished it —is that he puts too much faith into his own powers of observation.

The secret ego bursting out. Again and again, Crichton's skepticism of auras, of past-life regression, of voices from the beyond lasts only until he himself experiences them—or rather, thinks he does—usually guided by one of the Central Casting charlatans who are always found perpetuating this type of fraud.

Then he sits back, flutters his hands at the heavens and, drafting his previous skepticism to serve as further proof of the miracle, pronounces this new wonder a verified reality. He forgets the great value in sometimes distancing yourself from what you have seen when what you've seen clashes too strongly with the world as it is generally known.

In Haiti, I saw dancing mambos fill their mouths with hot coals they had scooped out of the fire. When they smiled, their mouths were a crescent of glowing orange, like a jack-o'-lantern. I saw it, and was impressed, but not convinced that there is a hidden spirit world of forbidden knowledge. There may be, but my witnessing the neat trick with the coals didn't add any evidence one way or the other. "No testimony," Hume wrote, "is sufficient to establish a miracle." Not even your own testimony. Maybe the mambos first filled their mouths with ice water, or Teflon. Maybe the coals were fake. Ersatz coals. I don't know. But I do know the experience didn't move me to start worshipping Erzulie Dantor or lighting the red candle.

Once I went to a palmist. Not out of desire to glimpse the yet-to-be, but for a story I was writing for the newspaper. I was getting married in a few months, and the idea behind the article was to visit various mediums to see if the pending Cecil B. DeMille–like carnival of nuptials would register on their psychic radar screens. Seismic reverberations were certainly going off in my inner spirit, and if anything was going to show up in the tea leaves, this would be it.

Most of the soothsayers and spiritualists I saw were hacks who ascertained nothing (one read my palm over the phone, instructing me to draw my hands slowly over the mouthpiece). Another palmist, however, a woman who had me coat my palms with black printer's ink and press them onto a card, was very good. She told me all sorts of things about myself. Secret things. Some were wrong, but a lot were right on the mark, enough to be eerie and unsettling.

But unlike Crichton, I did not then conclude she did it by connecting with the vast hidden mystery aether surrounding and enveloping us. Maybe, after I called and made the appointment, she took my name and phoned her friend at the credit bureau. Maybe she went through my garbage. Or could take a quick look at a stocky guy with rumpled clothes and thick glasses and make a few good guesses. Who knows? But I do know she didn't pull the information off the lines on my hands—at least I'm fairly certain. One must leave a little room for doubt—if nothing else, as a bulwark against zealotry and to give the impression of having an open mind. After all, as dumb as the lottery may be, as much as playing it is a statement of quiet personal despair, people do occasionally win.

THE BOX PUZZLE was not the only impossibility I toyed with as a schoolboy. Following a tradition that—unknown to me—was centuries old, I also dabbled in devising machines for perpetual motion. A chain of sponges, one side sodden, the other wrung out, traveling in an endless circle. Waterwheels attached to pumps, raising the water that flows over and drives them. That sort of thing.

Again, I was fact-checking life, making sure that the standard impossibilities were indeed impossible and not just waiting for a celestial talent such as myself to apply my skills to eternal problems.

The idea of sleeping in the still-warm beds of past failures is perfectly set out in the history of perpetual motion. The same over-balanced wheels that were carefully carved in medieval woodblock prints can be found described in U.S. patents of the 1830s. The flash of hoopla that accompanies announcements of engines running for hundreds of miles on a cup of weak tea—these seem to occur every few years—seldom mention the long line of previous disproven claims.

Modern readers may not realize what perpetual-motion enthusiasts were trying to do. It wasn't just getting something to move continuously—radiometers, those little glass bulbs with spinning black and white vanes, sold in museum gift shops, will do that, as will delicate clocks that run off atmospheric changes, and, for that matter, those bobbing bird toys, as least until their water evaporates.

Perpetual motion was supposed to *produce work*—drive mills, operate saws, pump water.

The futility of the dream of a perpetual-motion machine is not a recent discovery. For centuries, perpetual motion has been recognized as both intellectually enticing and physically impossible. "Not but there are sundry discourses concerning this subject, but they are rather *conjectures* than *experiments*," wrote John Wilkins, the future Bishop of Chester, in 1648. "And though many inventions in this kind may at first view bear a great shew of possibility, yet they will fail, being brought to trial, and will not answer in practice what they promise in speculation."

The gap between conjecture and experiment is a wide one, and though centuries pass, people continue to pour, lemming-like, into the breach. The fascinating thing about perpetual motion is that no amount of scientific data establishing its impossibility seem to affect the quest to discover it. "Those who occupy themselves with this chimera find nothing but embarrassment," the French mathematician M. de la Hire wrote in his *Démonstration de l'Impossibilité du Mouvement Perpétuel* in 1666. "When they propose their beautiful inventions to those who are versed in science, and who cannot immediately make them see or understand in what way their reasoning is false, they then publish to the world that the very cleverest men have been convinced of the truth of their perpetual motion."

Those inventing the machines were not the only ones taken in. The patent offices of the United States and European nations have all issued patents for perpetual motion, albeit in less critical days. During the South Sea Bubble mania in the early 1700s, when the entire population of Britain gave their life savings to Charles Keating–like financial wizards, one of the bogus prospectuses offered for sale was "for a Wheel of Perpetual Motion," even though decades had passed since Newton's second and third laws of motion contradicted the possibility of a perpetual-motion machine doing work. In 1775, the French Academy of Sciences had to pass a resolution banning the consideration of perpetual-motion proposals, since so much of its time was being taken up by those who felt they had done the impossible.

The great role that fraud played in the history of perpetual motion must be solemnly recognized. Lack of documentation makes it difficult to sort those who geniunely pursued the dream from those who sought to rig up clever fakes for personal gain, but cases where evidence still exists tend to fall into the second category.

What is most interesting about perpetual motionists is the surprising sameness with which they present their discoveries. Whether in 1400 or 1900, there is a sly, I've-got-something-wonderful-but-I-can't-quite-show-you-because-you'll-steal-it interplay that keeps the device itself just out of view of the skeptical observer.

As late as 1918, the United States Congress appointed a special commission to examine the claims of a particularly convincing proponent of perpetual motion.

What kept (and keeps) drawing people to such a foolhardy endeavor? Why do so many desirable impossibilities—raising the dead, levitation, time travel—lack perpetual motion's history of intensive struggle and failure to bring it into being? The answer, I believe, is a question of proximity. While you can't go backward in time, even a little bit, you can take a heavy flywheel on good bearings, give it a shove, and it will turn and turn and turn. Perpetual motion seems so near, just a tantalizing step away. Just beyond the frame of possibility.

Henry Dircks, in his massive 1861 study, *Perpetuum Mobile; or, A History of the Search for Self-Motive Power,* cites a "Mr. B—— of London, philosophical instrument maker," who spent thousands of pounds of his and others' money attempting perpetual motion. "Mr. B—— when speaking of their career would take up a scrap of paper, and tearing off a very small portion, exclaim, 'We got it—all but that,' throwing the paper to the table."

To this day, people still try to invent perpetual-motion machines. Every year, the U.S. Patent Office receives a number of attempts to patent perpetual motion. In order to discourage submissions, it requires that actual models of the devices be submitted, a requirement it abandoned for most patent applications years ago.

A good deal of the continuing interest must be put down as ignorant greed. Just as various lowlifes flushed themselves from the woodwork during the Pepsi tampering scare, sensing they could make money by dropping Grandpa's insulin syringe into the Pepsi Free, so various tinkerers, imagining untold wealth and fishing boats, cobble together a quick model, give it a spin, then trundle off to Washington to secure their place in history.

But one should not smirk too broadly when gazing at the perpetual motionists. It may be a quixotic quest, but as Dircks wisely points out, citing a forgotten tinkerer/suicide, so are a great many things: "If Hartmann of Leipsic hanged himself from despair at his vainly spent life in prosecuting this hopeless attempt, could not an equally sad tale be related of many a Poet and Artist?"

THE LUMPEN-PROLETARIAT shabbiness of perpetual motion would be good for merely a passing elitist smirk were it not also present at the very highest levels of intellectual life, as witnessed in the 1989 cold fusion incident, a treat for every fan of human folly and misapplication of effort.

Very briefly, fusion is the merging of atoms, releasing giant amounts of energy normally trapped within subatomic structures (as opposed to the more mundane fission, which involves breaking atoms apart).

Fusion occurs naturally in the center of stars such as the sun, supplying their power, and unnaturally on earth in the form of hydrogen bombs. Fusion requires incredible heat—upward of 100 million degrees—and has been achieved briefly by scientists using superheated plasmas, but not as yet in a way practical for producing energy commercially.

So imagine the fuss in March 1989 when a pair of respected chemists at the University of Utah, Martin Fleischmann and B. Stanley Pons, announced at a press conference that they had achieved cold fusion—that is, fusion not at millions of degrees but at room temperature—in a test tube in their Salt Lake City lab. The fusion was created electrochemically by running a current through palladium electrodes immersed in heavy water.

Pons and Fleischmann's press conference was the equivalent of two doctors at the Mayo Clinic announcing that the cure for cancer is a mixture of grape soda and rose water.

They hadn't created fusion, as many scientists around the country instantly knew. But others were sucked in, wistfully interpreting data from their own attempts to replicate the experiment. MIT jumped in with both feet, struggling to wrest away patent rights to the nonprocess. Stanford, Texas A&M and Georgia Tech also started cheering for cold fusion. (Texas A&M's researcher would later investigate the possibility of using the cold fusion process to transmute mercury into gold, briefly reviving the flagging spirits of alchemists everywhere.)

The state of Utah embraced cold fusion as a refutation of its self-perceived inferiority, with Utah newspapers waving paper pompoms and forming pyramids and the state legislature pressing $5 million into the itchy palm of the cold fusionists, almost unconcerned whether the thing worked or not. Lewis Thomas called the reaction to cold fusion "a collective derangement of minds in total disorder." In July, months after the rest of the nation had gotten tired of laughing at cold fusion and gone back to baseball, 67 percent of Utahans said they still believed in the chimerical phenomenon. Perhaps they still do.

In fact, Pons and Fleischmann hadn't even discovered anything new. The phenomenon they were observing was uncovered as early as 1956, when Luis Alvarez and his team at the University of California at Berkeley also thought they had found fusion. "For a few exhilarating hours, we thought we had solved mankind's energy problems forever," Alvarez wrote. Only Alvarez, unlike Pons and Fleischmann, did not immediately hold a press conference—he looked harder at the phenomenon, realized he had not really created fusion, and went on to study subatomic particles and win the Nobel Prize.

The entire three-ring cold fusion circus is definitively set out in Gary Taubes's *Bad Science*, a delightful and comprehensive, if slightly numbing, account of the episode. In Taubes's analysis, the key factor setting off the fiasco was that Pons and Fleischmann believed that a competitor, Steven Jones, at nearby Brigham Young University, was stealing their work. It was the image of Jones, peeking into their lab and breathing down their necks, that both reaffirmed cold fusion in the eyes of Pons and Fleischmann and prodded them into rushing their nondiscovery before the eyes of the public.

"If the electrolysis technique did not lead to nuclear fusion, why else would Jones be working so diligently to steal it?" Taubes muses, supplying the thinking for Pons and Fleischmann. "And why else would he be insisting that he had to publish it? What could be more self-evident?"

The first amazing thing about Pons and Fleischmann, according to Taubes, is that the cold fusion fiasco was only the capstone of a career marked by bungled research, which, incredibly, did nothing at all to tarnish their reputations. Their method was a blend of "sloppy experimental techniques combined with hubris," Taubes writes. Three years before cold fusion, they published a series of papers ranging "from dead wrong to recklessly interpreted." One of the papers claimed to have developed a process for oxidizing krypton and other noble gases, known to chemists as being so inert as to make it nearly impossible to get them to react to anything.

"That some of these [papers] were wrong, that his scientific claims seemed implausible to begin with, and in fact were downright impossible, was rarely discussed," Taubes writes, referring to Pons. "Chemists who were familiar with these errors refrained from mentioning them to the press even after the cold fusion announcement for the same reasons they had never mentioned them to the funding offices. It is considered in poor taste to point out that the experimental techniques of a competitor leave something to be desired."

Pons seized on the clever sophistry that anyone denying cold fusion was part of the old guard, just another bitter physicist who resented chemists swooping in and eating his lunch. The ploy worked, for a time. Cold fusion was also backed up by certain of the more credulous elements of the press. The *Los Angeles Times* called those who doubted cold fusion "small, petty people without vision or curiosity," and *The Wall Street Journal* practically became *The Cold Fusion Gazette,* declaring that "clearly, scientists have once again discovered something new under the sun." (Cold fusion was Good for Business; it had to be real.)

Cold fusion is a true emperor's new clothes story. A couple of guys stare into a test tube and say, Look, something's there. At once, a hundred other guys build their own test tubes and start staring. Most see nothing, but a few more see something as well. Look, it's right there! Cold fusion.

Most fascinating is the way that Pons (Fleischmann spent most of the affair lurking in the wings; he seemed the more *compos mentis* of the two, at one point admitting that cold fusion could be nothing more than a "horrible chain of misinterpretations and accidents") neatly reproduced the paradigm of perpetual-motion inventors, eager to both show off their devices and mask their fraudulence at the same time. Look at this wonderful device here, sayeth the inventor. But I can't quite show it to you, because you'll steal it. In fact, I need a bit more money to perfect my equipment. Then I'll show it to you. Maybe.

Pons was forever citing "secret agreements with the Defense Department" in refusing to release some germane bit of information, or bending the phenomenon to include whatever contrary results came from other labs, so as to use them to back up his claims for cold fusion.

The enigma at the heart of the story is what Pons and Fleischmann thought they were doing. Neither would talk to Taubes, so their thinking was caught by second parties in muttered phrases and dashed notes. Fraud has generously been ruled out by most analysts, who prefer to take the charitable view that Pons and Fleischmann had merely gone crazy, a temporary insanity induced by the initial miscalculation that led them to believe they had achieved cold fusion —actually, a madness of degrees, which began when the first, tentative negative results were ignored, and soon blossomed into a full-blown denial of reality, which clung to pathetic excuses and rationales as the criticism mounted.

I won't tell you what happened to Pons and Fleischmann— waiting for them to get their due was what got me through Taubes's rather lengthy book, which bogs down toward the end in a thick soup of labs and scientists and tritium. Suffice it to say that I was disappointed. No one was dragged through campus at midnight, a quivering ball of tar and feathers straddling a rail. No bands of undergraduates followed once-respected scientists to class, blowing horns and banging together garbage can lids. (I am joined in this thirst for ridicule by no less than the esteemed journal *Nature*, which regretted the general lack of "unrestrained mockery, even a little unqualified vituperation," in the cold fusion affair.)

SEVEN HUNDRED PAGES into *Remembrance of Things Past*, the Proust character, out for an evening carriage ride with a friend of his father's, spies a beautiful woman walking far ahead. "Jumping from the carriage without a word of apology," Marcel races off in hot pursuit of the vision. After chasing her down two streets, he finally "caught up with her again in a third, and arrived at last, breathless, beneath a street lamp, face to face with old Mme. Verdurin, whom [he] had been carefully avoiding for years."

This has happened to a lot of men (well, to me at least; I didn't take a poll). What makes the Proust passage stand out, however, is that he wonders what explanation there could be for this phenomenon. After all, you don't often see an old crone in the distance, only to find out on closer inspection that she is a beautiful woman.

The answer, Proust says, is that in our hearts we carry an image of beauty, of perfection, that we are always trying to match in reality. "If our imagination is set going by the desire for what we cannot possess, its flight is not limited by a reality perceived in these casual encounters in which the charms of the passing stranger are generally in direct ratio to the swiftness of our passage." Given half the chance, we layer that image over any convenient canvas: the fuzzy framework of a distant woman, or a shrub in the twilight, or whatever.

That image seems to me to lie at the heart of people like Pons and Fleischmann (to be charitable). They're looking for progress, for beauty and glory and perfection, and when they see it, or think they see it, boom, they lock in, throwing caution, reputation and millions of dollars in government funding to the winds.

Actually, I think such yearning dwells in the heart of most people. They will accept lives of blemish, disorder, compromise and cacophony, but in certain areas, or at certain times, they yearn for the impossibility of perfection.

This is what ruins a lot of weddings. People feel that because they've spent thousands of dollars and planned for months, they can therefore expect their weddings to turn out flawlessly.

But weddings never do, and the expectation of perfection turns things upside down. I was at a wedding once where the bride was weeping in the bathroom because the photographer they had hired had sent a substitute at the last minute. At other weddings, I have seen brides go ballistic over some detail of the service, or the tables. You'd have thought the groom didn't show.

The main advice I always give to people getting married is to view their wedding as a party and not a stage play. In a stage play, people have entrances and exits and lines they are supposed to say at certain times, and if someone is half a beat off, things are going wrong. Carried over to a wedding, the stage-play interpretation says that if the fountains don't geyser at the precise moment the bride walks in and the band swings into *Also Sprach Zarathustra* whilst a hundred white doves are released, then the wedding is "ruined."

In the party paradigm, you plan as much as you can and then step back and enjoy what happens. In this light, if the cake turns out to be vanilla and not French vanilla, or if Uncle Fyodor breaks into a *kazatski* during the vows, well, that's what has happened and you shrug and go on. I am proud that even though my wife's bouquet bore only slight resemblance to the one she spent an ungodly period of time planning with a florist, she didn't seem to mind. It was still a nice bouquet, and there was nothing to be done at that point.

My perfection mania is reserved not for events like weddings but for merchandise. I somehow feel that things should be in good condition, at least at the moment they are purchased. Sure, they will soon be chipped and dented and scratched, and become worn like everything else in this generally shabby man-made world. But you buy something with your hard-earned money, you deserve that initial moment of newness.

I bought a bike this year, after having not had a bike for my entire adult life. My perfection jones was made worse by the extra emotional baggage surrounding the concept of a new bicycle—king in the pantheon of traditional toys for boys: the train set, the first baseman's mitt, the bicycle. It was a big deal for me, and I approached the event with a certain solemnity, the good boy getting his deserved bike, the righting of an ancient wrong.

To make matters worse, I selected the bicycle purely on aesthetics. Rejecting complexities such as shiftable gears, and new developments such as mountain bikes, I picked out a one-speed black Schwinn Cruiser with fat whitewall tires and coaster brakes. Purchasing the bike, I took it for a spin around the parking lot and was at my car, with the trunk open, ready to load the bike in, when I noticed something: the little oval medallion at the front of the bike, a piece of metal reading "Schwinn Quality" and attached by two little screws. In tightening down the screws on the "Schwinn Quality" plate, somebody had obviously slipped with the screwdriver and put a deep gouge, half an inch or so, in the glossy black paint. Ironic, right? "Schwinn Quality."

It was night. I stood for a moment, in the lights of the parking lot, looking at that little mark. I tried convincing myself that it didn't matter, that I could live with the scratch. Then I sadly wheeled the bike back inside. They didn't have another in stock, so after I had a lengthy conversation with the manager, the store took the bike back. They would order another, the manager said, but he did not know when it would come in. Surely by summer.

That night I sulked. No bike for me. Fears began to grow that some sort of cosmic malevolence was keeping me from My New Bike. I decided prompt action was required. The next day, I went to a different Schwinn store and bought the same bike, with a properly installed plate. Saved twenty bucks in the process. Now the bike is dinged up and muddy, with chips that I have inexpertly tried to touch up and spots from the rain. But it was fine when it was new.

At least I can comfort myself with the thought that this sort of fixation on initial flawlessness is genetic. My father is the same way —or at least was, until the mellowing of age began to creep in. Twenty-five years ago, he bought a big metal desk. He had just constructed a study for himself, building a wing on the back of the house with his bare hands, and now ordered a black metal desk with a top resembling wood to go in it. The thing was huge. On the big delivery day, the department-store truck pulled up and two burly men wrestled the desk through the door and into the study. It nearly filled one wall of the room. My father sat down at the desk, running his splayed fingers happily over the metallic off-orange-passing-for-wood-grain top. Then he saw it. A dot. A white dot, in the center of the fake wood grain, as big as the head of a pin. He tried to rub it off, but it was a flaw, something in the fake wood-grain top itself. It was right in the center of that massive desktop. A blotter would have covered it completely.

No matter. Back came the department-store truck. Back came the burly men. Away went the white-dot desk, and a few days later a new, dotless desk arrived. And he was so happy, for a time.

I HAVE TIED perfection in with impossibility because generally perfection is impossible. The perfect vacuum, the perfect sphere, absolute zero, perpetual motion, the speed of light—all absolutes that remain a hairsbreadth, a micro-, nano-, pico-hairsbreadth, away from attainment.

The reason I hope for perfect things, rather than perfect moments, is that moments are much harder to achieve. You can find a bike that doesn't have any obvious flaws. But a day? Even an hour? That's more difficult.

I have had a couple of days that I consider perfect days because at the time they struck me so. None were in childhood. My childhood wasn't bad—nobody beat me, nobody had sex with me—it's just that childhood had a hostage quality, a suffocating sense of waiting, of marking off the days on the wall, marching through somebody else's routine, yearning toward some unspecific but eventual release.

Actually, only two perfect days come to mind. One was about ten years ago. I was visiting a friend in Boston, David Seldin, and we decided to drive to Cape Cod, where I had never been. I was amazed by the variety of natural settings—how quickly the landscape moved from seashore to desert, from pines around a secluded lake to the weather-worn clichés of Provincetown. We had dinner at some wharfside place, and I was happy to look out the window at a pelican sitting on a rotting pier, next to a weathered rowboat overturned and set up on sawhorses. The hackneyed scene in a thousand bad water-colors. But this time it was real.

Something about the day, the way I had expected this bland tourist haven and found instead a chain of natural beauty, resonated properly. In looking back on it, influenced by the morality conveyed in beer ads, I at first thought the day's single flaw was that I had been with another guy and not, for instance, Sherilyn Fenn. But if I had been with her, I would have had the added concern of our relation-ship. How was she feeling? Was she having fun? What would happen when we got to Provincetown? With David, I could charge shouting up the sand dunes, snooze sluggishly on the beach, and leave him to take care of himself. Perfect.

The other perfect day was at Eldora, a small ski resort just north of Boulder, Colorado, where my parents now live. I was visiting, and had announced beforehand that, for one day of the visit, I would go skiing. This was difficult, as my parents didn't see me much and hated to lose a day of my company. On the appointed morning, my father came downstairs and observed that it was 14 degrees below zero outside—far too cold for me to ski. I was disappointed. Then my mother bounded downstairs. Fourteen degrees below zero? So what? Go ahead. Dress warm. Have fun. Liberated, I took the bus to Eldora.

It was largely abandoned—who was crazy enough to ski in this cold? Since I hadn't skied in a few years, I signed up for a class. I was the only pupil, and the teacher was one Kirstin Severaid, a cute young woman with short blond hair. Class consisted of us chatting on the ski lift, making a single frosty run down the mountain, going into the lodge to warm up by the fire before making another run. At lunch, I asked what would happen if I signed up for the afternoon class. She said we'd keep skiing, so I did, and we did. At the end of the day, I sat in the lodge waiting for the bus, bruised and achy and tired and utterly happy, drinking coffee mixed with Jack Daniels. The guy playing the guitar was pretty good—he played R.E.M.'s "Don't Go Back to Rockville" and I gave him a couple of bucks. On the way out, I called for the manager. He came over, his face set with concern. "I just want you to know," I began seriously, "that every one of your employees, from the guy who fitted me for my boots, to the ski instructor, to the lunch servers, to the bartender in the lounge, treated me great. I had a perfect day at your place here today."

And so I did.

HELL HAS BEEN described in every detail, Mark Twain once pointed out, but nobody has ever written a good book about a day in heaven. Having set down two perfect days, I can see why—they aren't particularly interesting, certainly not funny.

While heaven itself does not get much literature (except for a few obscure tracts, written by giddy zealots who can't wait to get in), the idea of heaven-on-earth has spawned an entire literature. Countless utopian proposals, from Plato's vigorous autocracy, through centuries of homespun utopias, down to B. F. Skinner's bloodless *Walden Two*, have set out visions of a glorious world of perfect people living together flawlessly under an ideal system.

Far from being ideal, most utopias, viewed from the modern perspective, don't even seem like pleasant places to live, from the lack of privacy in Thomas More's *Utopia* ("every man may freely enter into any house whatsoever") to the distaste for Catholics in John Eliot's *Christian Commonwealth* (no contact is permitted with "that dirty Romish religion") to John Macnie's idea of a perfect world, in which engaged couples should be kept separate for a year to ensure they're really, really serious about getting married.

In general, utopian thought is probably the most addled soup of philosophy ever grouped under a single name. None of the utopias would work, but that hasn't seemed to matter. And there is a certain sameness to fictional utopias, the same banalities, set out in a breathless, de facto manner. We'll let Sylvester Judd's 1845 hymn to a Unitarian heaven-on-earth stand in for them all. In this tidbit, a committee from the state legislature visits the happy village of Mons Christi to study its secrets:

> They say our roads are in fine order, in fact none are better in the State; that the whole town has a striking aspect of neatness and thrift; that during all the time of their visit they saw not one drunken man . . . that the consumption of intoxicating drinks has diminished from six or eight thousand gallons annually to a few scores; that the amount paid for schools has risen from three or four hundred dollars to two thousand; that all taxes . . . have been promptly paid; that our poor have lessened three quarters . . .

And on and on and on. Never is any consideration given to the fact that a few unreformed sharpies would make off with the silver, or ravish the preacher's daughter while she is drawing at the well. In fact, the sense of unexamination that pervades utopian writing would lead one to fear that our ancestors were somehow retarded, were they not so roundly mocked in their own time by another thriving sub-genre, utopian satire.

Samuel Butler, to name just one author of utopian satire, found wild success with *Erewhon*, a biting critique of English society in the mid-1800s, written in the same yammering style of serious utopian fiction. A snippet, perhaps as apt today as it was then:

> . . . in that country if a man falls into ill health, or catches any disorder, or fails bodily in any way before he is seventy years old, he is tried before a jury of his countrymen, and if convicted is held up to public scorn and sentenced more or less severely as the case may be. There are subdivisions of illnesses into crimes and misdemeanours as with offences amongst ourselves—a man being punished very heavily for serious illness, while failure of eyes or hearing in one over sixty-five who has had good health hitherto is dealt with by fine only . . .

The sad part about utopianism is that certain people, caught in the spell of idealistic balderdash, have tried to establish actual perfect societies in the harsh setting of unvarnished reality, particularly in this country, which struck the wheezing idealogues in Europe as prime, unfurrowed ground in which to experiment.

The communities had names like Joyful, Freeland, Communia, Brotherhood, Celesta, Modern Times and Economy. There were two Harmonies, a New Harmony and a Harmonia. A community in Ohio called itself, with more optimism than originality, Utopia. Each had its own peculiarities: the Ephratans would use no metal; the Shakers would have no sex.

None of them worked. The Shakers died out for obvious reasons. The longest-lasting utopian experiment held out for a dozen or so years until internal squabbles and a range of mundane concerns destroyed the ideal dream. They all failed exactly for the same reason perpetual motion failed: friction. Perpetual motion assumed away the friction in every machine; utopianism ignored the petty selfishnesses in people, the squabbles, the despair. Utopias looked so good on paper, but in the real world, a tiny tiff was enough to bring an ideal system down.

Perfection, so attractive in the abstract, when sought in reality just places her hands on her slim hips and laughs elusively.

SIX

The Calamity of Long Life

—

Trouble in the Last Act

JAMES O'NEILL WAS a good actor, possibly a great actor. And successful too. His performance in the melodrama *The Count of Monte Cristo* was wildly popular. So much so that he bought the rights to the play and performed it over a thousand times, all across the country, for thirty years. It made him rich. It ruined him.

The ruin was self-assigned. O'Neill had fancied himself a great Shakespearian actor, on par with Henry Irving, with Edwin Booth. In old age, he expected to be applauded in the greatest roles. Instead he found himself endlessly replaying a hackneyed character in the backwaters of America, bound to the tar baby of the Count of Monte Cristo, that tear-jerking piece of dreck of which the public could not get enough. No one wanted to see him in anything else.

At the climax of the play, O'Neill's character, framed against a raging canvas sea, raises his arms toward the heavens and cries, in a strangled mixture of triumph and defeat; "The world . . . is . . . MINE!"

The role made a great impression on his son, who sometimes traveled with his father on the road. "I can still see [him] dripping with salt and sawdust, climbing a stool behind the swinging profile of dashing waves," recalled Eugene O'Neill. "The calcium lights in the gallery played on his long beard and tattered clothes, as with arms outstretched he declared that the world was his. This was a signal for the house to burst into a deafening applause."

After James O'Neill died—on his deathbed dismissing his life as "froth" and "rotten"—the image of the Count of Monte Cristo lingered on for his son, and he included it in his masterpiece, *A Long Day's Journey into Night*. There the father character, closely based on James O'Neill, denounces the vehicle that had made him a household name:

> That God-damned play I bought for a song and made such a great success in, it ruined me with its promise of an easy fortune . . . and by the time I woke up to the fact I'd become a slave to the damned thing and did try other plays, it was too late. I'd lost the great talent I once had through years of easy repetition.

THE PERIL OF easy success is an abstract, if not meaningless, concept to most people, whose failures are instead negations, voids, things that *didn't* happen.

As teenagers, my sister and I used to mock our ambitions to be a doctor and a novelist, respectively, by joking that she would end up titrating urine in the free clinic and I would end up writing the prose for the back of sugar packets. What we meant was that we would become normal people, a fate that we dreaded in the same way our parents dreaded being poor. We could joke about being ordinary because, in our hearts, it seemed so improbable.

We sincerely expected to be extraordinary, maybe even stars, at the very least to accomplish great things. It was an article of faith with me. I could hardly go into the school bathroom and take a pee without picturing Jacob Bronowski—who at the time was always popping up on PBS in some swamp, wearing hip boots and talking about the Battle of Agincourt—standing by the urinals in the boy's john at Roehm Junior High and intoning at the camera, "It was *here* that the young genius Steinberg first formed those revolutionary concepts which were later to stun a grateful world . . ."

The fact is that we did not accomplish great things. My sister, God bless her, actually did titrate urine—not in a free clinic, but as a technician in a hospital lab. She had tried to become a doctor, but was chewed up and spit out of medical school, ending up as a pathologist, analyzing bodily substances. If there was a more terrible fate for someone who once wrote her poetry in green India ink so as to better approach the Byronic romantic ideal, I can't imagine it.

For my part, I never wrote the prose for the back of sugar packets only because I never got lucky with a sugar packet company —during the years when I was writing anything that paid money, from a steel company's in-house newsletter to a handbook for girls' club leaders to the copy for a local car dealership's late-night TV ads, a lucrative sugar packet gig would have been most welcome.

Our younger brother, Sam, opted out of the quest for magnificence at a very early age. His first articulate phrase was "Plain Sam!" —a rebuke to all our cooings of "Good Sam!" and "Wonderful Sam!" He kept that attitude into adulthood, and thus could guiltlessly be a normal person, while my sister and I had to assume the pose of royalty in exile.

For a long while, our normality struck me as tragic, the withering of wondrous flowers that should have been allowed to bloom. But that was youthful ego. Now I see we were assuming our rightful spot in the great slurry of ordinary people, most of whom seem to want—at least at some point—to do some fabulous thing with their lives, to be glittering and special, only to eventually abandon their dreams and go on to mundane existences. We put our guitars in the attic, dump our novels in a drawer, store the paintings in the basement, and become actuaries. The ambition, if it remains, lingers on like a hidden tumor, usually benign, perhaps to flare up and cause trouble later in life.

To suggest that failure might still have come even if the novel had been published or the record issued, even if the brass ring had been grasped, is not something pretty to consider. It sounds like sour grapes: "Yeah, well, if I *had* finished architecture school, I would have probably designed one fantastic building when I was twenty-five and then spent the rest of my life bitterly trying to recapture that achievement."

Nobody says that, but it happens. A lot. There is mirror failure, waiting on the other side of success. That only a relative handful face this particular gorgon does not make it any less devastating. In fact, because it comes as such a surprise, the failure that bobs along in the wake of success can be worse than no success at all.

Or, to grit our teeth and quote Nietzsche: "There are two tragedies in a man's life. The first is to have failed to have reached your goal; the second is to have reached it."

The cruel reality is that no matter what you achieve, no matter how big a splash is created by the heartstopping magnitude of the sensation, unless you kill yourself shortly thereafter (and with everything going so well, who would?), the moment will pass, time will hurry onward, and you will have to cope with a new standard, based not on the benchmark of regular life, from which most people measure, but on the superheated fluke of your previous accomplishment.

Thus Michael Jackson, having already performed successfully, if with growing creepiness, in the public eye for twenty-five years, can turn out *Thriller* and sell 45 million copies, by far the most popular recording of all time, only to have a gang of piecework critics immediately sit back, make cathedrals with their fingertips, and speculate on whether his next album can top it.

It couldn't, of course, and the fact that *Bad* sold 20 million copies didn't prevent it from being labeled a disappointing flop. It was still among the all-time best-sellers. But it wasn't *Thriller* now, was it?

This was no subconscious act; people said it directly. "While many artists are overjoyed to sell one million, to Jackson, *Bad* and *Dangerous* failed by not approaching his previous number," a critic wrote in *Rolling Stone*.

This heightening of expectation after success happens constantly, even though failure to match exceptional past performance is almost a universal. There is even a mathematical principle—known as regression to the mean—that explains why it is so rare for one unprecedented achievement to be piled atop another in an upward staircase of ever-expanding glory.

Stated simply, regression to the mean says that if there is an average level of performance—say, most big-league batters hit .247, or most musical recordings sell diddly-squat—then a person who exceeds the average—by batting .406 one year, or by selling 45 million albums—will tend to perform closer to the norm the next time out, so as to help preserve the average.

This isn't a law—*Bad* could theoretically have sold 60 million copies. Rather, regression to the mean is a probability. A statistician, knowing nothing of the merits of *Bad* (assuming it has merits) and asked to predict the recording's sales, would have guessed it would sell somewhere between 45 million and diddly-squat, or about 20 million, which is exactly what it sold.

Despite the laws of probability reinforcing what we already

know from our experience to be true (whose life is a stepwise and unbroken progression of bigger and bigger successes?), for some reason—perhaps resentment, or a faulty understanding of the nature of life and creativity—there is a general assumption that one achievement will be followed by another, greater achievement, then another and another until . . . I don't know, you pop, I guess.

When Thomas Pynchon's *Gravity's Rainbow* was published in 1973, critics instantly recognized the book as a dazzling masterpiece —perhaps *the* masterpiece of the second half of the twentieth century. Nobody held their breath for Pynchon's next book—we recognize that masterpieces take time—but when a new Pynchon novel finally arrived, seventeen years later, there was a collective sigh of disappointment. *Vineland* was merely a good book, not the arrival of the millennium expected from the author of *Gravity's Rainbow*. Some clairvoyants suggested that *Vineland*, in its ordinariness, couldn't possibly be what Pynchon had been working on all those years, but must be some sort of by-product, a creative fart, an accident tossed out to occupy the public while Pynchon was busy crafting Dazzling Masterpiece Number Two. "Pynchon probably has interrupted work on a much longer novel-in-progress to write *Vineland*," guessed James McManus in the *Chicago Tribune*. I imagined the reclusive Pynchon, at his estate in Mexico (or on the subway in Manhattan or—my God!—*right over there!!!*), reading the reviews and thinking, Shit. I better come up with something.

There is a danger, when analyzing famous people, of mistaking public image for private fact. Michael Jackson and Thomas Pynchon might not care how critics view their work. It isn't as if you could call them up and ask. Some people don't mind a little public scorn, or even a lot of public scorn, so long as the checks still clear. Robert Goulet can ride *Camelot* into the vale of years, squeezing the old lemon in a way that would make James O'Neill blush, without any apparent remorse. It's a good gig, and he knows that a lot of people would jump at the chance. If you think we're not going to see William Shatner playing Capt. James T. Kirk in 2010, on the bridge of the *Enterprise* in a wheelchair, his knees covered by a plaid lap rug, then you're in for a surprise.

But the relentless weight of public opinion has a definite corrosive effect. Orson Welles's career was a dismal denouement only because the world viewed it from the lofty perspective of *Citizen Kane*, the classic movie he made at age twenty-five, which haunted him until his death at age seventy. Not only did the controversial movie make it more difficult for Welles to find backing for new movies, but it threw a pallor over future projects not up to the level of *Citizen Kane*—that is to say, everything he did for the rest of his life. "I am so tired of hearing only about *Citizen Kane*, Welles once wearily responded to a request that he participate in a scholarly analysis of the movie. "I have, you know, done other things in my lifetime."

Writers have a notoriously hard time following up on greatness, unnerved by the gaze of the world on their backs. Ralph Ellison never wrote another novel after *Invisible Man*. J. D. Salinger sentenced himself to internal exile after *Raise High the Roof-Beam Carpenters*. He has claimed to have never stopped writing, and some doe-eyed optimists believe him, holding out hope that all these great books are going to be found in a box upon his death. Fat chance. My bet is that they'll find stacks of typing paper with "My name is J. D. Salinger" typed hundreds of thousands of times, or maybe a pile of gray ash with the note, written in Salinger's hand: "This novel was better than *The Catcher in the Rye*, but I burned it up. Nyah-nyah-nyah." He seems to be that sort of guy.

My FIRST WRITING job almost ended my career as a writer. The summer after my sophomore year in college, I got a job working on the in-house newsletter for NASA's Lewis Research Center in Cleveland. I was proud because, though my father worked there, I didn't tell him I was going for the job until after I was hired.

The "Lewis News" came out every two weeks and consisted of a few small pages. I had a boss and a couple other guys helping me produce the newsletter. It was the easiest job in the world. They even let me draw a regular cartoon, satirizing life in state-sponsored science. My favorite featured a caricature of me sitting at the typewriter, my boss waving a piece of paper in my face. "In public relations, young man, we do our best to maintain a positive attitude," the caption reads. "Try saying that the rocket is a bright spot on the horizon, not that 'it blew up on the launch pad.'" They printed that.

Most of my day consisted of wandering around the facility, which was crammed with weird and interesting places—acoustically dead rooms with the walls, ceiling and floors made up of muffling cones of foam (you walked on a metal mesh suspended above the gray pointy rows); pressurized rooms where you had to go through airlocks to gain entrance; wind tunnels; drop towers; nuclear materials stations. The lab had a space museum, which was interesting to walk through. I got quite good at the lunar module simulator. And engineers were happy to stop what they were doing and talk to me. Guys who had spent decades in the same windowless cell studying some obscure aspect of fluid mechanics lit up in quivering delight at the sight of a human face, never mind one that expressed curiosity about their work.

The dreamy somnambulism of a life in the federal government cannot be overstated. At lunchtime, the PR staff would drag their metal desk chairs outside and, propping their feet on a rail, lean back, close their eyes and turn their faces toward the sun. Indeed, our efforts at times seemed to border on the vegetative, more like tropism than human activity. I once took off for lunch at 10:30 A.M., went swimming at Baldwin-Wallace College, caught a steak at the Brown Derby, then swung by home to take a nap and check the mail. I didn't get back until 2:30 P.M. Sometimes I signed out a government car and cruised the laboratory reservation; sometimes I just shrugged my shoulders and went home, or met my girlfriend, who lived nearby. There was something wonderful about enjoying amorous relations *and* being paid a hefty sum by the federal government at the same time.

Eventually, I got into trouble. My boss took me aside and gave me a talk. I was getting too much done. Rushing things. Making the others look bad. Ease up, he urged. Find a gentler pace. I promised I would try.

At the end of that golden summer, they offered me a full-time job—to this day, the only job I've ever been offered out of the blue and, the way I'm going, the only job I'm ever going to be offered out of the blue. I could finish my schooling at Cleveland State—the government would pay, of course. The job paid big money—a GS-12, I think. It was tempting. The lab was three miles from our home, and I could ride the entire distance on my bike through the verdant arch of the Metropark. It would be, I told myself, the sinecure I needed to write books.

But I couldn't do it. I wanted to, but something was stopping me. I was twenty years old. Taking the job seemed like surrender, easing myself into this bath of warm honey without ever challenging the world. Sure I would have time to write, but what would be my subject matter?

TORPOR!
A Tale of Lethargy in the Federal Government
by
N. Ira Steinberg

Slowly, my hand crept out to grasp the official requisition form.
. . . A pencil sharpener! I thought, wild with desperation. If my
office only had a pencil sharpener, then I wouldn't have to waste
precious energy always stepping next door to sharpen my pencils.
I could sharpen them right here—I'd be free, my own man!

My big fear, I believe, was that NASA was the Ohio equivalent
of Shangri-La in *Lost Horizon.* I would happily join this Eden, then, in
a flash, centuries would go by in the real world and I would be
trapped in Paradise. I would look up and my life would be over and
they would be handing me a watch.

"I can't do it," I told my dad, "I'm too young to retire." He
understood.

"Save yourself," he told me, clutching my lapel, his thin voice
cracking. "It's over for me. But you, you still have time . . ." (No,
actually, he didn't say that. Sorry, Dad. Just joking.)

So I moved on. The next summer I didn't go back to NASA—I
could have, but I took a job at Meldrum and Fewsmith, a big
Cleveland advertising agency. The internship paid a fraction of the
government paycheck, but I wanted to see if I liked advertising. I
didn't. The long boozy lunches with my office confreres were fine,
but I hated the part of the day that went before and after lunch. I
quit before the end of summer.

I've often thought of what would have happened had I stayed at
NASA. Berea, Ohio, is a lovely place to live. My parents would never
have gone to Colorado, so the family homestead would have been

nearby. I would have probably married my high school sweetheart, Sue, and been in some ways very happy. On bad days in Chicago, struggling through the *Sturm und Drang* of urban life, I imagine some parallel me, still back in Berea, sipping Genesee Cream Ale with Jim Sayler on a perfect summer afternoon, tending bratwursts on the Weber while Laura and Sue watch the kids and the wind whispers, quiet and zephyr-warm, through the weeping willows and aged oaks of the beloved little town.

PEOPLE CHANGE, sometimes for the better, usually for the worse. Either way, our past lives dog us, a pack of baying hounds we may lose sight of but which are never really that far behind.

William James Sidis is almost entirely forgotten today, which is ironic, since that was all he ever wanted to be when he was alive. Born in 1898, Sidis was the son of an eminent psychotherapist, Boris Sidis, who named his son after his friend and colleague, the famous psychologist William James.

Boris Sidis had a lot of theories about early cognition and learning, and he used his young son as a laboratory for testing out those theories, with dazzling results. Sidis the younger could read at two, write in French and English at three, and by five was writing compositions on anatomy and complex mathematical questions.

All of this was lapped up by the newspapers, which called Sidis "the wonder boy." The publicity was stoked by his proud father, who published a self-congratulatory book about his son—*Philistine and Genius*. The book, a "bitter and intemperate, often in grotesque, denunciation of everybody and everything connected with education in the United States at the present time," according to one reviewer, held the training of his son up as a model for the world to follow—a bit prematurely.

"It is not prudent to boast of youthful prodigies while they are still young," the *New York Times* sagely noted.

In the fall of 1909 William James Sidis, at age eleven, was admitted to Harvard University. His smiling, jug-eared countenance was splayed across the nation's newspapers. Readers of the *Times* debated whether Sidis was a miracle, a fraud, the reincarnation of Pythagoras, or perhaps a receptor for otherworldy wisdom. "Possibly the great minds of the past may be sending wireless vibrations to this sphere, in hopes that some minds here may be so attuned as to catch their message," speculated James H. Slipper, of Yonkers.

In January 1910, Sidis delivered a lecture on "Four-Dimensional Bodies" to about a hundred Harvard professors, advanced students and newspapermen, provoking another storm of attention. (The *Times,* in honor of the talk, dropped his age to ten.) Most of what he was saying flew over the heads of the audience, which nevertheless was spellbound by this little boy in black velvet knickers. They proclaimed him as the next great thing in mathematics.

And that was it. Almost immediately after the lecture Sidis had a breakdown and was rushed to his father's sanitarium, where he was sequestered for several weeks before returning to Harvard to quietly finish his education.

Classmates found him a changed prodigy. Where once he had confidently leapt into impromptu conversations, he was now shy, withdrawn. There were no more lectures. He next appeared in the public eye at the Harvard graduation of 1914, where, cornered by newspapermen, he made headlines across the country by proclaiming that he wanted to lead "the perfect life" of solitude, had no appreciation for feminine charms, and had vowed never to marry.

The press leapt to the defense of American womanhood, the beginning of what would be a cruel quarter-century public pillorying of Sidis, as if in retribution for the earlier praise. The *Chicago Journal* labeled the sixteen-year-old "an intolerable prig" and invited "some charming widow of about 28, some handsome, accomplished woman whose mourning has kept her out of the world just long enough to make her hungry to test her powers of conquest" to provide Sidis with some "incitements to propose" in the hopes of rendering him "almost fit for human society." The *Times* applauded the plan: "The profoundest psychotherapist could not prescribe a more promising regimen for anybody suffering as this wonder youth is said to be."

Instead of being granted solitude, Sidis was hounded by the papers, which tracked him to whatever temporary clerkship he managed to find for himself and exposed him—the wonder boy, the mathematical wizard—working at a mundane job! Any hints of sympathy were just so much preliminary throat-clearing before the knives were brought out and the joyous vivisection begun.

A 1924 *Times* editorial titled "Precocity Doesn't Wear Well" displayed Sidis, then twenty-six, as a comfort to "parents whose boys show no indications of being or becoming intellectual giants." Poohpoohing his salary ($23 a week) and his appearance ("dresses with carelessness"), the paper then tried to shrug off its assault with a show of evenhandedness. "While young Sidis is no more to be criticized adversely than anybody else for not wanting what he doesn't want," it opined, after doing just that, "it is hard not to regret that his marvels should have been confined to adolescence."

The worst was yet to come. In 1937, James Thurber, the brilliant humorist who was fascinated with the poignance of has-beens, was in the midst of writing a series for *The New Yorker* called "Where Are They Now?" He had already disinterred such one-trick ponies and flashes-in-the-pan as Gertrude Ederle, the first woman to swim the English Channel, and Virginia O'Hanlon, whose letter evoked the famous "Yes, Virginia, there is a Santa Claus" editorial from the *New York Sun*.

Beginning with Sidis's high point, the fabled Harvard lecture, Thurber, writing under the pseudonym Jared L. Manley, carefully tracked Sidis's early training, his moment of fame, his subsequent breakdown and long trek in obscurity, including an arrest for participating in the 1919 May Day riots, leading a parade of Communists and waving a red flag.

Thurber found that Sidis had utterly abandoned scholarship. His only passion, it seemed, was collecting streetcar transfers, which Thurber poignantly tied to Sidis's streetcar journeys taken back and forth to Cambridge as a young prodigy (his mother had insisted on accompanying him, seeing him off each morning at Harvard Gate). A self-published text written by Sidis, *Notes on the Collection of Transfers*, was liberally quoted from, with such characteristic passages as: "The peculiarities of the typical Stedman transfer are the tabular time limit occupying the entire right-hand end of the transfer (see Diagram in Section 47) and the row-and-column combination of receiving route (or other receiving conditions) with the half-day that we have already discussed in detail."

Sidis, at thirty-nine, was described as a "large, heavy man, with a prominent jaw, a thickish neck, and a reddish mustache" who told Thurber's researcher that he moved from one clerking job to another, quitting as soon as his coworkers found out who he was, or rather, who he had been. "All I want to do is run an adding machine," he said, "but they won't let me alone."

Thurber's story was both deadpan and ruthless, the damage conveyed quietly by the naked facts themselves, and differed only in its comprehensiveness from several other stories that had appeared over the years. But this time Sidis sued, claiming that *The New Yorker* had violated his right to privacy.

It became a landmark case, with Sidis representing himself and writing his own briefs. Eventually the case reached the Supreme

Court, which in 1940 declined to reverse a lower court decision in the magazine's favor. One of the judges described Sidis as an "insignificant clerk," an epithet that afterward stuck to Sidis like a title of royalty.

Sidis died in 1944, in a Boston rooming house. The *New York Times* allowed itself one last editorial sniff in the direction of his destiny. "Why wasn't it fulfilled?" the newspaper mused. "We can only conjecture. Perhaps his brain was tired and his interest dulled by long excessive stress on his intellectuals."

In struggling to contain its contempt, the *Times* missed the really interesting question: Why was anyone surprised at Sidis's early peak and long decline? Given the fact that his infancy was a lab experiment and his childhood a publicity circus, shouldn't his dismal adult life have been viewed as almost inevitable and perhaps evoked real sympathy from somebody?

After all, the root of Sidis's downfall was no fault of his own. Rather, his father's strutting pride set a trap for him to later become ensnared in. The way Sidis's initial success was used to lash the American educational system, it is not surprising that the browbeaten should have risen up at the first sign of the hero's faltering. And the general consensus is that it was Boris Sidis's harsh and inhuman training that left his son emotionally battered, not the boy's precocious knowledge.

John Radford, in his book on prodigies and early achievers, contrasts Sidis to prodigy Norbert Wiener, who attended Harvard at fourteen as a classmate of Sidis's, but went on to a brilliant career as the father of cybernetics. Wiener's father, Radford points out, stressed the boy's ordinariness, not his exceptional nature, and shielded him from publicity—both stark contrasts to Boris Sidis. Norbert Wiener had his troubles, too, but was helped by a supportive wife. Writes Radford:

Sidis never succeeded in forming a comparable stable relationship. This in turn probably reflects the inability of either of his parents to supply the emotional security a child, particularly such an odd and isolated one, must have needed. A combination of emotional starvation and parental exploitation exacerbated by continual hostile publicity, and not his original talents or even his education as such, produced the unhappy life of William James Sidis.

Perhaps Sidis's greatest legacy was as a cautionary tale for guardians of other bright children. When a group of brainy young panelists was featured on the radio show "The Quiz Kids," around the time of Sidis's death, the producers of the program made sure that publicity shots were printed showing the "Quiz Kid" boys doing typical "boy things"—painting a picket fence à la Huck Finn and washing a dog. The "Quiz Kids" girls were posed, one baking a cake, another scrubbing a floor "like girls her age are supposed to do." No geniuses here, just basic American children who happen to be very smart.

YOU DON'T NEED a critical world to make you regret unfulfilled promise. You can do that yourself. Something about the concept of frittered talent, of wasted precocity, whether it be *Citizen Kane* or the top prize in a high school writing contest, has a special ability to burn under a person's skin.

Expectations tend to gradually inflate over the years without any interference from the outside world. I remember the first time I had an article published in the *Chicago Sun-Times*. It was in the "Education Guide," a marginal section the paper published five times a year. The fact that I was able to get an article into it was a direct function of the section's insignificance. Nevertheless, I was in the big time, and I marked the occasion by dressing up and going to the Ritz Carlton garden bar to celebrate. Edie wore her hair up, the first time I had ever seen her that way. Drink in hand, I babbled the details of my success to the waitress. The world was mine.

Subsequent articles I insisted on dropping off at the newspaper, even though I could have mailed them. I wanted to walk through the enchanting commotion, greedily surveying the dizzying scene of ringing telephones, people typing at computers, reporters deep in thought, editors staring at glowing screens, intense conferences over important matters—a big-city paper. What a life. If only I could get myself on the paper. To work downtown, to belong; how exciting that would be!

Now the camera shot dissolves and I, ten years older and thirty pounds heavier, am slumped at a desk in the selfsame newsroom. Some ephemeral flap is burning in my craw. The bastards changed the lead. They sent Andy Herrmann on a wine-tasting cruise down the Seine. Some editor made a quip. The coffee's bad. I slowly raise my gaze and sweep around a room nearly identical to the one that inspired me a decade earlier and think, What am I doing in this dump? I could have been a contender, I could have had class. What series of missteps did I take to end up in this godforsaken backwater of talentless hacks and butt-nuzzling toadies? I've got to get out of here.

Fortunately, that feeling never lasts long. The aforementioned James Thurber probably summed up the problem best: "Even the most pleasurable of imaginable occupations, that of batting baseballs through the windows of the RCA Building, would pall a little as the days ran on." I was reminded of this during the 1993 American League playoffs, when the White Sox were battling the Blue Jays for the pennant and my assignment was to go to the games at Comiskey Park each evening and write something colorful. This took at least several minutes. My work done, I found myself with my face in a cup of beer, moaning to Rich Roeper, our star columnist, about how I had to go to these *baseball games* which ran on for *hours* and how terrible it all was.

HISTORY TENDS TO obscure the true arc of people's lives. We forget that even the most accomplished of famous figures maroon their flashes of brilliance in wide seas of mediocrity, seas that are then promptly ignored. Isaac Newton made three earth-shattering contributions to science—discovery of the universal law of gravitation, the spectral quality of sunlight, and the calculus—by the time he was twenty-six years old. We all know this.

But Newton lived to be eighty-five.

Less known is that he spent the last decades of his life running the Royal Mint, sniping with Leibnitz over who deserved credit for inventing the calculus (they both did, it seems, independently—shades of Bell and Gray), and furiously studying alchemy, a curious slop of beliefs revolving around the notion that the ancients knew the secrets of how everything works, including how to transmute metals and defy natural laws, but somewhere along the way everybody forgot.

Alchemy was no hobby for Newton—it was his life's true passion. Had Newton come up with a fourth major scientific contribution, it would have been "the vegetation of metals" or perhaps discovery of the Philosopher's Stone. He certainly tried hard enough.

Newton cannot be faulted for his alchemy. At the time, with the laws of science still dimly understood, the idea of turning lead into gold was no more incredible than, say, the thought of curing smallpox or flying to the moon. But what is incredible is the quick way in which Newton's biographers either ignored or minimized his interest in alchemy, a subject about which he wrote over a million words. The first few centuries of Newton scholarship studiously avoided the subject, a reluctance continuing to this day. The biographical essay on Newton in a recent edition of the Encyclopaedia Britannica never mentions the word "alchemy." While Newton's scientific papers were enshrined at Cambridge, his alchemical writings were deemed without "scientific merit" and allowed to drift into private hands, ending up sold at Sotheby's in 1936. (A horrified John Maynard Keynes, scandalized that his nation could let the heritage of one of her greatest sons scatter to the winds, tracked down roughly half the collection, buying up the manuscripts and eventually depositing them at the library at King's College.)

Charles Darwin, another godhead in the pantheon of science, took a detour late in his life analogous to Newton's alchemy. Coming as it did after *Origin of Species* and *The Descent of Man*, this swansong effort was quickly lost in the glare of Darwin's explosive evolutionary theories. You won't find it in bookstores. But if you poke around in a good library, you might just stumble upon a copy of Darwin's 1872 opus, *The Expression of the Emotions in Man and Animals*, a convoluted and in many ways incorrect attempt to show that human facial expressions evolved from muscular movements that once served specific organic purposes in animals. In other words, school audiences watching a play hiss at the entrance of the villain because baboons bare their teeth and exhale loudly to frighten off competitors.

This is not patently stupid. Fetuses have vestigial gills and tails, so why shouldn't laughter be connected to the screeching of tree monkeys? While not implausible, the theory isn't exactly true either, and Darwin, trying to prove his case from his observations of his own children and of animals at the London Zoo, plus the findings of scattered correspondents, ends up cobbling together a tortured and unintentionally amusing study in Victorian egocentrism and science-by-anecdote.

"Pouting does not seem very common with European children," Darwin concludes, citing "inquiries which I have made in several large families." Rather, he finds pouting "common and strongly marked with most savage races." He generally assigns negative expressions to foreigners, while finding the English a serene, pleasant-faced lot, despite their supposedly sharing a common ancestry.

Tossed in are a few true howlers, such as the idea that you can tell the insane by the "dryness and harshness" of their hair. "Dr. Browne attributes the persistently rough conditions of the hair in many insane patients, in part to their minds being always somewhat disturbed," Darwin writes, before launching into pseudoscientific babble comparing the hair of the insane to fear responses in lower animals. (True, we are smirking with the benefit of a century and a quarter of hindsight. But it doesn't take a modern sensibility to suspect that the rough hair of lunatics might somehow be due to the less than ideal tonsorial conditions found in British asylums.)

Darwin also argues that such complex behaviors as kneeling down to pray with one's face turned skyward is somehow a physiological phenomenon. "Devotion is chiefly expressed by the face being directed towards the heavens, with the eyeballs upturned," he writes. "Sir C. Bell . . . believes that 'when we are wrapt in devotional feelings and outward impressions are unheeded, the eyes are raised by an action neither taught nor acquired.' "

Other mannerisms, which Darwin describes as somehow being innate to humans, are revealed by the passing of time to be the tics of a particular age. "Under the feeling of contempt or disgust, there is a tendency from intelligible causes, to blow out of the mouth or nostrils, and this produces sounds like *pooh* or *pish*," writes Darwin. Evidently, evolution has been on the fast track in the past century and a quarter, and the physics of human facial muscles and disgust now produce sounds that would indeed surprise Mr. Darwin, and not just because they in no way resemble *pooh* or *pish.*

The Expression of the Emotions, made up largely of material Darwin had cut from *The Descent of Man* (a recent biography referred to the book as "the amputated head of *The Descent* that had assumed a life of its own"), was initially snapped up by a charmed public, but the theory was quickly rejected by the educated world and fell into oblivion. It is amusing to see how Darwin biographers hem and haw over the scientific merit of the volume, one calling the "long neglected" book "a classic first contribution to the subject."

While Darwin erred in his interpretation of the emotions, at least he was within the framework of the far-ranging scientific curiosity that had established his fame in the first place. Late failure commonly results when, having firmly established a reputation in one area, people decide they are now competent to leap into another, entirely unconnected area in which they have no knowledge or expertise.

Henry Ford, having made a lot of money building and selling cars, concluded in 1915 that his creation of the Model T endowed him with unique gifts to bring an abrupt end to World War I, which at that time was transforming in the American viewpoint from a colorful foreign spectacle into a stark and mind-boggling horror.

Ford was not alone. Many in the United States looked upon the accelerating carnage with a strange mixture of innocence and bluster —developing the notion that we both could and had to "do something" to stop the war.

The antiwar movement cannily approached Ford, who, with his combination of equally unlimited pocketbook and ego, took the abstract antiwar cry and tried to make it specific, chartering a ship and filling it with peace activists, though none of them his prominent pals who gave lip service to the effort. Talk was one thing, braving the U-boat–plagued icy waters of the North Atlantic another. Jane Addams waved from the dock. Thomas Edison turned down his old friend, though Ford begged him to come along and—it is reported—offered him a million dollars to make the journey.

The idea, touching in its naivete, was for the activists to serve as intermediaries between the warring nations, get them to open up, talk about their feelings, and put an end to this war business.

The reaction to what became known as the Peace Ship ranged from admiration to ridicule to combinations of the two. "Great War Ends Christmas Day; Ford to Stop It" read a *New York Tribune* headline on November 25, 1915. The activists and newsmen aboard the ship, used to scrounging around for crumbs, were positively mesmerized by the realization they were traveling on Ford's tab—one newsman's account of the odyssey contains chapters with titles such as "Running Wild on Ford's Dough" and "The Sneer Heard Round the World."

"Such extravagance gets into one's blood," said a participant. "One wants to rush to the rail and empty one's pockets in the sea and shout, 'What do we care for expense!' "

If this disturbed Ford, he did not show it. Instead he remained isolated in his suite of cabins during most of the voyage, poking his head out occasionally to speak to a favored member of the press. "I've got the facts," said Ford, whose "facts" referred to "International Jews," whom he felt to be the motivating force behind the war (all wars, as a matter of fact). In his railing against international capitalists, Ford sounded more like Eugene Debs than a Detroit tycoon. But then Ford spent his life deluded that he was some sort of displaced farmboy philosopher, rolling a hay stalk around in his mouth and observing the wickedness of the world.

Needless to say, Ford did not end the war. In fact, he bailed out of the voyage almost as soon as it hit Europe, leaving his passengers to flit around the continent, attending dinners and running up the tab for a few weeks before Ford's Dearborn accountants snapped shut the purse, bringing everybody home. Ford eventually realized why his peace mission failed: He wasn't Jewish. Jews, he told reporters in 1921 on the sixth anniversary of the ship's sailing, "controlled the world through control of gold and that the Jew, and no one but the Jew, could stop the war."

Ford's confident yet nonspecific pronouncements about how to end the war are reminiscent of a more recent tycoon, leaping Booth-like onto the political stage with a shout of "Death to Tyrants"— Ross Perot. Like Ford, Perot was instantly assumed to have the capability of tackling sticky national issues based on his proven ability to make a fortune. Like Ford, Perot got attention by promising to spend every penny of his bankroll, while actually hardly spending any money at all, relative to his huge wad. Like Ford, Perot got credit just for making the attempt.

Perot's quixotic quest for the presidency in 1992 is a classic example of the way failure can be a matter of perspective. If viewed simply as a bid for the White House, Perot's candidacy was a dismal comedy of errors—a three-steps-forward, two-steps-back, barn-dance kind of approach. But if seen as a transmutation of Perot from a shadowy Texas crank into a crank gleaming in the transfixed spotlight of national attention, then the effort was an unparalleled success.

There are two essential truths illustrated by the Peace Ship affair and by Perot's presidential bid. First, the failures of the very wealthy are usually mitigated, provided the wealth is left intact. Ford apologists without exception sloughed off the matter by pointing out that the half-million dollars spent on the Peace Ship enterprise was but a crumb by Ford standards (Ford spent ten times as much underwriting a rabidly anti-Semitic hate sheet, the *Dearborn Independent*). The drop-in-the-bucket defense was parroted by Perot operatives three quarters of a century later.

Second, the nobility of an effort also softens the sting of failure. Despite the empty pomp of Ford's words and the futility of his actions, he did get credit just for trying. "Even if he came to Berlin dressed like a clown in green tights, carrying peace placards and running up and down Wilhelmstrasse shouting 'Peace,' I would say he deserved praise," said J. W. Gerard, the U.S. Ambassador to Germany.

The clown-in-green-tights image might be the only derogatory metaphor not yet applied to Perot, whose menacing national presence poses something of a conundrum: Which is better, to sit simmering on the sidelines, convinced that you can run the country, or to leap into the fray and demonstrate that you cannot?

THERE IS NO question that a couple of billion dollars lessens the sting of failure. Without cash, failure is felt much more acutely. The last dozen years of Samuel Clemens's life were a tragic coda caused almost entirely by his desire to cap his fabulously successful writing career as Mark Twain by becoming a lion of industry on the scale of Andrew Carnegie or John D. Rockefeller, whom he mocked in public and envied in private.

Clemens started poorly, investing in the Paige typesetter, which bankrupted him in 1897 and forced him to go on a worldwide speaking tour to pay off his creditors. Still, Clemens perversely continued to toss away his money on a series of almost willfully stupid investments and Victorian contraptions—a skim milk derivative known as Plasmon; Kaolatype, a chalk engraving process; self-adjusting suspenders; self-pasting scrapbooks.

Needless to say, his true source of greatness (and income) suffered, and while Clemens continued to write diligently, if sporadically, his work between 1896 and his death in 1910 was on the whole a thin gruel. Ironically, the master storyteller was at his best making trenchant nonfictional observations on current events (he was an anti-imperialist before anti-imperialism was cool, and penned an open-minded defense of the Jews). But the majority of his other efforts fizzled, from a monumental *Autobiography* (which one scholar described as "trivial, self-indulgent and—what is most unfortunate coming from Mark Twain—dull") to sad attempts to resuscitate past heroes (*Tom Sawyer, Detective*).

Samuel Clemens's closing years of twilight—during which his wife, Olivia, often begged for him to stop frittering his talents away —recalls the other great literary decline, that of Leo Tolstoy, whose wife, Sonya, battled against the growing religious zealotry that led to his drecky final works, such as *Resurrection*, and ruined the ending of his great masterwork, *War and Peace*. Most people bail out of the epic halfway, never realizing that the book's appealing characters and engaging, if not quite snappy, plot evaporate during the last forty pages as the writing decays into a dense and incomprehensible tirade about free will and history.

But Sonya's efforts were thwarted by Tolstoy's band of fawning sycophants and rabid devotees, who grabbed control of his literary estate, emphasizing his nutbag political theories and not the great writing that had established his reputation in the first place. Isolated from his wife and in a state of near-madness, Tolstoy made a final, pathetic flight from his once-beloved home at Yasnaya Polyana, only to die in a rustic train station while his wife of forty-eight years, barred from being at his side, peered through the station windows.

To BE twenty-five and not to have done anything great was a terrible thing. Every day as I drove out to my job, as the opinion-page editor of the *Wheaton Daily Journal*, my pawnhood gnawed at me.

The newspaper was in a single-story, low, industrial-looking building on Schmale Road. It could have been a factory manufacturing boxes. After a few cups of coffee, I would head to the restroom. Above the urinal, some man had been sticking up snot, apparently for years, until it was like a galaxy, ten inches from my face. I made myself look at it, soaking in the horror of where I was: the *Wheaton Daily Journal*. I called it the Amityville Job, a takeoff on the movie *The Amityville Horror*, whose advertising tag line was the sepulchral cry "Get *out!!!*"

The definite low point of my stay in Wheaton was a visit by my classmate John Verbic. John was everything I was not. He was tall, handsome, well-connected—his father was the mayor of Rockford, Illinois. John was earning $150,000 a year on the commodities exchange; I was earning $14,000 at the *Journal.*

I had not known John in school, but when he advertised for a writer to help him polish his application to the Harvard Business School, I took the job. The pay was $75.

It was all above-board. Right off the bat, I insisted that I would not actually *write* his application essays—he would, then I would write a detailed critique to help guide his rewriting. He heartily agreed.

When he came by the *Journal* to drop off his preliminary application, I liked him immediately. Refined. A charcoal chesterfield coat with velvet collar tabs. Calfskin gloves. He had that natural leader-of-men quality. I felt he would go far.

Taking in the *Journal* offices for the first time, he was, I believe, disappointed. Holding an empty glove in his gloved hand, he gestured to the room. "You went to Northwestern," he said, with curiousity and not a trace of malice. "How did you end up *here?*"

The question was chilling, but I took a perverse pleasure from it, too. It had that schooldays clubiness to it, something a monocled explorer would say to a member of his old regiment, now gone native, found squatting beside a cook-fire in the Congo, his face painted like a death's head. "Why old boy, you were with me in the King's Royal Rifle Corps. How is it, dear chap, that you're now eating spiders and worshipping Damballa?"

Failure yes, but, like being pinned beneath the Flexible Flyer on a snowy lot in Berea, failure that could still be savored. Because the fact implicit in my enjoying both conditions was, I'm getting out. I wasn't really pinned beneath the sled—I could escape anytime I wanted. Ditto for Wheaton. As John Verbic implied with his question, I came from better stuff than this. Things change. At least, that is what I fervently hoped.

TOLSTOY ILLUSTRATES a second dictum, which, along with regression to the mean, should be recognized when evaluating failure against the span of a person's life: entropy. As any Pynchon fan knows, entropy is the physical truth that systems tend to run down, wear out, lose energy and deteriorate into a lukewarm nothingness. Planets do this. Stars do this. The entire universe will do this.

And people do this. They fail to meet past successes not only because of the intrinsic difficulty of superior work, but because the person is oftentimes in a reduced state as well. Had Tolstoy not been physically slipping, scholars maintain, he would never have let the "wall of Tolstoyites" come between himself and his family, and perhaps would not have ended up dying in the stationmaster's bed at Astapovo.

Thurber, too, after he went stone-blind and could no longer draw, even with a Zeiss loop and powerful lights, was never quite himself again. The work of his last ten years takes on a testy, annoyed tone, with more carping at fine points of grammar, parsing moot technicalities and wallowing in self-pity, than exploring the emerging modern sensibility that made him great. Thurber's slippage doesn't make him less great—if anything, it makes him greater, because we see, at the end, the terrible beast that his writing had kept at bay all those years.

Perhaps because I am thirty-three, one of the last years a man can be considered young, or youngish, on any scale except a geological one, I am still possessed with the giddy enthusiasm to try, in the end, to somehow refute the premise behind this chapter's title—the "calamity of so long life," one of the cruelties Hamlet ponders when debating whether he should be or not.

I happen to be lucky in that I have been progressing in reverse order when it comes to coping with the past. As a child I was depressed and nostalgic, feeling the best years had slipped away. This was when I was six, and would return to my old kindergarten classroom to enviously eye the new crop that had taken my place. For many years, I would have gratefully crawled back to kindergarten—heck, back home to the days before kindergarten, to slip between the bed and the wall and stay there until it was time to come out for a peanut butter sandwich and a bowl of Campbell's tomato soup.

As I grew older, I came to accept past highlights with a more reflective satisfaction. In *On the Waterfront*, Rod Steiger's Charlie, the older brother, has a great line. "You were beautiful," he says to Marlon Brando's Terry, the younger brother, in sincere admiration. That's about all you can do. My brother, Sam, and I used to be in pretty good shape, and once—just once—on a hot summer's day we ran up a long curving mountain road high into the flatirons over

Boulder, Colorado. The run would kill us both now. But thinking about us making it, in the burning sun, sweating like horses, bracing our hands on our knees when we finally reached the top, sucking air and looking down at the city far below us—I don't see how the memory can ever make me feel bad, just because I can't do it anymore. We were beautiful.

Anyway, Shakespeare was probably referring only to the specific infirmities of age, which, while often poignant, are also a kindness. Death would be doubly tragic if we lived out our full lives, then met it still vibrant, still beautiful, still young. By going through a long decline we are sort of eased out the door, transitioned into nothingness, so when death comes it is almost welcome and we can finally step down and give others a chance. If Dostoyevsky and Dickens and Henry James were still alive, now well into their second centuries, continuing to churn out great novels every five years, then Stephen King would still be living in a trailer and I would be running this book off on a mimeograph machine.

Since you can't always replicate your past successes, the key is to blunder forward as best you can, staring Death in the face as his puckering mouth lowers over yours. Having read *Death in Venice* makes it impossible to cling to the prerogatives of youth—all the toupees and facelifts and mod clothes smack too much of Gustav von Aschenbach, silly with his rouged cheeks and dyed hair, tripping down the beach after young Tadzio, his fading heart all aflutter.

I've fashioned a theoretical old age for myself, the prospect of which I can accept. I picture myself kissing my wife on her cool and powdered heavily lined cheek, putting on one of my well-preserved twenty-five-year-old suits, then toddling down to the library, shuffling among the stacks in a way not too far removed from the way I do now. I can see myself, lunching every day at the same little restaurant, just another watery-eyed old guy, smelling of mothballs, blowing on his soup, slowly chewing his food so he doesn't choke, a little box of pills set out on the tablecloth. In a scruffy briefcase at my feet will be the beginnings of my twenty-seventh volume of historio-comedio-autobio-something-or-other. If none of them have done very well—no big royalty checks, no *New York Times Book Review* with my image in squiggly scratchings and a gushing headline I've already written in my mind but can't reveal here out of the poignant hope that it may still come true—well, okay, it beats having worked in a foundry.

In my fantasy, I can taste the soup. I don't hope for much more. No one will shyly come up to me, eyes sparkling with recognition, and ask me to sign something. No one in the street will say, "Hey, isn't that Steinberg, the writer?" Rather, the oldster at the next table will shout, "Looks like it's warming up!" And I'll smile and nod and shout back, "My soup was fine, but the rolls aren't quite fresh."

SEVEN

The History of Babylon
Is Fraught with Sadness

—

Obscurity and Oblivion
Reconsidered

NORTHWESTERN UNIVERSITY'S main library is a hideous tri-towered mess of poured concrete, grayish beige in color. An outdated 1960s vision of the future, the stark and jagged building looks as if it should be orbiting Pluto rather than plunked down in the middle of the college's generally lovely tree-filled campus. It leaks, too, sending librarians scrambling to drape big sheets of plastic over shelves and roll garbage cans under dribbling ceilings whenever a hard rain falls.

Still, it is the best library around Chicago, a city where the central public library was stuck in an old warehouse until recently. When funds were finally scrounged up for a real library building, and a stunning red granite and terra-cotta edifice built, adorned with massive bronze froufrou and dedicated to the late mayor, Harold Washington, the city neglected to budget for any new books—none have been purchased for several years—making the Chicago Public Library one of the most impressive settings to study in, as long as you bring your own reading materials. And at the University of Chicago, the lights in the stacks are set on timers, so they snap off at inconvenient moments, plunging you into darkness while you are sitting cross-legged on the floor, scanning selections to see if they are worth being carried away. The librarians are mean, too.

So that leaves Northwestern. And despite the library's stained, threadbare carpeting and deadening, subterranean interior, I think I am at my happiest when I am trucking down one of its windowless corridors, hugging a big stack of sweet-smelling books, navigating via the Dewey decimal system. It's a geek joy; I know that. But hey, very few people have a job where they can shake off tackles and run the broken field, pumping their legs high, spiking the ball in the end zone as the stands erupt. You have to take your glory where you find it.

One of the great things about Northwestern's library is that despite the huge collection, it has open stacks. While at, say, the main branch of New York Public Library you get access only to the specific books you request, at Northwestern you can wander among the shelves—3.5 million volumes' worth—gazing at vistas of books related to the one you are looking for, stumbling upon discoveries that relate to nothing at all. Strange titles leap out: *Who Goes First?— The Story of Self-Experimentation*; *Rude Stone Monuments*; *The History of Human Error*. Happening upon an intriguing book is like finding a dollar bill on the ground.

Only at an open-stack library could a lowly undergraduate discover, as I did while still in college, a large black quarto book, hundreds of years old and set in German Gothic type, lying out on a table. The front plates featured weird engravings of a man with one eye open, one eye closed; a frightening and compelling visage. I copied the name of the author, Oswald von Wolkenstein, and asked my German literature professor, Rainer Rumold, about this Teutonic specter. He fixed me with a level stare. "Zee me after class," he said. I had fifty minutes to ponder what I had done, imagining I had inadvertently uttered some secret code word, and would be led down a sloping corridor, cut from the naked rock below campus, to find the assembled German department, decked out in their SS outfits, gathered before a big Lucite map of the world.

Finally, class ended. "Zo, how is it, Herr Shtayenbehg," the professor asked in his bass rumble, leaning back in his office chair and making a pyramid with his fingers, "zat you happen to know of Oswald von Wolkenstein?" I told him about stumbling upon the book, and he laughed his hearty beer-hall laugh. Oswald, it seems, was a homoerotic poet of the early fifteenth century, and not many people know of him. The one-eye-open/one-eye-closed business in the front plates, my professor explained, was some bit of medieval symbolism about being both inward- and outward-looking.

I admit that knowing about Oswald von Wolkenstein did not, in the ensuing decade, prove to be of immense practical value. But the discovery did have some worth as an amusing anecdote, and gave me an early indication of the value of conducting research randomnly.

A more recent discovery took place earlier this year on the fifth floor of the library's North Tower, in the American humor section —the 817s, by the Dewey decimal system. I was spending a good deal of time there, enough to become familiar with the neighborhood's more prominent residents.

Across the aisle from the wall of books by and about Mark Twain, on a top shelf, a grouping of a dozen books had caught my eye by virtue of the impressive net of cobwebs formed along the irregular heights of their richly ornate, finely gilded spines. The books were all by obscure nineteenth-century humorists—Josh Billings, Bill Nye, Artemus Ward, Petroleum V. Nasby—once-famous writers now utterly forgotten and unread by anybody. The books had joke titles: *Letters of Peregrine Pickle*; *Old Lim Jucklin*; *History and Records of the Elephant Club*; *Swingin Round the Cirkle*.

Nature takes her time assembling a good cobweb, and usually I'm loath to disturb one. But after passing the tableau several times, searching for various books, temptation got the better of me. Brushing away the creepy white tendrils, with that shuddering feeling associated with touching cobwebs, I snatched out one of the century-old volumes—*Remarks of Bill Nye*—blew a cinematic plume of dust off the top, and opened the book to a random middle page. I read the first sentence: "The history of Babylon is fraught with sadness." Then I closed the book and put it back on the shelf.

WANTING TO BE remembered is one of the true common denominators in the history of humanity. The reason why Babylonian cuneiform, Egyptian hieroglyphics and other ancient languages could be deciphered after being utterly forgotten for millennia is that most ancient monumental inscriptions say some version of the same thing: I am King Brapathrap, the Great King, the Mighty King, the King of Kings, whose kingish reign began on such-and-such a date and who can take full kingly credit for the following acts of kingliness . . .

It's almost funny, when reading accounts of the scholars who unscrambled ancient writings—whether from the jungles of Central America, the deserts of the Middle East, or the fjords of Norway—to note the number of times the academics, struggling by candlelight to make some sort of progress, suddenly have an inspiration: count up the number of times each symbol appears, label the most common one "king," and go on from there. A breakthrough!

Both Georg Friedrich Grotefend, the German schoolteacher who began deciphering cuneiform—on a barroom bet, so the story goes —and Henry Rawlinson, trying to do the same thing, independent of Grotefend and thirty years later, made the same assumption. Of course, Rawlinson almost had no choice: he was working to translate Kurdistan's *Rock of Behistun*, a gigantic figure of a man with a bow, his foot crushing the neck of an enemy, hewn into a cliff and covered with over a thousand lines of tiny, wedge-shaped writing. One might safely assume that nobody would polish the face of a cliff and carve a message sixty feet wide except for a king in the mood for some serious boasting.

That such painstakingly carved tributes to royal ego lionize tyrants whose achievements inevitably come to nothing, or practically nothing, has long been commented on. Ideally, I wouldn't insult my readership by quoting from the famous sonnet of Shelley. But since most people were watching MTV during the two minutes their grandfathers and great-grandfathers devoted to reading "Ozymandias," I'll pause to reprint the poem, in recognition that it will be a fresh discovery for many:

> I met a traveller from an antique land
> Who said: Two vast and trunkless legs of stone
> Stand in the desert. Near them, on the sand,
> Half sunk, a shatter'd visage lies, whose frown,
> And wrinkled lip, and sneer of cold command,
> Tell that its sculptor well those passions read
> Which yet survive, stamp'd on these lifeless things,
> The hand that mock'd them and the heart that fed:
> And on the pedestal these words appear:
> "My name is Ozymandias, king of kings:
> Look on my works, ye Mighty, and despair!"
> Nothing beside remains. Round the decay
> Of that colossal wreck, boundless and bare,
> The lone and level sands stretch far away.

Swell poem, but Shelley made a poor choice, historically, in picking Ozymandias out of the two hundred or so Egyptian pharaohs he could have chosen. Ozymandias, the Greek name for Ramses II, is perhaps the best known of the whole lot, from the many

monumental works of his sixty-seven-year reign that remain in existence to this day, such as the Temple at Abu Simbel, to his major
role in the Bible (he is the pharaoh who had the run-in with Moses).
Even his mummified corpse is on display, in the Cairo museum. He
looks sort of like Sadat—the same high cheekbones.

All told, Shelley would have done better with Pepi II Neferkare.

But what did Shelley know? Few of Ramses's monuments had
been dug up in 1817, when Shelley wrote the poem. The hieroglyphics that had been found could not be read; Champollion
wouldn't announce his breakthrough with hieroglyphics for another
five years. Shelley never went to Egypt, but lifted his description of
Ozymandias's boastful mutterings from Diodorus of Sicily, an ancient writer who himself never saw the monument, but was para-
phrasing Hecataeus of Abdera (one of the many authors whose
works are utterly lost, existing only as quoted by catfish historians
such as Diodorus).

In this game of telephone, carried out over the centuries, it is
only natural that veracity suffers. Like failure, obscurity is a relative
thing. Ramses II is among the most documented and celebrated men
in history, yet in Shelley's hands he becomes an avatar of oblivion.
To me, Bill Nye is an obscure humorist—you might be writing your
thesis on him.

While obscurity is relative, oblivion is absolute. The enigma of
oblivion, however, is that we can seldom know with authority what
exactly it is we no longer have. Montaigne says he has "regretted a
thousand times that we have lost the book that Brutus had written
on virtue," before going on, tongue in cheek, to question whether
Caesar's assassin was the best person to discourse on the subject.

The phrase "the burning of the library of Alexandria" has always
created a twinge in my heart. What great works were destroyed?
What philosophical tools obliterated? I imagined the arsonists—

Turks? Mongols? Arabs?—wickedly stacking the dry papyrus scrolls, the flames leaping from the white marble edifice, illuminating the terrified faces of the scholars, huddling nearby, transfixed by the atrocity.

The event itself didn't actually happen like that. Or maybe it did. The truth is, we don't know, today, exactly what the library at Alexandria was, where it was, or even who burned it. Ptolemy I Soter set out to collect "the books of all the peoples of the world" in a library at Alexandria. Scrolls aboard ships stopping in port were hurriedly copied, and pleas for books were sent to the known countries of the earth. Galen tells the probably fictional story of Ptolemy III's convincing Athens to loan him the official scrolls for the works of Sophocles, Euripides and Aeschylus so that copies could be made for the library. Copies were made, and then sent to Athens, with the precious originals remaining in Ptolemy III's possession. An impressive collection was amassed, though it was more an act of patriotism than of scholarship. The role of the library was to show the glory of the nation—another monument. (To thwart rival libraries, Egypt banned the export of papyrus.)

The first candidate for burning the library was Julius Caesar, whose troops torched the Alexandrine ships to distract attackers during a raid. Some sources consider this the burning of the library at Alexandria, but others feel it was just the burning of 40,000 scrolls stored in a dockside warehouse containing "grain and books," and not the royal library.

If there was in fact a library. Historian Luciano Canfora speculates that belief in the existence of a royal library comes from the mistranslation of a single word in Hecataeus—*bibliotheke*, usually read as "library," but in the context Hecataeus used it more logically meaning "shelf." Somehow, "the burning of the bookshelf at Alexandria" doesn't pack the same emotional punch.

The next candidate is Caliph Omar I, whose Moslem armies captured the city on December 22, 640. Omar, reasoning that the books in the library were superfluous if they contained material in keeping with the Koran, and blasphemous if they didn't, ordered the library destroyed, though what sort of library it was by then is also a question. Nearly a thousand years had passed since the library's founding. "The delicate scrolls of old were gone," writes Canfora. "Their last remnants had been cast out as refuse or buried in the sand, and they had been replaced by more substantial parchment, elegantly made and bound into thick codices—and crawling with errors, for Greek was increasingly a forgotten language."

Whatever the library was—whether a bunch of shoddy copies or the chapbooks of Aristotle—it was put to the torch, used to fuel the fires of the public baths of Alexandria. "They say," wrote historian Ibn al-Caught, "that it took six months to burn all that mass of material."

THOSE OF US who are not kings, and cannot dragoon the forces of a country to perpetuate our glory (not only did Nebuchadnezzar construct a palace for himself, but his name was stamped on every brick), must be a little more diligent in nudging our names toward immortality.

One way is to create our own little monuments—gravestones— just to make sure our names are preserved somewhere. Often, in a very few words, they give a pretty good sense of what a person must have been like. I remember a gravestone my wife and I discovered in Deer Island, Maine, which reads in its entirety: "Burt Dow—Deep Water Man." I could almost squint and picture Dow—heavily lined face, oiled coat, enjoying a pipe at the warfside, his seasoned eye measuring the swelling of the sea.

The strong urge to perpetuate one's name is reflected in oddball schemes that pop up from time to time. Remember the guy who was offering to take metallic, cold pill–sized containers of people's ashes, with their names inscribed on the side, and shoot them into space?

In a man's lifetime, a Russian proverb goes, he should plant a tree, have a son, and write a book. Most people ignore the book part (though perhaps not as many as would be ideal) and plant trees with only ornamentation in mind. But the son part still carries weight. The idea that this person, a minor impression of you, will go on, carrying exactly half your gene pool and more or less half your biases and opinions, is a great comfort.

I know that I feel a flashing genetic kinship with my father on the rare occasions when I break into a run, an exact imitation of the awkward, arm-flapping, change-jingling trot that passed for running when he was in a hurry, or when I do that sort of ruminative, dragging sniff-pinch of the nose (a near copy of his arching porpoise of a nose, at that). While I don't have a son yet, I hope someday to have one, a son who will carry on my heritage. A son who will hate his job the way my father hated his, the way I hate mine, and find satisfaction working on his own side projects, the way my father did, the way I do. A son who will subscribe to *The New Yorker*, and have a fondness for that brightly colored, geometric English licorice. A son who will, when making store-bought cheese fondue, hold the open foil pouch to his nose, inhale deeply, then thrust the pouch under his wife's nose and command that she do the same, barking, "Smell the wine in that!" The way my father did. The way I do.

Sadly, while the hope for a male descendant is probably attainable, the hope for an unbroken family chain of any considerable length is actually quite slim, particularly a chain with my name attached to it.

Most family lines die out over time. Thomas Malthus mentions this little-known fact in his classic *Essay on the Principle of Population,* though it gets overlooked in the glare of the book's greater doomsday message. He cites the meticulous records of the town of Berne, Switzerland, whose sovereign council granted official "bourgeoisie" approval to 487 families between 1583 and 1654. During the next century and a third, 379 of the families became extinct, and by 1783 only 108 of the original family names remained, despite the steady increase in population that so troubled Malthus.

This makes sense when you think about it. One result of the act of marriage is that two individuals with different surnames become a family with one surname (usually—I'm ignoring the unfortunate recent practice of pairing surnames, which works only for a generation or two and raises the specter of every name eventually sounding like faded English nobility: "Hi, this is Roger Blanding-Randall-Kepworth-Feldman. Roger, meet my friend, Susan Goldman-Minsky-Lopez." Maybe by ignoring it, it will go away). And so while more individuals are being created, they draw from fewer and fewer last names. Thus four grandparents, with four different last names, produce two parents, with two different last names, who can then have four more kids, all with the same name. The extinction of last names is common; their creation, unusual.

So the secret hope of your name being carried forward into perpetuity by your descendants is largely a vain one. Someday everyone in the world will be named Johnson, Smith, Mendez, Yang or one of a few dozen other names. I must admit that much as I'd like to imagine some band of as-yet-unconceived Steinbergs gathering in a Martian pub and raising their glasses of alphajuice, a hush falling as wise old Sirilious B-12 Zaphtek Steinberg invokes my name and heritage in a toast, I can't put much stock in it. Far more likely is the image of Murble Stenbeg searching through stacks of boxes, hoping to find canned food but, instead, discovering a yellowed, moldy and disintegrating copy of one of my books. Dully recognizing a vaguely familiar pattern to some symbols on the cover, he'll give the decaying mass an exploratory sniff before shrugging and tossing it into the crackling cook-fire. And thus exits my intellectual legacy from the world.

AND WHY NOT? Aren't decay and loss and oblivion the way of the world? Science tells us that, no matter who wins the National Book Award next year, eventually we'll all be part of the same lukewarm, uniformly distributed soup. The fact that Mick Jagger was big, and Andy Pratt wasn't, won't matter a lot then. Nothing will matter.

The Buddhists have the right idea, creating their gorgeous mandalas of colored sand, singing a little song, then brushing them away with brooms. There is something pathetic about all our curators, with their Zeiss loops and sable brushes, lovingly restoring the work that some Dutchman slapped together in between bottles of kvass.

Things have to be destroyed, to return to dust. That's what makes the little we save precious. If we had this huge, ever-growing mass of antiquities and valuable artifacts, all complete, all in perfect condition, we'd go nuts trying to house and care for it all. There'd be no room for anything new.

Edward Gibbon doesn't shed many tears for the library at Alexandria in his *Decline and Fall of the Roman Empire*. Uncertain whether the flames were sparked by Caesar, or by the Moslems, or maybe even by "the mischievous bigotry of the Christians who studied to destroy the monuments of idolatry," Gibbon shrugs his shoulders and says, whichever way, no matter. It was no big loss: "If the ponderous mass of Arian and Monophysite controversy were indeed consumed in the public baths, a philosopher may allow, with a smile, that it was ultimately devoted to the benefit of mankind."

What strikes Gibbon is not the mystery and tragedy of the loss at Alexandria, but the marvel that anything at all has survived to this day from the ancient world:

> I sincerely regret the more valuable libraries which have been involved in the ruin of the Roman empire; but when I seriously compute the lapse of the ages, the waste of ignorance, and the calamities of war, our treasures, rather than our losses, are the object of my surprise . . . we should gratefully remember, that the mischances of time and accident have spared the classic works to which the suffrage of antiquity had adjudged the first place of genius and glory.

He has a point. You don't see a lovely Egyptian soup bowl, preserved for 5,000 years and now on display at the Met, and immediately wonder what happened to the salad plate.

On the other hand, Gibbon does make a touchingly human error in his logic. The lost materials are a bunch of tedious Monophysite hooey. The things that we still have are the cherished treasures. He goes so far as to state confidently that nothing important has been lost at all: "Nor can it fairly be presumed that any important truth, any useful discovery in art or nature, has been snatched away from the curiosity of modern ages."

Now what makes him say that? Even Shakespeare's plays, written in the relative yesterday of Elizabethan England, arrive to us in a tattered, secondhand, almost accidental form. Gibbon's argument springs from his inability to accept the fact that rare works of surpassing merit, treasures which would enrich us to this day, valuable thoughts, have been ground into nothing by the rumble of history. In this way, his view resembles the poignant faith of the families of soldiers missing in Vietnam. Our boys must still be there, prisoners, the logic goes. We loved them so much, they couldn't just *disappear*.

Gibbon can doubt the loss of potential classics because he lived in an age when writers might sit in their studies and hope for the perfectibility of civilization. There is still time. Nothing has yet been lost, not really. Let us then hold hands and walk into the promised land together.

We in the twentieth century, given a crash course in the obliterating hand of history, know better. Not only is there terrible loss, but we weary even of the task of calculating the toll. Nuclear obliteration hasn't been a peril for, gee, almost five years now. Somehow not quite long enough to make us confidently look to the founding of the New Jerusalem. Too much has happened, is happening. The Titians seem to be in the museum now only because nobody has blown them up yet; the books in the library quietly await the day when they are pulled from the shelves and burned in the street.

I MOVED INTO a new apartment in Oak Park a decade back, and my housekeeping being what it is, I kept a few paper bags of possessions —old toys, blocks, dolls, junk, mostly—in the kitchen for a few months. I meant to put them away but never got around to it.

One day part of the kitchen ceiling caved in. Water damage. Some workmen came around in a day or two to fix the ceiling. They piled their garbage around the bags of old possessions, and the building superintendent came in and threw the whole lot out.

That evening, I discovered what had happened and confronted the super, who brought me to the Dumpster where the bags had been deposited. The Dumpster was chock-full—stuffed with plastic bags spilling greasy chicken boxes, dirty rags, broken eggshells, wet paper sacks oozing glop. The toys were not on top. I was tormented by vestigial thoughts that I should "save" the dolls—Raggedy Andy, his face worn away by kisses; Lucky Pup, with a bell in its ear, held by my chubby fist almost since birth. They were all in there, under that garbage. All I had to do was wade in and find them.

I didn't. I let them go. I figured it was meant to be—*bashert*, as they say in Yiddish. It was time. Still, until the Dumpster was hauled away, I felt tension, qualms buzzing around my resolve. But then the Dumpster was emptied and I felt a little better. I still had a few toys left—a lovely Steiff mohair lobster. The teddy bear, his face eaten away by moths.

Sure, in the ensuing years, I've had doubts, regrets. Times when I could have used that Lucky Pup. I worry I let them down, tweak myself with the thought that they were alone and cold in that Dumpster, waiting for me to rescue them, and I never came. Perhaps readers will think less of me for standing back, letting them go. Cold-hearted bastard betrayed his toys. Or, more likely, they'll smirk at me for caring at all. Be a man, they'll say, without taking too hard a look at the general condition of men.

My decision at the Dumpster was quite out of character. I am what Thurber called "an analyzer, a rememberer." I would have happily kept every toy I ever touched, in gray archival boxes, if I could have. Every garment, every shirt, I'd have worn out, then wrapped in acid-free tissue and placed in a pure nitrogen atmosphere. White-gloved curators would have used wooden tongs to snatch up the crumpled papers from around my desk, placing them carefully into glass reliquaries. My mother would have been like Franklin Delano Roosevelt's mother, saving his baby clothes, certain of his eventual fame.

As a child, I hated the thought of things being forgotten, being lost. I would pity a missing sock. I would jot down the names of strangers I sat next to on planes, not because I found them significant, but because I was troubled by the thought that I might want to recall the name someday and be unable to.

I was forever burying time capsules, hiding papers between the leaves of books, beginning journals, mentally telegraphing messages to myself in the future. It is no accident that, to this point, my writing has consisted of documenting the obscure, of sniffing into the deep recesses of libraries, putting my back into cranking open the movable shelving in long-term basement storage rooms.

I take comfort that I am not alone in this mania. The Mormons, for instance, place genealogy as a cornerstone of their religion, burying their familial records in deep vaults designed to survive Apocalypse. Knowing your history is the key to heaven. Similarly, in his *Utopia*, Thomas More noted that the perfect country kept its records "preserved with an exact care, and run backward 1,760 years." Mmmm, nice.

Blaming one's mother is the easy way, but I do suspect that I am so fixated on preserving things because my mother was a vigorous cleaner, and would ruthlessly throw out whatever crossed her path. Perhaps that's what made me a keeper, squirreling away cherished possession—doodlings, folders, letters—in certain drawers she knew to be sacrosanct, safe zones of immunity.

She will protest this, claiming that she tried to respect our possessions. I did manage to save a lot despite her zeal (which, I'm sorry, Ma, at the time struck me as just shy of Torquemada's). I'm the only person I know who still has his baseball-card collection, his old baseball mitt, his comic books. Though I can only gaze, uncomprehendingly, at people who chirp that the baseball cards, or the comic books, must be "worth something." I suppose my kidneys are worth something, too, but I don't plan to unload them anytime soon.

Pulling open a file drawer, I find work sheets from elementary school. Tests from high school. Notes passed in class. None of the stuff is precocious. A diary entry from November 27, 1968: "Today was a pack meeting. Are [sic] den, den 6, put on a skit. I got a trophy for the cub scout of the month. But I can only keep it for a month." Still, I suppose I will store the mass, somewhere, for the rest of my life, giving my wife a very melancholy afternoon over a large garbage can someday around the year 2035. In those terms, I sometimes wish my mother had gotten to more.

We savers should take heart. The curve of civilization is generally moving toward more preservation, not less. Images have been crudely recorded for tens of thousands of years. Thoughts have been accurately set down for, roughly, the past 5,000. Five hundred years ago, movable type was invented, followed by photography (167 years ago), sound recording (125) and moving pictures (100), until today, when people can, and do, record the smallest events of their lives.

I see the accelerating documentation in my own family. My grandparents took a single wedding portrait. My parents' wedding was recorded in eighteen black-and-white photographs, bound in a white leather album. My wedding was videotaped. I could have had a tape professionally produced, with romantic songs (perhaps the first song Edie and I ever danced to, that lush ballad "Bela Lugosi's Dead" by Bauhaus) and shots of our baby pictures in heart-shaped frames. But I didn't want that—it seemed crass, violating my sense of propriety. Perhaps mired in old ways, I like to have a bit left out, the tantalizing mystery of my parents' wedding photographs. I wanted our wedding video, I told Edie, "to look like the Zapruder film," so we had her sister-in-law videotape it from behind a plant. The results were satisfying, while still retaining a somewhat amateurish, spare and documentary air, filled with voids, giving a mystery to something that, if filmed professionally and completely, might risk appearing insipid. She did not film the reception, however, which in my mind was the best part, though those two facts might not be unrelated. In my mind's eye, I wistfully recall myself at the reception, a dapper, tuxedoed groom making an eloquent and moving toast, later dancing like a gazelle, and wish my sister-in-law had captured it. But had she filmed the actual event, perhaps I would now shudder at the thought of my reception, haunted by the documented and unde-niable image of a red-faced, sweaty blockhead mumbling some asi-nine remarks into a microphone, or writhing awkwardly on the dance floor, bow tie vertical, steatopygic rump gyrating grotesquely.

Society has taken a much more serious attitude about preserving ephemera, at least in certain areas. Television—ironically, consider-ing its content—does better at preserving itself even than publishing. If I wanted to track down a popular book from my childhood—Lois Lenski's *Policeman Small* or one of those Dan Frontier books I learned to read with—it would be quite a task, either dragging through an endless perdition of used-book shops or hiring a wildly expensive book-search firm.

On the other hand, if the memory of a certain episode of "McHale's Navy" began calling to me, enticingly, back over the years, I'm sure I could troop down to Blockbuster and find it on laser disc (maybe in a boxed "Classic Golden Episodes of 'McHale's Navy' " set, complete with restored lost footage, "The Making of 'McHale's Navy' " tacked on at the end, old commercials, plus an alternate sound track with Ernest Borgnine providing reminiscences and commentary).

This ready availability of shows and films, oddly enough, dimin-ishes their value. When the only way to see old movies was to wait to see them on television, or in a revival house, there was a certain sense of moment when an obscure favorite—*The President's Analyst, The Russians are Coming! The Russians are Coming!, Twelve O'Clock High*—would pop up in the listings. I'd never miss a chance to see one. Now that I can own tapes of the movies and watch them whenever I want to, I never have to worry about being denied, and thus never watch them at all. That's why a mediocre stage play is better than a good movie —because the play is real, in front of you, occurring for a short spell, then disappearing into the void, like life itself.

Loss does tantalize. The burning of the library at Alexandria intrigued me, even though I was not particularly interested in ancient studies. The problem wasn't that I had read the length and breadth of antiquity and now regretted there were no new worlds to conquer. Rather, it was the image of loss—of crackling scrolls, of playwrights whose names are unknown, characters, passions, love, all flying skyward in a plume of smoke—that affected me.

It's sort of obscene, now that I think of it, in light of all the more recent destruction and holocaust, the sorrow of the world, to fix on this ancient, perhaps even mythical incident and feel bad about it. A fake, theatrical emotion.

But that's how people are. They like to focus on small, manageable objects for their pity. I don't think it's a conscious act—the idiots rallying to the defense of some deprived porpoise at Chicago's Shedd Aquarium didn't first decide that world hunger was too big an issue to tackle. But I think that's exactly what goes on, unconsciously. Human beings are so messy; you help them and they ask for more. How awkward. Animals just gaze gratefully with those big, lovely eyes. As with Proust's image of beauty, we can read gratitude or nobility or anything we please into the fathomless depths of those sparkling orbs.

I found myself giving more money to beggars in France, and realized it was because the beggars there equip themselves with cats. I can scorn most human beggars, with effort, making myself imagine the loved ones they hurt on their journey to the gutter. But a cat earns my sympathy, automatically, and I cough up a few coins. Cat pity is not a particularly noble attitude, but it is common nevertheless.

NOT ONLY DOES loss tantalize, but by creating rarity it creates value. This is apparent on an economic level—there are forty-seven extant Gutenberg Bibles, and any one of them could be sold tomorrow for $5 million. If, however, the Vatican finds five hundred more Gutenberg Bibles, stacked in a forgotten papal warehouse, and decides to unload them, then the price will no doubt fall.

This holds intellectually as well. I have read Darwin's *Expression of the Emotions* but not his *Descent of Man,* because the former is an odd, obscure work, while the latter is part of every educated person's intellectual background, if only in outline form.

There is more than a tinge of elitism in this, a reluctance to flatter the rank breath of popularity. If everybody started reading Thomas Pynchon's impenetrable *Gravity's Rainbow,* discussing it on the bus, calling in radio talk shows to offer insights ("Yes, Lester from Plainfield, you have a comment . . ." "Thank you, Bobo, I do. First, I love your show. Second, I've always considered the use of song in Pynchon more a mimicry of the Greek chorus than an acerbic comment on modern music . . ."), I might profess to be pleased, but deep down, I know I'd feel threatened, as if people were invading my turf. In this same way, my brother tells me that his coworkers in Japan were very pleased when he could speak a bit of Japanese, but became increasingly cool to him as his command of the language improved. They define themselves by their language, he explained, and while they are flattered to see foreigners try, it begins to encroach on their private domain if they get too good.

There is pleasure in discovering something that is both good and unknown. Obscurity makes a thing seem private, a small garden you discover yourself, as opposed to a big public park, chocked with skateboarders and scary men.

There is also a sense of rescue in enjoying the obscure. I have the ten-volume set of the writings of William Cowper Brann, the fiery editor of the Waco *Iconoclast* who was shot in the back in 1898 by one of the victims of his acid pen. I've never read the books in any methodical way, but when I need a dose of witty bile, I'll pull down a random volume and read a bit, my pleasure increased by the thought that nobody else has read what I'm reading, possibly for years. Of course, the sixteen graduate students presently working on theses on various aspects of Brann's life will no doubt object. But I said it was a thought, not a verified reality. Not only are there probably sixteen graduate students, but also fifty other smug assholes, referring to *their* cherished sets of Brann, simultaneously. I try not to think about it.

Underlying it all is the random quality of popular success. Those who languish in obscurity are not necessarily lesser than those who bask in fame. Rather, the dice tumbled against them, or, as Twain wrote: "Fame is a vapor, popularity an accident. The only earthy certainty is oblivion."

Much of oblivion is deserved. So much garbage gets published, recorded, painted, filmed, videotaped. New books arriving at the *Chicago Sun-Times* are piled on tables and sold when they are no longer needed (and the vast majority are never needed). Pay two bucks to a scholarship fund and you can take almost any book you like—art books cost a bit more. The sad part is that even at a fire-sale price, hundreds of books go untouched and are carted off to a charity at regular intervals. What the charity does with the shunned books is a mystery—maybe they go into the furnace to warm baths for the poor. Gibbon would like that.

Oblivion comes in many guises. Artistic works do not have to be heaped into a fire to be rendered meaningless. If nobody reads a book, or listens to a piece of music, or sees a picture, the end result is the same, whether the tangible artifact exists or not. "Of what use are books without number and complete collections if their owner barely finds time in the course of his life even to read their titles?" Seneca asks.

The burden of oblivion rests only with the living. Those whose posthumous reputations crumble are beyond caring. This point sometimes gets overlooked. Our reluctance to recognize death makes us imagine that longevity of reputation somehow reflects back on the incarnate person, as if Samuel Clemens is happier in heaven than Bill Nye because his books are still in print. That a person's works will live on, whatever the field, cannot bring happiness after death, particularly since it doesn't seem to do much for people while they are alive. Having written *War and Peace* did not comfort Tolstoy in his last years, just as F. Scott Fitzgerald wrote *This Side of Paradise* and *The Great Gatsby* and still drank himself into the grave, forty-four years old, his pudgy mistress helping him make fudge to sooth his ravaged stomach.

A FEW DAYS before I finished this book, I went back to the North-western library. Errors have a way of creeping into any book pur-porting to be fact, and I wanted to eliminate as many as I could before critics had the chance to gleefully discover them and pin them on me like holiday ornaments. It was Christmas break, and the library was nearly empty. Just before it closed, I found myself back in the 817s, back in front of the obscure humorists. I was exhausted after a long day of fact checking. Months had passed since I pulled down the Bill Nye book and opened to that particular page, and I couldn't remember which volume it was. But I made a judgment call —the gaudiest spine, the one with silver ink, with the engraving of a feather pen on the green cover, and a dapper gent in bow tie and tails, and Bill Nye's florid, curlicued signature. That had to be it. I took it from the shelf. I opened to a random page. "The history of Babylon is fraught with sadness." The spine of the book was broken there. It fell open naturally to that page.

Nye's prose has stood up about as well as the cheap, acidy paper, now turned a deep golden brown, especially around the page edges, closer to the oxidizing air. Well on its way to dust. I had read only the single sentence, but it captured the tone of the entire piece. "Thus Babylon," Nye wrote, "with 3,000 years the start of Minne-apolis, is to-day a hole in the ground, while Minneapolis socks her XXXX flour into every corner of the globe, and the price of real estate would make a common dynasty totter on its throne."

There are a few good lines. He points out that "while Cheyenne has the electric light and two daily papers, Babylon hasn't got so much as a skating rink," and he quotes Rawlinson, the translator of Babylonian cuneiform, on the irony of Babylon's present state of utter ruin: "When we turn from this picture of the past to contem-plate the present condition of these localities, we are at first struck with astonishment at the small traces which remain of so vast and wonderful a metropolis. The broad walls of Babylon are utterly broken down. God has swept it with the besom of destruction."

But in general, it's pretty choppy stuff. Nye goes on too long, and throughout displays too little craft, such as this joke following mention of the fall of the tower of Belus: "I am glad I was not contiguous to it when it fell, and also that I had omitted being born prior to that time." Yet, I suppose, squinting, it might almost sound like Mark Twain, on a very bad day. Though I am a fine one to talk. Nye was obviously hot stuff in his time. It will be quite a while before I appear on the cover of a book, wearing a bow tie and tails or anything else.

THE FIRST WRITING I ever had published in a book was a humor piece I wrote in college called "Let's Capitulate to the Russians"— based on how stupid I found the right-wing fears that the Russians would "take us over." The piece was a series of single statements, following the logical impossibility of the Russians running this country to its obvious conclusion (nothing works; the Russians declare the entire endeavor a success and go home). The statements were illustrated by Robert Leighton, the brilliant cartoonist, writer, deep-sea diver, concert pianist and autodidact.

A guy named Joey Green was putting together an anthology of American college humor and approached us with this deal: I'll print the piece and give you nothing. If you don't give your permission, I won't print your work but will find somebody else's work to print. "Best," after all, is a broad umbrella. After carefully determining just how little pride we had, we went for the deal.

By the time the book came out, I had graduated and was twirling in the flaming hell of my first job, at the Bohle Company, a Los Angeles public relations concern. My primary task was to write promotional material for low-level publicity stunts—a series of biographies of twelve-year-old BMX bicycle racers sticks in mind—the sort of breathless pap that today I don't take the energy to wad up into a ball before throwing away; instead, I use one efficient motion when sliding the press releases from the envelope under my gaze and into the garbage.

I found the book, *Hellbent on Insanity,* in a Waldenbooks in Century City. Our names weren't printed along with the piece, but were stuck at the end of the book in a small-type index. I ran my finger down the list of contributors, all in this ridiculously tiny type, until it rested on my minuscule name, occupying a scant handful of square millimeters, a few molecules of ink. Then I directed my gaze up, and around, at the huge Waldenbooks bookstore, jammed floor to ceiling with flashy volumes, shelves stuffed with best-sellers vectoring off in all directions. My contribution seemed nothing. "It's like a twig snapping," I thought, "in a bonfire the size of a barn."

The thought of the barn-sized bonfire returned as I trod through the Northwestern library, looking for book 378.19802 S819—my first book, a history of college pranks. Since learning that the library was acquiring a copy, I had been tracking its progress for months through the computer system—the book's pending acquisition, arrival, cataloging, journey to the bindery, processing. Now it was on the shelves, in the section devoted not to humor but to colleges, the very aisles where I had researched a good part of the book, yanking out three-inch-thick college histories, searching through their mind-numbing tedium for a few nuggets of whimsy.

I was worried, as I made my way toward the proper shelf, walking briskly through the confusing circular maze, that the experience would be depressing—to find my book, the product of three years of increasingly intensive work, jammed among the old alumni registers and dusty, forgotten volumes celebrating defunct academic institutions.

There it was, hardbound, in one of those sponge-clean, clear-plastic library covers. I took it down and opened it. Nobody had yet cracked the spine. I read the dedication to my father, considered checking the book out, then rejected the idea. The book should be available to scholars who might want to consult it, I thought. The bright two-thirds-inch ribbon of spine should be a flashing beacon to anyone whose eye—perhaps a weary eye in need of a little soothing—might notice it. The book should be there on the shelf, waiting to be stumbled upon, taken down, checked out, read, balanced against a scarred wooden table, wrestled with in bed, balanced on a knee on the bus, cracked open at dinner, its white pages eventually flecked with traces of Cabernet and tomato soup. That's what books are for.

Walking away, I was relieved not to feel the snapping-twig-in-a-bonfire sensation. There really isn't a word for how I felt—a calming "on the shelf" feeling. I figured, Okay, all these ideas, millions of authors, billions of books. Everybody standing on soapboxes, screaming into microphones, the laser printers and mimeograph machines and offset web presses chugging away, full blast, endlessly churning out material. Five hundred channels, vomiting into the aether, radio signals hurtling into the measureless void. And now me, my ideas, my voice, for fifty years or a hundred, depending on the quality of the paper, on the shelf, adding my particular twist. No one had requested it, there was no pressing need, but nevertheless it was there, *I was there.*

The next time I ran the book through the computer, to make sure it was still there, it wasn't. Somebody had checked it out.

ACKNOWLEDGMENTS

—

THIS BOOK IS dedicated to Bill Thomas, my editor at Doubleday, not only because he suggested its subject—failure—but because he then had the faith to stand back and let me do with it what I would, guiding my progress with great subtlety and understanding.

I have the great good fortune to be in the hands of a marvelous agent, David Black, and his energetic staff. If you learned of this book through a magazine excerpt, you have Susan Raihofer to thank for it, as do I.

The support staff at Doubleday—the graphic artists, the designers, the production team—transformed the stack of typing paper I delivered to them into the beautiful volume you have in your hands. The sales staff batted away a dozen competitors' books to get this volume into bookstores. Particular thanks to Rob Robertson, for his boundless enthusiasm, and to Bob Daniels, "an absolute knave" whose copy editing prevented the book from becoming a vague and ungrammatical swamp of error.

Many others helped in the writing of this book, and some may not even know it. Robert Davis kept my spirits high at the *Chicago Sun-Times*, never letting me give up on the prospects for quality in daily journalism; Robert and Jean McMath trusted me enough to give me free reign in their product showcase; Perry Grover, of Glendale, California, set me straight on Varaflame candles; Chris Stec; Larry Doyle, my editor in the balmy days of the old *National Lampoon*, pointed me in a fruitful direction, toward a helpful toy company executive whom I will thank but not name. Bill Buford honored the book by including an exerpt from it in his peerless magazine, *Granta*.

The spelling bee chapter owes its existence to Sruti Nadimpalli and her family, good people who I hope do not regret their participation in this endeavor.

My family—sister Debbie, brother Sam and my parents, Robert and June Steinberg—all consented to let me drag their good names into the dirt. I also want to thank the various friends, both past and present, who were swept up in my reminiscences, particularly Esther Otterson. I hope that my writing about that summer wasn't a creepy, Bob Greene thing to do. Special thanks to Richard Roeper, my constant friend, who eats Mike Royko's lunch five days a week and makes it look easy. Finally, thanks to Dennis Britton, editor of the *Chicago Sun-Times*, both for granting me a vital leave of absence and for his interest beyond the call of duty.

As always, the staffs at Northwestern University Library, the New York Public Library and the Oberlin College Archive were particularly helpful in responding to my strange requests.

On a personal note, I'd to thank all the friends—Kier Strejcek, Robert Leighton, Cate Plys, Didier Thys, Jim and Laura Sayler, Carol Weston, Rob Ackerman, Bill Zwecker, Larry and Ilene Lubell —who buoyed me up in the past year, plus others who are unnamed but not forgotten. And as always, a special, kiss-laden thanks to my wife, Edie, who helped me in a thousand ways, small and large, the largest being the gift of her fierce and unwavering love, the sort of love most people search for their entire lives and never find.

BIBLIOGRAPHY

—

"I DO NOT COUNT my borrowings," Montaigne wrote, "I weigh them." One of the joys of writing this book was getting a chance to read the works of many wonderful authors. To recognize some of the most important sources used in this book, and to point readers toward more detailed accounts of subjects they may wish to investigate further, here is a selective list of vital texts:

INTRODUCTION: The Siren Beauty of Ruin

Remembering the Future. New York: Rizzoli, 1989. A big book, filled with photographs, that recounts not only the 1964 New York World's Fair but the 1939 fair as well, comparing and contrasting them in interesting ways.

I.   TRAGICALLY DEFUNCT—Product Failure

Baker, Nicholson.   *The Mezzanine.* New York: Vintage Books, 1988. A guy's shoelace breaks and he goes to buy another. That's the entire plot. The rest, as Hillel says, is commentary.

Gershman, Michael.   *Getting It Right the Second Time.* Reading, Mass.: Addison-Wesley, 1990. Written for use by those in business, but a lot of fun for civilians, too. A must for fans of consumer-product history.

Sacharow, Stanley.   *Symbols of Trade.* New York: Art Direction Book Company, 1982. The only place you're going to find the three other cigarettes test-marketed along with Camels in 1913 (Osman, Red Kamel and Reyno). Origins of all manner of brand symbols, tainted only with an occasional burst of enthusiastic corporatese.

Stern, Sydney Ladensohn, and Schoenhaus, Ted.   *Toyland: The High-Stakes Game of the Toy Industry.* Chicago: Contemporary Books, 1990. Filled with good stories and insider dope.

2.   WERE THE MOUNTAIN SMALLER—Pointless Failure

Holzel, Tom, and Salkeld, Audrey.   *First on Everest: The Mystery of Mallory and Irvine.* New York: Henry Holt, 1986. A recent and complete thorough account of the enigma of Mallory and Irvine.

Hunt, Sir John.   *The Conquest of Everest.* New York: E. P. Dutton, 1954. The official version—still a gripping read, even if Tenzing does get short shrift.

Ullman, James Ramsey, ed.   *Kingdom of Adventure: Everest.* New York: William Sloane, 1947. A nice collection of Everest writing by Mallory, Norton, Noel and all the early crew.

Younghusband, Sir Francis.   *The Epic of Mount Everest.* New York: Longmans, Green, 1926. The first three expeditions, in all their pith-helmeted glory.

3.   SHIVER LIKE RHESUS MONKEYS—Institutionalized Failure

If there are any books at all about spelling bees, I missed them.

4.   MYTHS OF TELEPHONE HISTORY—Bad Timing

Gray, Elisha.   *Experimental Researches in Electro-Harmonic Telegraphy and Telephony.* Russel Brothers: 1878. Gray's story in his own words—and dignified, slightly injured words they are.

Institute of Electrical and Electronic Engineers. *Bell and Gray: Contrasts in Style, Politics and Etiquette.* 1977. A monograph explaining how each man's personality affected his chances for success.

5.   IT CAN'T BE DONE—The Lure of Impossible

Crichton, Michael. *Travels.* New York: Ballantine, 1988. Don't take my word for it; read it yourself. The first half is actually very thought-provoking.

Davis, Philip J., and Park, David, eds. *No Way: The Nature of the Impossible.* New York: W. H. Freeman, 1987. Not all the authors display equal skill in addressing the subject of the impossible in fields from chemistry to law to music, and a few have axes to grind. But a broad and intriguing primer for this rarely addressed topic.

Ord-Hume, Arthur W. J. G. *Perpetual Motion: The History of an Obsession.* New York: St. Martin's Press, 1977. A good basic source, much more accessible than Dircks's thousand-page *Perpetuum Mobile.*

Parrington, Vernon Louis, Jr. *American Dreams: A Study of American Utopias.* New York: Russell & Russell, 1964. A very satisfying guide to literary utopias.

Taubes, Gary. *Bad Science: The Short Life and Weird Times of Cold Fusion.* New York: Random House, 1993. My primary source for the account of cold fusion. Taubes covers the material so expertly and thoroughly, it's hard to imagine anything else—other than a mea culpa by Pons and Fleischmann—adding to the story.

vos Savant, Marilyn. *The World's Most Famous Math Problem.* New York, St. Martin's Press, 1993. A fun little book. Amazingly broad for its short length and the speed with which it must have been written.

6.   THE CALAMITY OF LONG LIFE—Trouble in the Last Act

Hersey, Burnet.   *The Odyssey of Henry Ford and the Great Peace Ship.* New York: Taplinger, 1967. Written with a lot of ginger by a newspaperman who was on board.

Scheaffer, Louis.   *O'Neill: Son and Artist.* Boston: Little, Brown, 1973. Information about the end of James O'Neill's life is from this second volume of Sheaffer's peerless and heartbreaking two-part biography of Eugene O'Neill.

Wallace, Amy.   *The Prodigy.* New York: E. P. Dutton, 1986. A sympathetic and complete portrait of William James Sidis, filling in all the holes that are going to be filled in. Had I found this volume before my book was nearly done, I'd probably not have addressed Sidis's case at all, since Wallace does such a nice job of it.

7.   THE HISTORY OF BABYLON IS FRAUGHT WITH SADNESS— Obscurity and Oblivion Reconsidered

Canfora, Luciano.   *The Vanished Library.* Translated by Martin Ryle. Berkeley: University of California Press, 1989. A fascinating account of what is known—and not known—of the burning of the library at Alexandria. Canfora directed me to the sources I cite on the library.